1000 GREAT
rail-trails
A Comprehensive Directory

The Official Rails-to-Trails Conservancy Directory

Second Edition

The
Globe
Pequot
Press

Guilford, Connecticut

Cover design by Jane Sheppard
Text design by Lisa Reneson

Library of Congress Cataloging-in-Publication Data.

1000 great rail-trails : a comprehensive directory : the official Rails-to-Trails Conservancy directory.–2nd ed.
　　　p. cm.
　　ISBN 0–7627–0928–6
　　　1. Rail-trails—United States—Directories. 2. Railroads—Right of way—Multiple use—United States. I. Title: One thousand great rail-trails. II. Rails-to-Trails Conservancy.

GV191.35 .A18 2001
917.304'931–dc21

2001018186

Printed on recycled paper
Manufactured in the United States
Second Edition/First Printing

RAILS
- to -
TRAILS
CONSERVANCY

Dear Trail Enthusiast,

Rails-to-Trails Conservancy proudly offers you the second edition of *1000 Great Rail-Trails*. As a nonprofit membership organization dedicated to connecting people and communities, Rails-to-Trails Conservancy enriches America by creating a nationwide network of public trails from former rail lines and connecting corridors.

Today, over 1,000 rail-trails in all 50 states totaling over 11,000 miles are open to the public. There are approximately 1,200 additional trail projects underway.

Thanks to thousands of volunteers and professionals throughout America, trails and greenways are transforming our lives.

If you are looking for maps, photos and detailed narratives to guide you along the top rail-trails, order our new guidebooks. The order form is in the back of this book. Choose from guidebooks for California, Florida, New England (CT, RI, VT, ME, MA, NH) and Mid-Atlantic (MD, DE, VA, WV). We will be adding more states in the future, so watch for announcements on our Web site, www.railtrails.org, in the fall of 2001, or in our quarterly membership magazine, *Rails to Trails — A Celebration of Trails and Greenways*.

Whether you walk, use a wheelchair, bike, skate, ride horses, or cross-country ski, enjoy the trails in our new directory.

Yours sincerely,

Keith Laughlin

Keith Laughlin
President
Rails-to-Trails Conservancy

1100 Seventeenth Street, NW
10th Floor
Washington, DC 20036
202-331-9696
FAX: 202-331-9680
www.railtrails.org

100% Recycled Paper

1996 Recipient of Presidential Award
for Sustainable Development

Member of

Earth Share.

Contents

The Rail-Trails

Introduction

Across America there are more than 1,000 rail-trails now open for public use. With the help of this directory, you can embark upon 1,000 diverse and exciting trail adventures, such as hiking the recently completed Lake Wobegon Trail in Minnesota, bicycling through nearly a dozen tunnels on West Virginia's 60-mile North Bend Rail-Trail, hiking along the spectacular Katy Trail State Park that parallels the Missouri River and the Lewis and Clark expedition route, or riding horseback through the Badlands and rugged canyons of the Caprock Canyons Trailway in Texas.

Explore the remains of once-thriving coal mining communities by visiting the Ghost Town Trail in Pennsylvania. Trace history along the Minuteman Bikeway outside of Boston, following the route marched by British soldiers in 1776. Discover the scenic beauty of the Black Hills along South Dakota's George S. Mickelson Trails. Wander along the sparkling Susan River against a backdrop of jagged canyon cliffs on Northern California's Bizz Johnson Trail. To learn more about these trails and the others in this directory, visit www.TrailLink.com, Rails-to-Trails Conservancy's new online trail directory. Whether you walk, use a wheelchair, bike, skate, ride a horse, or cross-country ski, rail-trails are for you!

Because they are built on abandoned railroad corridors, rail-trails offer gentle grades and easy access for all types of recreation enthusiasts. Reflecting the booming railroad system of yesteryear, rail-trails connect urban hubs with sprawling suburbs, traverse small towns, and stretch through state and national forests.

In 1916 the United States boasted the largest rail system in the world, with nearly 300,000 miles of steel connecting every large city and small town in a massive transportation network. Today that impressive system has shrunk to less than 145,000 miles, taking a back seat to cars, trucks, and airplanes. As more than 2,000 miles of track are abandoned each year, unused corridors (with tracks and ties removed) offer a perfect backbone for another type of transportation network and a new recreation system—rail-trails.

The rail-trail movement began in the Midwest in the mid-1960s. In 1963 the late Chicago naturalist, May Theilgaard Watts, wrote a letter to the editor of the *Chicago Tribune* proposing the constructive reuse of an abandoned right-of-way outside of Chicago.

"We are human beings," she wrote. "We are able to walk upright on two feet. We need a footpath. Right now, there is a chance for Chicago and its suburbs to have a footpath—a long one." She evoked images of a trail rich in maple trees with stretches of prairie open to walkers and bicyclists. This practical letter inspired thousands of citizens to undertake the 20-year creation of the 55-mile Illinois Prairie Path, complete with hand-built bridges, prairie remnants, and wildlife-rich wetlands.

The idea spread slowly, with some of today's most well-used trails serving as cornerstones for the new movement. Wisconsin opened the Elroy Sparta Trail in 1967. Seattle cut the ribbon on the Burke-Gilman Trail in 1978. The first half of Virginia's Washington and Old Dominion Trail became available in 1981. In 1986, when the Rails-to-Trails Conservancy opened its doors and began helping communities see their dreams become reality, we knew of only 100 open rail-trails and another 90 projects in the works. Today, 1,000 trails in all 50 states serve the public, and nearly 1,200 additional projects are underway. When completed, these rail-trails will cover 38,000 miles, or almost 90 percent of the current 43,000 miles of interstate highway.

While the Rails-to-Trails Conservancy does not promote the curtailment of railroad service or the abandonment of tracks, we work to keep abandoned rights-of-way in public ownership as trails. Also, rail-trails provide a means of preserving our nation's valuable corridor system for possible future rail use.

The invaluable benefits of rail-trails speak for themselves. When the Little Miami Scenic Trail opened in southern Ohio, wheelchair-bound Sandy Stonerock traveled to a local department store on her own for the first time ever. An Iowa couple initially opposed a trail project that spanned the length of their farm but completely changed their outlook after the trail was built. They even opened a bed-and-breakfast for trail users. An abandoned corridor between Baltimore and Annapolis was notorious for its vandals and open-air drug market until the B&A Trail turned the route into the pride of the community and the most popular park in the county's system—not to mention a model rail-trail for the rest of the nation.

The success of our movement depends on thousands of volunteers and professionals across the United States. So whatever your time allows, get involved by joining the Rails-to-Trails Conservancy. Together we will make our dream of a coast-to-coast system of rail-trails a reality.

How to Use Rail-Trails

By design, rail-trails accommodate a variety of trail users. While this is generally one of the many benefits of rail-trails, it can also lead to occasional conflicts among trail users. Everyone should take responsibility to ensure trail safety and harmony by following a few simple trail etiquette guidelines.

One of the most basic rules of etiquette is, "Wheels yield to heels." Bicyclists (and in-line skaters) yield to other users; pedestrians yield to equestrians.

Generally, this means that you need to warn other users (to whom you are yielding) of your presence. If, as a bicyclist, you fail to warn a walker that you are about to pass, the walker could step in front of you, causing an accident that could have been prevented. Similarly, it is best to slow down and warn an equestrian of your presence. A horse can be startled by a bicycle, so make verbal contact with the rider and be sure it is safe to pass.

Here are some other guidelines you should follow to promote trail safety:

- Obey all trail use rules posted at trailheads.
- Stay to the right except when passing.
- Pass slower traffic on the left. Yield to oncoming traffic when passing.
- Give a clear warning signal when passing. For example, call out, "Passing on your left."
- Always look ahead and behind when passing.
- Travel at a reasonable speed.
- Keep pets on a leash.
- Do not trespass on private property.
- Move off the trail surface when stopped to allow others to pass.
- Yield to other trail users when entering and crossing the trail.
- Do not disturb any wildlife.

How to Use This Book

At the beginning of each state, you will find a map showing the general location of each rail-trail listed in that state. The description of every rail-trail begins with the following information:

Trail name: The official name of the rail-trail is stated here.

Endpoints: This heading lists the endpoints for the entire trail, usually identified by a municipality or a nearby geographical point.

Mileage: This heading lists the total trail mileage (including mileage that is not on former railroad right-of-way).

Surface: The materials that make up the surface of the rail-trail vary from trail to trail. This heading describes the surface or surfaces you will find, ranging from asphalt to crushed stone to the significantly more rugged original railroad ballast.

Location: The county or counties through which the trail passes are stated here.

Contact: The name, address, telephone number, and e-mail and Web site address (when available) are listed here. The selected contacts are generally responsible for managing the trail and can provide additional information about the trail and its condition.

Many trail managers have maps or other descriptive brochures available free or for a small fee. Managers can answer specific questions about their trails. If a trail is not yet fully developed, the manager can provide information about which sections are presently open and usable.

Legend: Every trail also has a series of icons depicting the activities allowed on the trail.

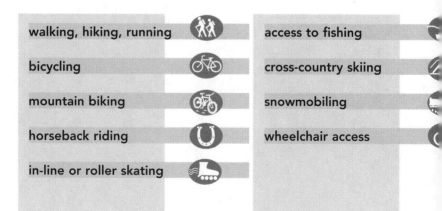

walking, hiking, running	access to fishing	
bicycling	cross-country skiing	
mountain biking	snowmobiling	
horseback riding	wheelchair access	
in-line or roller skating		

the

rail-trails

ALABAMA

1 Chief Ladiga Trail

Endpoints:
Maxwellborn to Calhoun/
Cleburne county line
Mileage: 22.1
Surface: asphalt, gravel

Location: Calhoun; Cleburne
Contact: Tommy Allison
Trail Manager
City of Piedmont
109 North Center Avenue
P.O. Box 112
Piedmont, AL 36272-2013
(256) 447–9007
www.calhounconews.com

2 Limestone Trails

Endpoints: Athens, Alabama
state line
Mileage: 10.8
Surface: crushed stone

Location: Limestone
Contact: Richard Martin
Coordinator for Rail-Trails
Limestone County Parks and
Recreation Board
Athens Road Runners
P.O. Box 945
310 West Washington Street
Athens, AL 35612-0945
(205) 230–9010

3 Marion Walking Trail

Endpoints: Marion
Mileage: 1
Surface: asphalt

Location: Perry
Contact: Carolyn Thomas
City Clerk, City of Marion
P.O. Box 959
Marion, AL 36756-0959
(334) 683–6545

4 Monte Sano Railway Trail

Endpoints: Monte Sano,
Huntsville
Mileage: 2
Surface: ballast

Location: Madison
Contact: Jill Gardner
Executive Director
Huntsville Land Trust
P.O. Box 43
Huntsville, AL 35804-0043
(205) 534–5263
www.landtrust-hsv.org
hsvland@landtrust-hsv.org

5 Robertsdale Trail

Endpoints: Robertsdale
Mileage: 2.1
Surface: concrete, asphalt

Location: Baldwin
Contact: Jackie Lipscomb
City of Robertsdale
P.O. Box 429
Robertsdale, AL 36567-0429
(334) 947–7354

ALASKA

1 Tony Knowles Coastal Bicycle Trail

Endpoints: Anchorage, Kinkaid park
Mileage: 11
Surface: asphalt

🚶 🐎 🚲 ♿

Location: Anchorage
Contact: Dave Gardner
Municipality of Anchorage
Department of Culture and Recreation
Parks and Beautification Division
P.O. Box 196650
Anchorage, AK 99519-6650
(907) 343–4474

ARIZONA

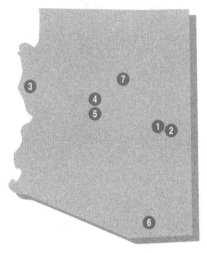

1 Apache Railroad Multi-Use Trail

Endpoints: Route 260, Big Lake
Mileage: 21
Surface: cinder, crushed stone

Location: Apache
Contact: Kathy Moore
U.S. Forest Service
Springerville Ranger District
P.O. Box 760
Springerville, AZ 85938-0760
(520) 333–4372

2 Indian Springs Trail

Endpoints: Apache Sitgreaves
National Forest, Springerville
Mileage: 7.5
Surface: ballast

Location: Apache
Contact: Barbara Romero
Recreation/Lands Assistant
U.S. Forest Service
Springerville Ranger District
P.O. Box 760
Springerville, AZ 85938-0760
(520) 333–4372
bromero/r3_apachesitgreaves@
fs.fed.us

3 Mohave and Milltown Railroad Trails

Endpoints: Oatman (near), Mohave Valley (near)
Mileage: 7
Surface: ballast

Other use: ATV
Location: Mohave
Contact: Bruce Asbjorn
Outdoor Recreation Planner
BLM, Kingman Field Office
2475 Beverly Avenue
Kingman, AZ 86401
(520) 692–4400
basbjorn@az.blm.gov

4 Peavine Trails

Endpoints: Peavine Park
Mileage: 5.7
Surface: ballast, cinder

Location: Yavapai
Contact: Ron Grittman
Director, Chino Valley Dept. of
Public Works
P.O. Box 406
Chino Valley, AZ 86323-0406
(520) 636–2646

5 Prescott Peavine Trail

Endpoints: Highway 89A, Prescott
Mileage: 5.5
Surface: crushed stone, dirt

Location: Yavapai
Contact: Eric Smith
Trails and Open Space
City of Prescott
Prescott, AZ 86302
(520) 445–5880
esmith@ci.prescott.az.us

6 Railroad Trail

Endpoints: Patagonia/Sonoita Creek Preserve
Mileage: 1
Surface: dirt

Location: Santa Cruz
Contact: Edward Wilk
Preserve Assistant
The Nature Conservancy
P.O. Box 815
Patagonia, AZ 85624-0815
(520) 394–2400

7 University Heights to Fort Tuthill Trail

Endpoints: Flagstaff
Mileage: 3
Surface: crushed stone

Location: Coconino
Contact: Paul Jones
City of Flagstaff
211 W. Aspen Avenue
Flagstaff, AZ 86001
(520) 779–7632

ARKANSAS

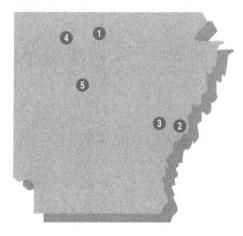

1 Big Spring Nature Trail

Endpoints: Cotter, White River
Mileage: 2.5
Surface: crushed stone, ballast

Location: Baxter
Contact: J.D. Pratt
Mayor, Town of Cotter
P.O. Box 9
Cotter, AR 72626
(870) 435–6325

2 Levee Walking Trail

Endpoints: Helena
Mileage: 4.7
Surface: asphalt

Location: Phillips
Contact: Sandi Ramsey
Mayor's Assistant, City of Helena
226 Perry Street
Helena, AR 72342-3338
(501) 338–9831

3 Marvell Bike Trail

Endpoints: Marvell
Mileage: 1.3
Surface: asphalt

Location: Phillips
Contact: Barbie Washburn
Administrative Assistant
City of Marvell
City Hall
P. O. Box 837
Marvell, AR 72366-0837
(501) 829–2573
Marvell@nnb.com

4 Old Railroad Trail

Endpoints: Gilbert (Buffalo National River)
Mileage: 1.7
Surface: ballast, grass, dirt

Location: Searcy
Contact: Lowell Butts
Chief of Maintenance
Buffalo National River
P.O. Box 1173
Harrison, AR 72602-1173
(870) 741–5444
Lowell_Butts@nps.gov

5 Ozark Highlands Trail

Endpoints: Ozark–St. Francis National Forest
Mileage: 155 (2.7 are Rail-Trail)
Surface: ballast

Location: Franklin; Johnson; Newton; Searcy; Crawford
Contact: Joe Wallace
Recreation Staff Officer
Ozark–St. Francis N.F.
Russellville, AR 72801
(501) 968–2354

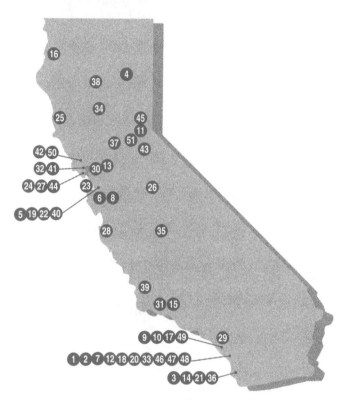

1 Alton to Bristol Bike Trail

Santa Ana, CA 92702-1988
(714) 571–4211

Endpoints: Santa Ana
Mileage: 1.8
Surface: asphalt

Location: Orange
Contact: Paul Johnson
Senior Parks Supervisor
City of Santa Ana Recreation &
Community Services Agency
P.O. Box 1988 M-23

2 Atchison, Topeka and Santa Fe Trail

Endpoints: Irvine
Mileage: 3
Surface: asphalt

Location: Orange

Contact: Katie Berg
Associate Transportation Analyst
City of Irvine Dept. of Public
Works
P.O. Box 19575
Irvine, CA 92623-9575
(949) 724–7347

3 Bayshore Bikeway

Endpoints: Coronado, Imperial
Beach
Mileage: 9
Surface: asphalt

Location: San Diego
Contact: Joel Rizzo
Bicycle Coordinator
City of San Diego
1010 Second Avenue, Suite 800
San Diego, CA 92101
(619) 533–3110
r8h@sddpc.sannet.gov

4 Bizz Johnson Trail

Endpoints: Susanville, Westwood
Mileage: 30
Surface: gravel, ballast

Location: Lassen
Contact: Stan Bales
Outdoor Recreation Planner
Bureau of Land Management
Eagle Lake Resource Area Office
2950 Riverside Drive
Susanville, CA 96130
(530) 257–0456
www.ca.blm.gov/eaglelake

5 Black Diamond Mines Regional Preserve RR Bed Trail

Endpoints: Black Diamond
Mines Regional Preserve
Mileage: 1
Surface: dirt

Location: Contra Costa
Contact: Steve Fiala
Trails Specialist
East Bay Regional Park District
2950 Peralta Oaks Court
P.O. Box 5381
Oakland, CA 94605-5381
(510) 635–0135

6 Bol Park Bike Path

Endpoints: Palo Alto
Mileage: 1.25
Surface: asphalt

Location: Santa Clara
Contact: Gayle Likens
Senior Planner
City of Palo Alto
Transportation Division
P.O. Box 10250
Palo Alto, CA 94303-0250
(650) 329–2520
gaylelikens@city.palo-alto.ca.us

7 Bud Turner Trail

Endpoints: Fullerton
Mileage: 3.8
Surface: wood chips, dirt

Location: Orange
Contact: Greg Meek
Engineering Department
303 West Commonwealth
Avenue
Fullerton, CA 92632-1710
(714) 738–6590

8 Creek Trail

Endpoints: San Jose
Mileage: 2.4
Surface: asphalt, dirt

Location: Santa Clara
Contact: Mike Will
Park Ranger
Alum Rock Park
16240 Alum Rock Avenue
San Jose, CA 95127-1307
(408) 259–5477

9 Culver City Median Bikeway

Endpoints: Culver City, Los
Angeles
Mileage: 1.4
Surface: asphalt

Location: Los Angeles
Contact: Pam Keyes
Deputy Public Works
Director/Engineer
Public Works Dept.
P.O. Box 507
Culver City, CA 90232-0507
(310) 253–6420

10 Duarte Bike Trail

Endpoints: Duarte
Mileage: 1.6
Surface: asphalt, dirt

Location: Los Angeles
Contact: Donna Georgino
Director
Duarte Parks & Recreation
1600 E. Huntington Drive
Duarte, CA 91010-2592
(626) 357–7931

11 El Dorado Trail

Endpoints: Camino, Placerville
Mileage: 2.5
Surface: asphalt

Location: El Dorado
Contact: Ron Mueller
Recreation and Parks Director
City of Placerville
549 Main Street
Placerville, CA 95667-5609
(916) 642–5232

12 Electric Avenue Median Park

Endpoints: Seal Beach
Mileage: 0.5
Surface: concrete, grass

Location: Orange
Contact: Barry Curtis
Planning Assistant
City of Seal Beach
211 Eighth Street
Seal Beach, CA 90740-6305
(562) 431–2527

13 Fairfield Linear Park

Endpoints: Fairfield
Mileage: 4
Surface: asphalt, concrete

Location: Solano
Contact: Sandra Reece-Martens
Assistant Comm. Services
Director
City of Fairfield
1000 Webster Street
Fairfield, CA 94533-4883
(707) 428–7420

14 Fay Avenue Bike Path

Endpoints: San Diego, La Jolla
Mileage: 0.8
Surface: asphalt

Location: San Diego
Contact: Joel Rizzo
Bicycle Coordinator
City of San Diego
1010 Second Avenue, Suite 800
San Diego, CA 92101-4101
(619) 533–3110
r8h@sddpc.sannet.gov

15 Fillmore Trail

Endpoints: Fillmore
Mileage: 2
Surface: asphalt

Location: Ventura
Contact: Bert Rapp
City Engineer
The City of Fillmore
250 Central Avenue
Fillmore, CA 93015-1907
(805) 524–3701

16 Hammond Trail

Endpoints: McKinleyville
Mileage: 3
Surface: asphalt, crushed stone

Location: Humboldt
Contact: Bob Walsh
Parks Supervisor
Humbolt County Department of
Public Works
1106 Second Street
Eureka, CA 95501-0531
(707) 445–7652

17 Hermosa Valley Greenbelt

Endpoints: Hermosa Beach,
Manhattan Beach
Mileage: 3.7
Surface: wood chips

Location: Los Angeles
Contact: Mike Flaherty
Public Works Superintendent
City of Hermosa Beach
1315 Valley Drive
Hermosa Beach, CA 90254-3884
(310) 318–0214

18 Hoover Street Trail

Endpoints: Westminster
Mileage: 2
Surface: asphalt

Location: Orange
Contact: Dennis Koenig
Engineering Technician
City Hall–Engineering
Department
8200 Westminster Blvd.
Westminster, CA 92683-3395
(714) 898–3311

19 Iron Horse Regional Trail

Endpoints: Concord (Monument
Blvd.), Dublin/Pleasanton
Mileage: 17
Surface: asphalt, concrete

Location: Alameda; Contra
Costa
Contact: Steve Fiala
Trails Specialist
East Bay Regional Park District
2950 Peralta Oaks Court
P.O. Box 5381
Oakland, CA 94605-5381
(510) 544–2611
www.ebparks.org

20 Juanita Cooke Greenbelt

Endpoints: Fullerton
Mileage: 3.5
Surface: wood chips, dirt

Location: Orange
Contact: Greg Meek
Engineering Department
303 West Commonwealth
Avenue
Fullerton, CA 92632-1710
(714) 738–6590

21 King Promenade Trail

Endpoints: San Diego, El
Camino Real, Vista
Mileage: 12
Surface: crushed stone, gravel,
dirt

Location: San Diego
Contact: Paul Fiske
Planning and Development
City of San Diego
202 C Street, M.S. 4A
San Diego, CA 92101-4806
(619) 533–7125

22 Lafayette/Moraga Regional Trail

Endpoints: Lafayette, Moraga
Mileage: 7.6
Surface: asphalt, concrete

Location: Contra Costa
Contact: Lane Powell
Publication Coordinator
East Bay Regional Park District
2950 Peralta Oaks Court
Oakland, CA 94605
(510) 635–0135

23 Lands End Trail

Endpoints: San Francisco
Mileage: 2
Surface: crushed stone

Location: San Francisco
Contact: Don Giovanetti
Golden Gate National Recreation
Area
Fort Mason Building 201
San Francisco, CA 94123
(415) 561–4511

24 Larkspur Path

Endpoints: Corte Madera,
Larkspur
Mileage: 1
Surface: asphalt

Location: Marin
Contact: Ben Berto
Associate Planner
Town of Corte Madera
300 Tamalpais Drive
Corte Madera, CA 94925-1417
(415) 927–5064

25 MacKerricher Haul Road Trail

Endpoints: Fort Bragg, Ten Mile
River
Mileage: 7
Surface: asphalt

Location: Mendocino
Contact: Greg Picard
Superintendent
California Department of
Parks and Recreation
P.O. Box 440
Mendocino, CA 95460
(707) 937–5804
gpica@parks.ca.gov
www.mcn.org/1/10milecoastal-
trail/

26 Merced River Trail

Endpoints: Briceburg
Mileage: 8
Surface: ballast, dirt

Location: Mariposa
Contact: Jeff Horn
Outdoor Recreation Planner
Department of Interior USDI
Bureau of Land Management
63 Natoma Street
Folsom, CA 95630
(916) 985–4474

27 Mill Valley–Sausalito Path

Endpoints: Mill Valley, Sausalito
Mileage: 3.5

Surface: asphalt

Location: Marin
Contact: Don Dimitratos
Director
Parks, Open Space & Cultural
Services Department
Marin County Civic Center
San Rafael, CA 94903
(415) 499–6387

28 Monterey Peninsula Recreational Trail

Endpoints: Pacific Grove,
Seaside
Mileage: 7
Surface: asphalt

Location: Monterey
Contact: Tim Jenson
Program Manager
Monterey Peninsula Regional
Park District
700 West Carmel Valley Road
Carmel Valley, CA 93924-9457
(831) 659–6068
jenson@mprpcl.org
www.mprpd.org

29 Mt. Lowe Railroad Trail

Endpoints: Angeles National
Forest, Echo Mountain to Mt.
Lowe Trail Camp
Mileage: 4
Surface: ballast, dirt

Location: Los Angeles
Contact: Donald Gilliland
Supervisor
Angeles National Forest
Arroyo-Seco District
4600 Oak Grove Drive
Flint Ridge, CA 91011-3757
(818) 790–1151

30 Ohlone Greenway

Endpoints: Berkeley, Richmond
Mileage: 3.8
Surface: asphalt

Location: Alameda; Contra
Costa
Contact: Beth Bartke
Management Assistant
City of El Cerrito
10890 San Pablo Avenue
El Cerrito, CA 94530-2321
(510) 215–4382
BBARTKE@ci.el-cerrito.ca.us

31 Ojai Valley Trail

Endpoints: Ojai, Ventura
Mileage: 9.5
Surface: asphalt, grass, wood
chips

Location: Ventura
Contact: Andrew Oshita
Parks Manager
GSA Parks
800 South Victoria
Ventura, CA 93009-0001
(805) 654–3945

32 Old Railroad Grade

Endpoints: Mill Valley, Mt. Tamalpais State Park
Mileage: 9
Surface: ballast, dirt

Location: Marin
Contact: Eric McGuire
Environmental Services Coordinator
Marin Municipal Water District
220 Nellen Avenue
Corte Madera, CA 94925-1105
(415) 924–4600

33 Pacific Electric Bicycle Trail

Endpoints: Santa Ana
Mileage: 2.1
Surface: asphalt

Location: Orange
Contact: Ron Ono
Design Manager
Recreation & Community Services Agency
P.O. Box 1988
Santa Ana, CA 92702-1988
(714) 571–4200

34 Paradise Memorial Trailway

Endpoints: Paradise
Mileage: 5.5
Surface: asphalt

Location: Butte
Contact: Al McGreehan
Community Development Director
Town of Paradise
5555 Skyway
Paradise, CA 95969
(916) 872–6291

35 Reedley Rail-Trail Community Parkway

Endpoints: Reedley
Mileage: 1
Surface: asphalt, crushed stone

Location: Fresno
Contact: Andrew Benelli
Public Works Director/City Engineer
City of Reedley
1733 Ninth Street
Reedley, CA 93654
andrew.benelli@reedley.com
www.reedley.com

36 Rose Canyon Bicycle Path

Endpoints: San Diego
Mileage: 1.3
Surface: asphalt

Location: San Diego
Contact: Joel Rizzo
Bicycle Coordinator
City of San Diego
1010 Second Avenue, Suite 800
San Diego, CA 92101-4101
(619) 533–3110
r8h@sddpc.sannet.gov

37 Sacramento Northern Bike Trail

Endpoints: Sacramento, Rio Linda
Mileage: 8
Surface: asphalt

Location: Sacramento
Contact: Gayle Totton
Landscape Architecture Section
Department of Public Works
1023 J Street, Room 200
Sacramento, CA 95814
(916) 264–5540

38 Sacramento River Trail

Endpoints: Redding
Mileage: 9.5
Surface: asphalt, concrete

Location: Shasta
Contact: Terry Hanson
Community Projects Manager
City of Redding Planning Department
760 Parkview Ave.
Redding, CA 96001-3318
(916) 225–4095
t.hanson@ciredding

39 Santa Maria Valley Railroad Multi-Purpose Trail

Endpoints: YMCA at Skyway Drive, Santa Maria Country Club
Mileage: 1.2

Surface: asphalt

Location: Santa Barbara
Contact: William H. Orndorff
Director of Commercial Development
City of Santa Maria
110 South Pine Street, Suite 101
Santa Maria, CA 93454
(805) 925–0951, x240
borndorff@ci.santa-maria.ca.us

40 Shepherd Canyon Trail

Endpoints: Oakland
Mileage: 3
Surface: asphalt

Location: Alameda
Contact: Martin Matarrese
Parkland Resource Supervisor
Oakland Parks and Recreation
3590 Sanborn Drive
Oakland, CA 94602
(510) 482–7857

41 Sir Francis Drake Bikeway (Cross Marin Bike Trail)

Endpoints: Samuel P. Taylor State Park, Lagunitas
Mileage: 6
Surface: asphalt, ballast

Location: Marin
Contact: Lanny Waggoner
State Park Ranger

Samuel P. Taylor State Park
P.O. Box 251
Lagunitas, CA 94938-0251
(415) 488–9897

42 Sonoma Bike Path

Endpoints: Sonoma
Mileage: 1.5
Surface: asphalt

Location: Sonoma
Contact: Sandra Cleisz
Assistant Planner
City of Sonoma
No. 1 The Plaza
Sonoma, CA 95476-9000
(707) 938–3794
sandra@sonomacity.org

43 Sugarpine Railway Trail (Westside Trail)

Endpoints: Twain Harte
Mileage: 16.5
Surface: gravel, dirt

Location: Tuolumne
Contact: Mike Cook
Recreation Technician
Mi-Wuk Ranger District
P.O. Box 100
Mi-Wuk Village, CA 95346-0100
(209) 586–3234

44 Tiburon Linear Park

Endpoints: Tiburon
Mileage: 3.7

Surface: asphalt

Location: Marin
Contact: Tony Iacopi
Director
Tiburon Public Works
Department
1155 Tiburon Boulevard
Tiburon, CA 94920-1550
(415) 435–7399

45 Truckee River Bike Trail

Endpoints: Tahoe City, Squaw
Valley
Mileage: 4
Surface: asphalt

Location: Placer
Contact: Cindy Gustafson
Director, Resource Development
Tahoe City P.U.D.
P.O. Box 33
Tahoe City, CA 96145-0033
(916) 538–3796
TCPUD@sierra.net

46 Tustin Branch Trail— Esplanade

Endpoints: Tustin
Mileage: 1
Surface: crushed stone

Location: Orange
Contact: Sherri Miller
Trails Planner
Harbors, Beaches and Parks

EMA/County of Orange
P.O. Box 4048
Santa Ana, CA 92702-4048
(714) 834–3137

47 Tustin Branch Trail– Newport Avenue

Endpoints: Tustin
Mileage: 1
Surface: asphalt

Location: Orange
Contact: Sherri Miller
Trails Planner
Harbors, Beaches and Parks
EMA/County of Orange
P.O. Box 4048
Santa Ana, CA 92702-4048
(714) 834–3137

48 Tustin Branch Trail– Wanda Road

Endpoints: Villa Park
Mileage: 0.5
Surface: asphalt

Location: Orange
Contact: James Konopka
Assoc. Environmental Planner
Caltrans
Lake Forest, CA 92630
(714) 724–2224

49 Watts Towers Crescent Greenway

Endpoints: Los Angeles
Mileage: 0.2
Surface: asphalt, crushed stone,
grass, wood chips

Location: Los Angeles
Contact: Dale Royal
Project Manager
Metropolitan Transportation
Authority
P.O. Box 194
Los Angeles, CA 90053-0194
(213) 244–6456

50 West County Trail (Joe Redota Trail)

Endpoints: Sebastopol, Santa
Rosa, and Granton
Mileage: 6.5
Surface: asphalt

Location: Sonoma
Contact: Mickey Karagan
Administrative Aide
Sonoma County Regional Parks
2300 County Center Drive
Suite 120-A
Santa Rosa, CA 95403-3013
(707) 527–2041
Trailnet88@aol.com
www.sonoma-county.org

51 Western States Pioneer Express Recreation Trail

Endpoints: Auburn, American
River
Mileage: 100 (2.0 are Rail-Trail)
Surface: gravel, dirt

Location: El Dorado; Placer
Contact: Greg Wells
Trails Coordinator
California Department of Parks
and Recreation
P.O. Box 3266
Auburn, CA 95604-3266
(916) 885–4527

COLORADO

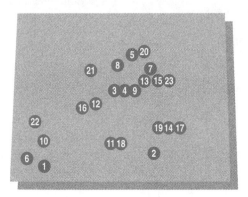

1 Animas River Trail

Endpoints: Durango
Mileage: 3
Surface: asphalt, gravel, concrete

Location: La Plata
Contact: Kathy Metz
Parks and Recreation Director
Durango Parks and Recreation Department
949 East Second Avenue
Durango, CO 81301
(970) 385–2959

2 Arkansas Riverwalk Trail

Endpoints: Canon City
Mileage: 3.5
Surface: crushed stone

Location: Fremont
Contact: Jeff Jackel
Executive Director
Canon City Metropolitan
Recreation and Park District
P.O. Box 947
Canon City, CO 81215
(719) 275–1578
canrec@ris.net

3 Blue River Bikeway

Endpoints: Breckenridge, Dillon Reservoir (Farmer's Corner)
Mileage: 6
Surface: asphalt

Location: Summit
Contact: Summit County

Chamber of Commerce
P.O. Box 215
Frisco, CO 80443
(800) 530–3099
info@summitchamber.org

4 Boreas Pass

Endpoints: Breckenridge, Como
Mileage: 21.7
Surface: crushed stone, gravel

Location: Summit Park
Contact: Scott Hobson
Open Space & Trails Manager
Summit County Community
Development Department
P.O. Box 68
Breckenridge, CO 80424-0068
(970) 547–0681

5 Corridor Trail

Endpoints: Lyons
Mileage: 0.8
Surface: crushed stone, ballast,
concrete

Location: Boulder
Contact: Kurt Carlson
Parks, Recreation & Cultural
Director
Town of Lyons
P.O. Box 49
Lyons, CO 80540-0049
(303) 823–6640

6 East Fork Trail

Endpoints: San Juan National
Forest
Mileage: 7.5
Surface: ballast

Location: Dolores
Contact: John Reidinger
Trails Specialist
San Juan National Forest
Dolores Ranger District
P.O. Box 210
Dolores, CO 81323-0210
(970) 882–7296

7 Fowler Trail

Endpoints: Eldorado Canyon
State Park
Mileage: 0.7
Surface: crushed stone

Location: Boulder
Contact: Tim Metzger
Park Manager
Eldorado Canyon State Park
Box B
Eldorado Springs, CO 80025-
0010
(303) 494–3943

8 Fraser River Trail

Endpoints: Fraser, Winter Park
Mileage: 6.3
Surface: asphalt

Location: Grand
Contact: Tom Russell
Director
Public Works Department
Town of Winter Park
Winter Park, CO 80482
(970) 726–8011

9 Frisco-Farmer's Corner Recreation Trail

Endpoints: Frisco, Dillon
Reservoir
Mileage: 2.5
Surface: asphalt

Location: Summit
Contact: Summit County
Chamber of Commerce
P.O. Box 215
Frisco, CO 80443
(800) 530–3099
info@summitchamber.org

10 Galloping Goose Trail

Endpoints: Telluride, Lizard
Head Pass
Mileage: 15
Surface: gravel, ballast

Location: San Miguel
Contact: Bill Dunkleberger
Recreation Specialist
U.S. Forest Service

Norwood Ranger District
P.O. Box 388
Norwood, CO 81423-0388
(970) 327–4261

11 Midland Bike Trail

Endpoints: Pike and San Isabel
National Forest, Buena Vista to
Trout Creek Pass
Mileage: 12
Surface: dirt

Location: Chaffee
Contact: Jeff Hyatt
Recreation Forester
Salida Ranger District
325 West Rainbow Blvd.
Salida, CO 81201-2233
(719) 539–3591

12 Mineral Belt Trail

Endpoints: Leadville
Mileage: 7
Surface: asphalt

Location: Lake
Contact: Director
Lake County Parks and
Recreation Board
901 South Highway 24
Leadville, CO 80461
(719) 486–4226

13 Narrow Gauge Trail

Endpoints: Pine Valley Ranch Park
Mileage: 2
Surface: crushed stone

Location: Jefferson
Contact: Mark Hearon
Trail Planner
Jefferson County Open Space
700 Jeffco County Parkway
Suite 100
Golden, CO 80401
(303) 271–5925

14 New Santa Fe Regional Trail

Endpoints: Palmer Lake, Colorado Springs
Mileage: 14
Surface: gravel

Location: El Paso
Contact: Susan Johnson
Supervisor of Planning
El Paso County Park Department
2002 Creek Crossing
Colorado Springs, CO 80906-1200
(719) 520–6375

15 Platte River Trail

Endpoints: Commerce City, Chatfield Reservoir
Mileage: 28.5

Surface: concrete, cinder

Location: Arapahoe; Adams
Contact: Chad Anderson
Trails Coordinator
Denver Parks and Recreation
945 South Huron
Denver, CO 80223-2805
(303) 698–4903

16 Roaring Fork Trail

Endpoints: Basalt, Woody Creek
Mileage: 12
Surface: asphalt, gravel

Other use: llamas, skateboards
Location: Garfield, Pitkin
Contact: John Kruger
Trails Supervisor
Aspen Parks Department
130 South Galena
Aspen, CO 81611-1902
(970) 920–5120

17 Rock Island Trail

Endpoints: Falcon, Payton
Mileage: 10
Surface: gravel, dirt, concrete

Location: El Paso
Contact: Susan Johnson
Supt. of Planning and Resource Mgmt.

El Paso County Parks
2002 Creek Crossing
Colorado Springs, CO 80118
(719) 520–6992
sue_johnson@co.el-paso.co.us

18 Salida Trail System

Endpoints: Salida
Mileage: 7
Surface: asphalt, concrete

Location: Chaffee
Contact: Donna & John Rhoads
Chairpersons
Salida Trail System
317 West Second
P.O. Box 417
Salida, CO 81201-1613
(719) 539–6738

19 Shooks Run Trail

Endpoints: Colorado Springs
Mileage: 1.8
Surface: asphalt

Location: El Paso
Contact: Fred Mais
Design and Development
Manager
City of Colorado Springs
Parks and Recreation
P.O. Box 1575, Mail Code 1200d
Colorado Springs, CO 80901-1575
(719) 385–6522

20 Switzerland Trail

Endpoints: Glacier Lake,
Sugarloaf Mountain
Mileage: 5.5
Surface: gravel, dirt

Location: Boulder
Contact: Brent Wheeler
Open Space Ranger
City of Boulder Open Space
66 South Cherryvale Road
Boulder, CO 80303-9717
(303) 441–4495

21 Ten Mile Canyon National Recreation Trail

Endpoints: Frisco, Vail
Mileage: 24
Surface: asphalt

Location: Summit; Eagle
Contact: Summit County
Chamber of Commerce
P.O. Box 215
Frisco, CO 80443
(800) 530–3099
info@summitchamber.org

22 Uncompahgre River Trail Bikepath—Montrose RiverWay

Endpoints: Montrose
Mileage: 4.5
Surface: concrete

Location: Montrose
Contact: Dennis Erickson
Parks Superintendent
City of Montrose
P.O. Box 790
Montrose, CO 81402-0790
(970) 240–1481

23 Union Pacific Trail

Endpoints: Thornton
Mileage: 0.5
Surface: asphalt, concrete

Location: Adams
Contact: Lynn Lathrop
Parks Supervisor
Thornton Parks & Recreation
Department
2211 Eppinger Boulevard
Thornton, CO 80229-7656
(303) 255–7875

CONNECTICUT

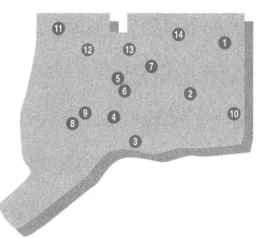

1 Airline North State Park Trail

Endpoints: Windham, Putnam
Mileage: 27
Surface: ballast, dirt

Location: Windham
Contact: John Folsom
Park Supervisor
Mashamoquet Brook State Park
147 Wolfden Drive
Pomfret Center, CT 06259
(860) 928–6121

2 Airline South State Park Trail

Endpoints: East Hampton, Windham
Mileage: 22.7

Surface: crushed stone, gravel, ballast

Location: Hartford; Middlesex; New London; Windham
Contact: William Mattioli
Trails Coordinator
Department of Environmental Protection
79 Elm Street
Hartford, CT 06106-1632
(860) 424–3202

3 Branford Trolley Trail

Endpoints: Pine Orchard, Stony Creek
Mileage: 1
Surface: crushed stone, gravel, concrete

Location: Branford
Contact: John Moss
Planning and Zoning Department
P.O. Box 150
Town Hall Drive
Branford, CT 06405-0150
(203) 488–1255

4 Farmington Canal Linear State Park Trail

Endpoints: Cheshire, Hamden
Mileage: 6
Surface: asphalt, gravel, grass

Location: New Haven
Contact: Vincent McDermott
Vice President
Landscape Architecture and
Planning
Milone & MacBroom, Inc.
716 South Main Street
Cheshire, CT 06410-3415
(203) 271–1773
www.viewzone.com/bikepath.
html

5 Farmington River Trail (Farmington River Fishing Access Area)

Endpoints: Farmington to
Collinsville, Collinsville to
Stratton Brook State Park
Mileage: 7
Surface: asphalt, crushed stone,
gravel

Location: Hartford
Contact: Daniel Dickinson
Park & Forest Supervisor
State of Connecticut
Department of Environmental
Protection
178 Scott Swamp Road
Farmington, CT 06032
(860) 677–1819

6 Farmington Valley Greenway

Endpoints: Farmington, Suffield
Mileage: 25
Surface: asphalt, gravel

Location: Hartford
Contact: Glenn Marston
Director Parks and Recreation
Town of Avon
60 West Main Street
Avon, CT 06001
(860) 409–4332

7 Hop River State Park Trail

Endpoints: Manchester,
Willimantic
Mileage: 20
Surface: ballast

Location: Hartford; Tolland
Contact: Joseph Hickey
Environmentalist
Department of Environmental
Protection
79 Elm Street
Hartford, CT 06106-1632
(860) 424–3202

8 Larkin Bridle Trail

Endpoints: Southbury, Naugatuck
Mileage: 10.7
Surface: gravel, ballast, cinder

Location: New Haven
Contact: Tim O'Donoghue
Supervisor
Southford Falls State Park
175 Quaker Farms Road
Southbury, CT 06488-2750
(203) 264–5169

9 Middlebury Greenway

Endpoints: Middlebury
Mileage: 6
Surface: asphalt, crushed stone, gravel

Location: New Haven
Contact: Edward St. John
Middlebury Public Works
Department
1212 Whittemore Road
P.O. Box 392
Middlebury, CT 06762

10 Moosup Valley State Park Trail

Endpoints: Moosup, Rhode Island border
Mileage: 8
Surface: ballast

Location: Windham
Contact: Scott Dawley
Park Supervisor
Pachaug State Forest
Headquarters
P.O. Box 5
Voluntown, CT 06384-0005
(860) 376–4075

11 Railroad Ramble

Endpoints: Salisbury, Lakeville
Mileage: 1
Surface: grass, dirt

Location: Litchfield
Contact: Mary Alice White
President
Salisbury Association
P.O. Box 553
24 Main Street
Salisbury, CT 06068-0553
(860) 435–0566

12 Stillwater Greenway (Winsted Riverfront Recapture)

Endpoints: Winchester, Torrington
Mileage: 5
Surface: gravel

Location: Litchfield
Contact: Art Matiella
Stillwater Greenway
40 Yale Avenue
Torrington, CT 06790
(860) 482–8792

13 Stratton Brook Trail

Endpoints: Simsbury, Stratton Brook State Park
Mileage: 3
Surface: asphalt, gravel, dirt

Location: Hartford
Contact: Gerard Toner
Director
Simsbury Dept. of Culture, Parks and Recreation
P.O. Box 495
Simsbury, CT 06070-0495
(860) 658–3255
Toner@simsbury.th.ccmail.
compuserve.com

14 Vernon Hop River Rail-Trail

Endpoints: Rockville, Vernon
Mileage: 5.7
Surface: crushed stone

Location: Tolland
Contact: Bruce Dinnie, Director
Vernon Parks and Recreation
120 South Street
Vernon, CT 06066-4404
(860) 872–6118

DELAWARE

1 Brandywine Park Trail

Endpoints: Wilmington, Brandywine Park
Mileage: 0.75
Surface: crushed stone

Location: New Castle
Contact: Kyle Gulbronson
Grants & Community Assistance
Delaware Division of
Parks & Recreation
89 Kings Highway
Dover, DE 19901
(302) 739–5285
k.gulbronson@state.de.us

2 Pomeroy Line Trail

Endpoints: Newark
Mileage: 2
Surface: crushed stone

Location: New Castle
Contact: Susan Moerschel
Division of Parks & Recreation
P.O. Box 1401
Dover, DE 19903-1401
(302) 739–5285
smoerschel@state.de.us

DISTRICT OF COLUMBIA

1 Capital Crescent Trail

Endpoints: Silver Spring, MD,
Washington, D.C.
Mileage: 12
Surface: asphalt, crushed stone

Location: Montgomery
Contact: William Gries
Montgomery County Department
of Parks
9500 Brunett Avenue
Silver Spring, MD 20901-3299
(301) 495–2535

FLORIDA

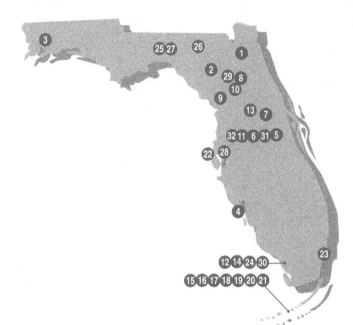

1 Baldwin to Jacksonville Trail

Endpoints: Baldwin, Jacksonville
Mileage: 14.5
Surface: asphalt

Location: Duval
Contact: Louie Jenkins Jr.
Department of Parks and
Recreation
851 North Market Street
Jacksonville, FL 32203
(904) 630–3596

2 Bell Trail

Endpoints: Bell
Mileage: 0.5
Surface: grass, dirt

Location: Gilchrist
Contact: Mark Gluckman
Consultant
Development Advisory Services,
Inc.
P.O. Box 160
Bell, FL 32619-0116
(352) 463–7185

3 Blackwater Heritage State Trail

Endpoints: Milton, Whiting
Mileage: 9
Surface: asphalt

Location: Santa Rosa
Contact: Robert Barlow
Park Manager
Blackwater River State Park
7720 Deaton Bridge Road
Holt, FL 32564-9005
(904) 983–5363
brsp_bob@erec.net
www.bikesplus.com/rails

4 Boca Grande Bike Path

Endpoints: Gasparilla Island
Mileage: 6.5
Surface: asphalt

Location: Lee
Contact: Andy Getch
Bicycle/Pedestrian Coordinator
Lee County Department of
Transportation
15 Monroe Street
Fort Myers, FL 33901-3643
(941) 479–8900
getchan@bocc.co.lee.fl.us

5 Cady Way Trail

Endpoints: Winter Park, Orlando
Mileage: 3.6
Surface: asphalt

Location: Orange
Contact: Dan Gallagher
Chief Planner
City of Orlando
400 South Orange Avenue
Orlando, FL 32801-3317
(407) 246–3395
dgallagh@ci.orlando.fl.us
www.ci.orlando.fl.us/
departments/planning_and_
development/rtc.html

6 Clermont Trail

Endpoints: Clermont
Mileage: 1.14
Surface: asphalt, concrete

Location: Lake
Contact: Clermont City Hall
P.O. Box 120-219
Clermont, FL 34712-0219
(407) 394–4081

7 Cross Seminole Trail

Endpoints: Oviedo
Mileage: 3.7
Surface: asphalt

Location: Seminole
Contact: Ginger Hoke
Senior Greenways & Trails Plan
Seminole County Government
Comp. Planning
1101 East First Street
Sanford, FL 32771-1468

(407) 665–7395
ghoke@co.seminole.fl.us

8 Depot Avenue Rail-Trail

Endpoints: Gainesville
Mileage: 2
Surface: asphalt

Location: Alachua
Contact: Linda Dixon
Transportation Planning Analyst
City of Gainesville
Public Works Department
P.O. Box 490, MS 58
Gainsville, FL 32602-0490
(352) 334–5074
dixonlb@ci.gainesville.fl.us

9 Dixie-Levy-Gilchrest Greenway (Nature Coast Greenway)

Endpoints: Chiefland, Trenton
Mileage: 4
Surface: asphalt

Location: Dixie, Gilchrest, Levy
Contact: Manatee Springs State
Park
11650 NW 115th Street
Chiefland, FL 32626
(352) 493–6738

10 Gainesville-Hawthorne State Trail

Endpoints: Hawthorne,
Gainesville

Mileage: 17
Surface: asphalt

Location: Alachua
Contact: Tim Vitzenty
Park Ranger
Florida DEP
Route 2, Box 41
Micanopy, FL 32667
(904) 466–3397
geotim1@aol.com

11 General James A. Van Fleet State Trail

Endpoints: Mabel, Polk City
Mileage: 29.2
Surface: asphalt, ballast, grass,
dirt

Location: Lake; Polk; Sumter
Contact: Robert Seifer
Trail Manager
Division of Parks & Recreation
12549 State Park Drive
Clermont, FL 34711-8667
(352) 394–2280
wstvft@juno.com

12 Jones Grade Trail

Endpoints: Fakahatchee Strand
State Preserve
Mileage: 6
Surface: grass

Location: Collier
Contact: Mike Hart
Park Ranger
Fakahatchee Strand State
Preserve
P.O. Box 548
Copeland, FL 33926-0548
(941) 695–4593

13 Lake Minneola Scenic Trail

Endpoints: Minneola, Clermont
Mileage: 4
Surface: asphalt

Location: Lake
Contact: Noradell-Mae Hess
City Clerk
P.O. Box 678
Minneola, FL 34755-0678
(352) 394–3598

14 Mud Tram Trail

Endpoints: Fakahatchee Strand
State Preserve
Mileage: 1
Surface: grass

Location: Collier
Contact: Mike Hart
Park Ranger
Fakahatchee Strand State
Preserve
P.O. Box 548
Copeland, FL 33926-0548
(941) 695–4593

15 Overseas Heritage Trail— Channel 5 Fishing Bridge/ Pedestrian Path

Endpoints: Fiesta Key, Craig Key
Mileage: 1
Surface: asphalt

Location: Monroe
Contact: Silvia Vargas
Parks and Recreation Planner
Monroe County Planning
Department
2798 Overseas Highway
Suite 410
Marathon, FL 33050-4277
(305) 289–2500

16 Overseas Heritage Trail— Cudjoe Key Pedestrian Path

Endpoints: Cudjoe Key
Mileage: 2
Surface: asphalt, dirt

Location: Monroe
Contact: Silvia Vargas
Parks and Recreation Planner
Monroe County Planning
Department
2798 Overseas Highway
Suite 410
Marathon, FL 33050-4277
(305) 289–2500

17 Overseas Heritage Trail— Long Key to Conch Key

Endpoints: Long Key, Conch Key
Mileage: 2.3
Surface: asphalt

Location: Monroe
Contact: Silvia Vargas
Parks and Recreation Planner
Monroe County Planning
Department
2798 Overseas Highway
Suite 410
Marathon, FL 33050-4277
(305) 289–2500

18 Overseas Heritage Trail– Lower Matecumbe Boardwalk

Endpoints: Lower Matecumbe
Key
Mileage: 4.4
Surface: asphalt

Location: Monroe
Contact: Silvia Vargas
Parks and Recreation Planner
Monroe County Planning
Department
2798 Overseas Highway
Suite 410
Marathon, FL 33050-4277
(305) 289–2500

19 Overseas Heritage Trail– Marathon Key to Pigeon Key Bridge

Endpoints: Marathon Key,
Pigeon Key
Mileage: 2.3
Surface: asphalt

Location: Monroe

Contact: Silvia Vargas
Parks and Recreation Planner
Monroe County Planning
Department
2798 Overseas Highway
Suite 410
Marathon, FL 33050-4277
(305) 289–2500

20 Overseas Heritage Trail– Missouri Key to Ohio Key

Endpoints: Missouri Key, Ohio
Key
Mileage: 0.5
Surface: asphalt

Location: Monroe
Contact: Silvia Vargas
Parks and Recreation Planner
Monroe County Planning
Department
2798 Overseas Highway
Suite 410
Marathon, FL 33050-4277
(305) 289–2500

21 Overseas Heritage Trail– Tom's Harbor Walkway

Endpoints: Grass Key, Walker's
Island
Mileage: 5
Surface: asphalt, dirt

Location: Monroe
Contact: Silvia Vargas
Parks and Recreation Planner
Monroe County Planning
Department
2798 Overseas Highway
Suite 410
Marathon, FL 33050-4277
(305) 289–2500

22 Pinellas Trail

Endpoints: St. Petersburg, Tarpon Springs
Mileage: 47
Surface: asphalt

Location: Pinellas
Contact: Brian Smith
Bicycle Pedestrian Planner
Pinellas County Planning
Department
14 South Ft. Harrison Avenue
Clearwater, FL 33756
(813) 464–4751
bsmith@co.pinellas.fl.us
www.co.pinellas.fl.us/mpo

23 South Dade Trail

Endpoints: Miami-Dade, Florida City
Mileage: 19.6
Surface: asphalt

Location: Dade
Contact: Jeffrey Hunter
Bicycle/Pedestrian Coordinator
Miami Dade County MPO
111 NW First Street, Suite 910
Miami, FL 33128-1999
(305) 375–1647
jhunter@co.miami-dade.fl.us

24 South Main Trail

Endpoints: Fakahatchee Strand State Preserve
Mileage: 3
Surface: crushed stone, grass

Location: Collier
Contact: Greg Toppin
Fakahatchee Strand State
Preserve
P.O. Box 548
Copeland, FL 34137
(941) 694–4593
fssp@mindspring.com
www.floridastatepark

25 Stadium Drive Bikepath

Endpoints: Tallahassee
Mileage: 1.5
Surface: asphalt

Location: Leon
Contact: Gregory Wilson
Bike/Ped Coordinator
Tallahassee Traffic Engineering
Division
City Hall
300 S. Adams Street
Tallahassee, FL 32301-1731
(904) 891–8090
wilsonG@ch.ci.tlh.fl.us

26 Suwannee River Greenway

Endpoints: Branford, Ichetucknee River
Mileage: 15
Surface: asphalt

Location: Columbia, Suwannee
Contact: Eddy Hillhouse
President
Suwannee County Chamber of
Commerce

P.O. Drawer C
Live Oak, FL 32060
(904) 362–3071

27 Tallahassee–St. Marks Historic Railroad State Trail

Endpoints: Tallahassee, St. Marks
Mileage: 18.5
Surface: asphalt

Location: Wakulla; Leon
Contact: Wes Smith
Park Manager
Division of Parks & Recreation
Florida DNR, Environmental
Protection Department
1022 Desoto Park Drive
Tallahassee, FL 32301-4555
(904) 922–6007
www.dep.state.fl.us:80/parks/big-
bend/stmarks.html

28 Upper Tampa Bay Trail

Endpoints: Citrus Park
Mileage: 3
Surface: asphalt

Location: Hillsborough
Contact: Tina Russo
Trail Manager
Hillsborough County Parks and
Recreation Department
7508 Ehrlich Road
Tampa, FL 33625
(813) 264–8511

29 Waldo Road Trail

Endpoints: Gainesville
Mileage: 3
Surface: asphalt

Location: Alachua
Contact: Linda Dixon
Transportation Planning Analyst
City of Gainesville Department of
Public Works
P.O. Box 490, MS 58
Gainesville, FL 32602-0490
(352) 334–5074
dixonlb@ci.gainsville.fl.us

30 West Main Trail

Endpoints: Fakahatchee Strand
State Preserve
Mileage: 3
Surface: grass

Location: Collier
Contact: Mike Hart
Park Ranger
Fakahatchee Strand State
Preserve
P.O. Box 548
Copeland, FL 33926-0548
(941) 695–4593

31 West Orange Trail

Endpoints: Apopka,
Orange/Lake county line
Mileage: 20
Surface: asphalt, concrete, dirt,
wood chips

Location: Orange
Contact: Tim Bucher
Orange County Parks and
Recreation
501 Crown Point Crossroad
Winter Garden, FL 34787
(407) 654–1108

32 Withlacoochee State Trail

Endpoints: Citrus Springs, Trilby
Mileage: 46
Surface: asphalt

Location: Citrus; Hernando;
Pasco
Contact: Robert Seifer
Trail Manager
Florida Division of
Recreation & Parks
Division of Parks & Recreation
12549 State Park Drive
Clermont, FL 34711-8667
(352) 394–2280

GEORGIA

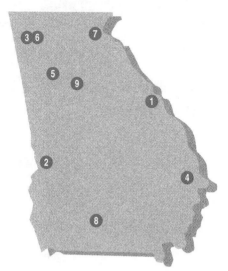

1 Augusta Canal Trail

Endpoints: Headgates, Turning
Basin
Mileage: 7
Surface: dirt

Location: Richmond
Contact: Thomas Robertson
Augusta Canal Authority
P.O. Drawer 2367
Augusta, GA 30903
(706) 722–1071

2 Chattahoochee Trail

Endpoints: Columbus, Ft.
Benning
Mileage: 1
Surface: asphalt

Location: Muscogee
Contact: Richard Bishop
Director
Columbus Parks and Recreation
Department
P.O. Box 1340
Columbus, GA 31902-1340
(706) 653–4175

3 Heritage Park Trail

Endpoints: Rome
Mileage: 6
Surface: asphalt, grass

Other use: skateboarding
Location: Floyd

Contact: Tim Banks
Assistant Director
Rome-Floyd Parks & Recreation
Authority
300 West Third Street
Rome, GA 30165-2803
(706) 291–0766
rfprp@rfpa.com

4 McQueens's Island Historic Trail (Old Savannah–Tybee Rail-Trail)

Endpoints: Savannah,
McQueen's Island
Mileage: 6.5
Surface: asphalt

Location: Chatham
Contact: Jim Golden
Director
Chatham County Parks,
Recreation and Cultural Affairs
P.O. Box 1746
Savannah, GA 31402-1746
(912) 652–6785

5 Silver Comet Trail

Endpoints: Smyrna, Rockmart
Mileage: 37
Surface: asphalt, concrete

Location: Cobb, Paulding, Polk
Contact: Ed McBrayer
Executive Director

PATH Foundation
P.O. Box 19327
Atlanta, GA 30324
(404) 875–7284
pathf@ix.netcom.com
www.pathfoundation.org

6 Simms Mountain Trail (Pinhoti Trail)

Endpoints: Lavender, Armuchee
Mileage: 4.5
Surface: cinder

Location: Chattooga; Floyd
Contact: Tim Banks
Assistant Director
Rome-Floyd Parks & Recreation
Authority
300 West Third Street
Rome, GA 30165-2803
(706) 291–0766
TBank@fc.peachnet. edu

7 Tallulah Falls Rail-Trail — Short Line Trail

Endpoints: Tallulah Gorge State
Park
Mileage: 3
Surface: Asphalt

Location: Habersham, Rabun
Contact: Tallulah Gorge State
Park
P.O. Box 248
Tallulah Falls, GA 30573
(706) 754–7970

8 Tom 'Babe' White Linear Park

Endpoints: Lower Meigs Road,
Municipal Airport (Moultrie)
Mileage: 5
Surface: asphalt, gravel, wood
chips

Location: Colquitt
Contact: Rick Gehle
Director
Moultrie-Colquitt Co. Parks and
Recreation
P.O. Box 3368
Moultrie, GA 31776
(912) 890–5428

9 Trolley Trail

Endpoints: Atlanta, Decatur
Mileage: 12
Surface: asphalt, concrete

Location: Dekalb; Fulton
Contact: Alycen Whidden
Assistant
Atlanta City Hall Bureau of
Planning
68 Mitchell Street, SW
Suite 3350
Atlanta, GA 30335
(404) 330–6145

1 Kapa'a Bike Path

Endpoints: Kauai
Mileage: 2
Surface: asphalt

Location: Kauai
Contact: Mel Nishihara
Kauai County Parks and
Recreation
4444 Rice Street, Suite 150
Lihue, HI 96766
(808) 241–6670

2 Pearl Harbor Bike Path

Endpoints: Ewa, Pearl Harbor
Mileage: 10
Surface: asphalt

Location: Honolulu
Contact: Michael Medeiros
Bike/Ped Coordinator
Department of Transportation
HWY-T
601 Kamokila Boulevard,
Room 602
Kapolei, HI 96707
(808) 692–7675

IDAHO

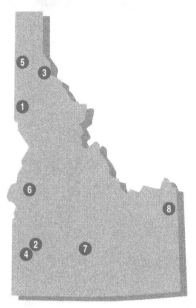

1 Bill Chapman Palouse Trail

Endpoints: Pullman, WA, Moscow, ID
Mileage: 7.5
Surface: asphalt

Location: Whitman, Latah
Contact: Roger Marcus
Whitman County Parks
310 North Main Street
Colfax, WA 99111
(509) 397–6238
ranger@co.whitman.wa.us

2 Greenbelt Trail

Endpoints: Lucky Peak Reservoir, Boise
Mileage: 12
Surface: asphalt

Location: Ada
Contact: Donna Griffin
Parks & Waterways Director
Ada County Parks & Waterways
4049 South Eckert Road
Boise, ID 83706-5721
(208) 343–1328

3 Mullan Pass–Lookout Pass Loop (Route of the Hiawatha)

Endpoints: Lookout Pass, Mullan
Mileage: 13
Surface: ballast

Other use: ATV
Location: Shoshone
Contact: Jaime Schmidt
Idaho Panhandle National Forest
Avery Ranger Station
HC Box 1
Avery, ID 83802
(208) 245–4517

4 Nampa to Stoddard Trail

Endpoints: Nampa, Stoddard
Mileage: 1.5
Surface: asphalt, gravel, sand

Location: Ada; Canyon
Contact: Alan Caba
Parks and Recreation Director
411 Third Street South
Nampa, ID 83651-3721
(208) 465–2220

5 North Idaho Centennial Trail

Endpoints: Coeur d'Alene, Idaho
state line
Mileage: 18
Surface: asphalt

Location: Kootenai
Contact: Sheryl Ward
Administrative Supervisor
Kootenai County Commissioner
P.O. Box 9000
Coeur d'Alene, ID 83816-9000
(208) 769–4450
kcbbcc@kootenai.co.id.us

6 Weiser River Trail

Endpoints: Cambridge
Mileage: 7
Surface: gravel, ballast

Location: Adams; Washington
Contact: Dick Pugh
Friends of the Weiser River Trail
2165 Seid Creek Road
Cambridge, ID 83610-5019
pugh@cyberhighway.com

7 Wood River Trails

Endpoints: Ketchum, Bellevue
Mileage: 22
Surface: asphalt

Location: Blaine
Contact: Mary Austin Crofts
Director
Blaine County Recreation District

P.O. Box 297
Hailey, ID 83333-0297
(208) 788–2117

8 Yellowstone Branch Line Trail

Endpoints: Warm River, Montana
State Line
Mileage: 34
Surface: ballast

Location: Fremont
Contact: Bart Andreasen
Landscape Architect
420 North Bridge Street
P.O. Box 208
St. Anthony, ID 83445-1425
(208) 624–3151

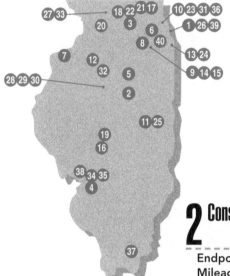

2 Constitution Trail

Endpoints: Bloomington, Normal
Mileage: 13.5
Surface: asphalt

Location: McLean
Contact: Keith Rich
Director
Bloomington Parks and
Recreation Department
109 East Olive Street
Bloomington, IL 61701-5219
(309) 823–4260

1 Burnham Greenway

Endpoints: 106th Street, William
Powers Conservation Area;
142nd Street, Little Calumet River
Mileage: 4
Surface: asphalt

Location: Cook
Contact: Calumet-Memorial Park
District
P.O. Box 1158
626 Wentworth Avenue
Calumet City, IL 60409
(708) 868–2530

3 Dekalb Nature Trail

Endpoints: Dekalb
Mileage: 1.3

Location: Dekalb
Contact: Terry Hannan
Superintendent
Dekalb County Forest Preserve
110 East Sycamore Street
Sycamore, IL 60178-1448
(815) 895–7191

4 Delyte Morris Trail

Endpoints: Edwardsville, Madison
Mileage: 2.6
Surface: asphalt, crushed stone, dirt, cinder

Location: Madison
Contact: Anna Schonlau
Southern Illinois University at Edwardsville
Recreation Department
P.O. Box 1157
Edwardsville, IL 62026
(618) 650–3235
aschonl@siue.edu

5 El Paso Walking Trail

Endpoints: El Paso
Mileage: 5
Surface: crushed stone

Location: Woodford
Contact: Ted Gresham
City Administrator
Town of El Paso

475 West Front Street
El Paso, IL 61738-1422
(309) 527–4005
dfever@elpaso.net

6 Fox River Trail

Endpoints: Aurora, Crystal Lake
Mileage: 35
Surface: asphalt

Location: Kane; McHenry
Contact: William Donnell
Landscape Architect
Fox Valley Park District
712 S. River Street
Aurora, IL 60506-5911
(708) 897–0516

7 Great River Trail

Endpoints: Rock Island, Savanna
Mileage: 28
Surface: asphalt, crushed stone

Location: Rock Island; Whiteside; Carroll
Contact: Patrick Marsh
Bikeway Coordinator
Bi-State Regional Commission
1504 Third Avenue
Rock Island, IL 61201-8646
(309) 793–6300

8 Great Western Trail

Endpoints: St. Charles, Sycamore
Mileage: 17
Surface: asphalt, crushed stone

Location: Kane; DeKalb
Contact: Jon Duerr
Director of Field Services
Kane County Forest Preserve
719 Batavia Avenue
Geneva, IL 60134-3077
(708) 232–5981

9 Great Western Trail (Dupage Parkway Section)

Endpoints: Villa Park, West Chicago
Mileage: 12
Surface: crushed stone

Location: DuPage
Contact: Ruth Krupensky
Principal Planner
DuPage County DOT
130 North County Farm Road
Wheaton, IL 60187-3957
(603) 682–7318

10 Green Bay Trail

Endpoints: Highland Park, Wilmette
Mileage: 9.5
Surface: asphalt, crushed stone

Location: Lake; Cook
Contact: Bill Lambrecht
Superintendent of Parks/Planning
Wilmette Park District
3555 Lake Avenue
Wilmette, IL 60091-1016
(847) 256–6100
blambrecht@wilpark.org

11 Heartland Pathways

Endpoints: Seymour, Clinton and Cisco
Mileage: 33
Surface: ballast

Other use: ATV
Location: Champaign; De Witt; Piatt
Contact: David Monk
President
Heartland Pathways
115 North Market Street
Champaign, IL 61820-4004
(217) 351–1911

12 Hennepin Canal Parkway

Endpoints: Atkinson, Rock Falls
Mileage: 96
Surface: grass

Location: Bureau; Henry; Lee; Whiteside
Contact: Steve Moser
Site SuperintendentIllinois
Department of Natural Resources
Hennepin Canal Parkway

RR 2, Box 201
Sheffield, IL 61361-9571
(815) 454–2328

13 Illinois & Michigan Canal NHC

Endpoints: Joliet, La Salle
Mileage: 68.5
Surface: asphalt, gravel

Location: DuPage; Grundy; La Salle; Will
Contact: Vincent Michael
Associate Director
Canal Corridor Association
220 South State Street
Suite 1880
Chicago, IL 60604-2001
(312) 427–3688

14 Illinois Prairie Path

Endpoints: Maywood to Wheaton, spurs to Aurora, Batavia, Elgin and Geneva
Mileage: 55
Surface: crushed stone, dirt

Location: Cook; DuPage; Kane
Contact: Ruth Krupensky
Principal Planner
DuPage County DOT
130 N. County Farm Road
Wheaton, IL 60187-3997
(630) 682–7318
www.mcs.net/~msc/IPP/

15 Illinois Prairie Path— Geneva Branch

Endpoints: Geneva, West Chicago
Mileage: 9
Surface: crushed stone

Location: DuPage; Kane
Contact: Ruth Krupensky
Principal Planner
130 North County Farm Road
Wheaton, IL 60187-3997
(630) 682–7318
www.mcs.net/~msc/IPP/

16 Interurban Trail

Endpoints: Chatham, Springfield
Mileage: 3
Surface: asphalt

Location: Sangamon
Contact: City of Springfield
300 South 7th Street
Springfield, IL 62701
(217) 789–2000

17 Libertyville Trail

Endpoints: Libertyville
Mileage: 3
Surface: crushed stone

Location: Lake

Contact: Steve Magnusen
Director of Public Works
Town of Libertyville
200 East Cook Avenue
Libertyville, IL 60048-2090
(708) 362–2430

18 Long Prairie Trail

Endpoints: Winnebago county line, McHenry county line
Mileage: 14.6
Surface: asphalt

Location: Boone
Contact: John Kremer
Executive Director
Boone County Conservation District
7600 Appleton Road
Belvidere, IL 61008-3076
(815) 547–7935

19 Lost Bridge Trail

Endpoints: Rochester, Springfield
Mileage: 5
Surface: asphalt

Location: Sangamon
Contact: Linda Shaw
Village Manager
Village of Rochester
P.O. Box 618
Rochester, IL 62563
(217) 498–7192
lindas@rpls.lib.il.us

20 Lowell Parkway Bicycle Path

Endpoints: Dixon, Lowell Park
Mileage: 3.5
Surface: asphalt, wood chips

Location: Lee
Contact: Dave Zinnen
Director of Administration and Recreation
Dixon Park District
804 Palmyra Avenue
Dixon, IL 61021-1960
(815) 284–3306

21 McHenry County Prairie Trail

Endpoints: Kane county line, Wisconsin state line
Mileage: 25
Surface: asphalt, ballast

Location: McHenry
Contact: Steve Gulgrer
Planning Manager
McHenry County Conservation District
6512 Harts Road
Ringwood, IL 60072-9641
(815) 678–4361

22 McHenry County Prairie Trail–North

Endpoints: Ringwood, Wisconsin state line
Mileage: 7.5

Surface: gravel, ballast

Location: McHenry
Contact: Mary Eysenbach
Assistant Director
McHenry County Conservation
District
6512 Harts Road
Ringwood, IL 60072-9641
(815) 678–4431

23 North Shore Bike Path

Endpoints: Lake Bluff, Mundelein
Mileage: 8
Surface: asphalt, crushed stone

Location: Lake
Contact: Bruce Christensen
Transportation Coordinator
Lake County Division of
Transportation
600 West Winchester Road
Libertyville, IL 60048-1381
(847) 362–3950
bchristensen@co.lake.il.us

24 Old Plank Road Trail

Endpoints: Park Forest, Joliet
Mileage: 23
Surface: asphalt

Location: Cook, Will
Contact: Forest Preserve District
of Will County
P.O. Box 1069

Joliet, IL 60434
(815) 727–8700

25 O'Malley's Alley

Endpoints: Champaign
Mileage: 0.5
Surface: concrete

Location: Champaign
Contact: James Spencer
Director of Operations
Champaign Park District
706 Kenwood Drive
Champaign, IL 61821-4112
(217) 398–2550

26 Palatine Trail

Endpoints: Palatine
Mileage: 28
Surface: asphalt

Location: Cook
Contact: Cheryl Scensny
Landscape Architect
Palatine Park District
250 E. Wood Street
Palatine, IL 60067-5332
(847) 705–5140

27 Pecatonica Prairie Path

Endpoints: Freeport, Rockford
Mileage: 20
Surface: ballast

Location: Stephenson;
Winnebago
Contact: Rick Strader
Manager of Planning &
Development
Rockford Park District
1401 North Second Street
Rockford, IL 61107-3086
(815) 987–8865

28 Pimiteoui—Rock Island Trail

Endpoints: Peoria, Alta
Mileage: 7.5
Surface: asphalt, crushed stone

Location: Peoria
Contact: Peoria Park District
2218 N. Prospect Road
Peoria, IL 61603-2126
(309) 682–1200

29 Pioneer Parkway (Rock Island Trail Extension)

Endpoints: Peoria, Alta
Mileage: 2.5
Surface: crushed stone

Location: Peoria
Contact: Peoria Park District
2218 N. Prospect Road
Peoria, IL 61603-2126
(309) 682–1200

30 River Trail of Illinois

Endpoints: East Peoria, Morton
Mileage: 7
Surface: asphalt

Location: Tazewell
Contact: James Coutts
Director
Fon Du Lac Park District
201 Veterans Drive
East Peoria, IL 61611-2798
(309) 699–3923
www.fondulacpark.com

31 Robert McClory Bike Path

Endpoints: Winthrop Harbor,
Lake Bluff
Mileage: 11
Surface: asphalt, crushed stone

Location: Lake
Contact: Bruce Christensen
Transportation Coordinator
Lake County Division of
Transportation
600 West Winchester Road
Libertyville, IL 60048-1381
(847) 362–3950
bchristensen@co.lake.il.us

32 Rock Island Trail State Park

Endpoints: Alta Toulon
Mileage: 28.3
Surface: crushed stone

Location: Peoria; Stark
Contact: Melinda Kitchens
Site Superintendent
Illinois Department of Natural
Resources
P.O. Box 64
Wyoming, IL 61491
(309) 695–2225

33 Rock River Recreation Path

Endpoints: Rockford, Love's Park
Mileage: 8.5
Surface: asphalt

Location: Winnebago
Contact: Rick Strader
Planning & Development
Manager
Rockford Park District
1401 North Second Street
Rockford, IL 61107-3086
(815) 987–8865
rpdmail@inwave.com

34 Ronald J. Foster Heritage Trail

Endpoints: Glen Carbon
Mileage: 3.2
Surface: asphalt, gravel

Location: Madison
Contact: Bill Kleffman
Village Treasurer
Village of Glen Carbon
151 North Main Street

R151 North Main
Glen Carbon, IL 62034-0757
(618) 288–1200
(314) 606–3167 (cell phone)
www.glen-carbon.il.us

35 Sam Vadalabene Great River Road Bike Trail

Endpoints: Alton, Pere
Marquette State Park
Mileage: 21
Surface: asphalt

Location: Jersey; Madison
Contact: James Easterly
District Engineer
Illinois Department of
Transportation
1100 Eastport Plaza Drive
P.O. Box 988
Collinsville, IL 62234-6198
(618) 346–3100

36 Skokie Valley Bike Path

Endpoints: Lake Forest,
Highland Park
Mileage: 5
Surface: asphalt, crushed stone

Location: Lake
Contact: Bruce Christensen
Transportation Coordinator
Lake County Division of
Transportation
600 West Winchester Road
Libertyville, IL 60048-1381
(847) 362–3950
bchristensen@co.lake.il.us

37 Tunnel Hill State Trail

Endpoints: Harrisburg
Mileage: 2.3
Surface: asphalt

Location: Saline
Contact: Kimberly Watson
Excecutive Director
Southeastern Regional Planning
and Development Commission
P.O. Box 606
Harrisburg, IL 62946-0606
(618) 252–7463

38 Vadalabene Nature Trail (Madison County Nature Trail)

Endpoints: Edwardsville,
Pontoon Beach
Mileage: 7.9
Surface: asphalt, ballast

Location: Madison
Contact: George Arnold
Madison County Trail Volunteers
1306 St. Louis Street
Edwardsville, IL 62025-1310
(618) 656–3994

39 Village Bike Path

Endpoints: Dundee Road,
Northbrook
Mileage: 1.1
Surface: asphalt

Location: Cook
Contact: Carl Peter
Village Engineer
Village of Northbrook
1225 Cedar Lane
Northbrook, IL 60062
(847) 272–5055

40 Virgil Gilman Nature Trail

Endpoints: Blisswoods Forest
Preserve, Montgomery
Mileage: 14
Surface: asphalt, crushed stone

Location: Kane; Kendall
Contact: William Donnell
Landscape Architect
Fox Valley Park District
712 South River Street
Aurora, IL 60506-5911
(708) 897–0516

INDIANA

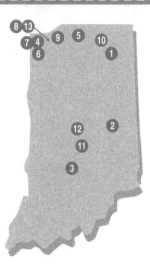

1 Auburn to Waterloo Bike Trail

Endpoints: Auburn, Waterloo
Mileage: 4
Surface: concrete

Location: De Kalb
Contact: Andrew Jagoda
Superintendent
Auburn Parks Department
P.O. Box 506
1500 South Cedar
Auburn, IN 46706-0506
(219) 925–8245

2 Cardinal Greenway

Endpoints: Muncie
Mileage: 10
Surface: asphalt, dirt

Location: Delaware
Contact: Bruce Moore
Director of Operations
Cardinal Greenway, Inc.
614 East Wysor Street
Muncie, IN 47305–1945
(765) 287–0399

3 Clear Creek Rail Trail

Endpoints: Bloomington, Victor
Mileage: 2.5
Surface: ballast

Location: Monroe
Contact: Dave Williams
Operations and Development
Director

Bloomington Parks & Recreation
P.O. Box 848
Bloomington, IN 47402-0848
(812) 349–3700

4 Cross-Town Trail

Endpoints: Griffith, Highland
Mileage: 3.1
Surface: asphalt

Location: Lake
Contact: Highland Parks and
Recreation Department
2450 Lincoln Street
Highland, IN 46322
(219) 838–0114

5 East Bank Trail

Endpoints: South Bend,
Roseland
Mileage: 0.5
Surface: asphalt, cinder

Location: St. Joseph
Contact: Betsy Harriman
South Bend Parks Department
301 South St. Louis Boulevard
South Bend, IN 46617-3092
(219) 235–9401

6 Erie Lackawanna Trail Linear Park

Endpoints: Merrillville, Lake
County Line
Mileage: 10
Surface: asphalt

Location: Lake
Contact: John Novacich
Superintendent
Schereville Parks and Recreation
833 West Lincoln Highway
Suite B-20-W
Schererville, IN 46375-1600
(219) 853–6378

7 Erie Lackawanna Trail, Linear Park— Hammond Section

Endpoints: Hammond, Little
Calumet River
Mileage: 4.7
Surface: asphalt

Location: Lake
Contact: Kathy Kazmierczak
Parks Chair
Hammond Parks Department
5825 Sohl Avenue
Hammond, IN 46320-2358
(219) 853–6378

8 Iron Horse Heritage Trail

Endpoints: Portage
Mileage: 5
Surface: gravel

Location: Porter
Contact: Carl Fisher
Superintendent
City of Portage Parks &
Recreation

2100 Willowcreek Road
Portage, IN 46368-1596
(219) 762–1675

9 Lake George Trail

Endpoints: Hammond, Whiting
Mileage: 1.5
Location: Lake
Contact: 504 North Broadway
Suite 418
Gary, IN 46402

10 Mill Race portion of the Maple City Greenway

Endpoints: Goshen
Mileage: 2.7
Surface: asphalt, crushed stone

Location: Elkhart
Contact: Richard Fay
Goshen Park and Recreation
Department
607 West Plymouth Avenue
Goshen, IN 46526
(219) 534–2901

11 Monon Trail

Endpoints: Indianapolis
Mileage: 7.5
Surface: asphalt

Location: Marion
Contact: Ray Irvin
Administrator

Indianapolis Greenways
151 South East Street
Indianapolis, IN 46202
(317) 327–7431
rayrirvin@indygov.org
www.indygov.org/parks/
greenways

12 Nancy Burton Memorial Trail

Endpoints: Zionsville
Mileage: 1.1
Surface: ballast

Location: Boone
Contact: Albert Smith
Parks Superintendent
Zionsville Town Hall
110 S. Fourth Street
Zionsville, IN 46077-1611
(317) 733–2273
zparks@iserve.net

13 Prairie-Duneland Trail (Oak Savannah Trail)

Endpoints: Portage, Chesterton
Mileage: 9
Surface: asphalt

Location: Porter; Lake
Contact: Carl Fisher
Superintendent
City of Portage Parks &
Recreation
2100 Willowcreek Road
Portage, IN 46368-1596
(219) 762–1675
woodland@netnitco.net

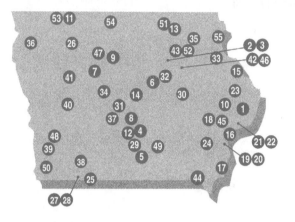

1 Brookfield Wildlife Refuge Trail

Endpoints: Brookfield Wildlife Refuge
Mileage: 2
Surface: grass, dirt

Location: Clinton
Contact: Al Griffiths
Director
Clinton County Conservation Board
P.O. Box 161
Grand Mound, IA 52751-0161
(319) 847–7202
cccb@netins.net

2 Cedar Prairie Trail

Endpoints: Cedar Falls
Mileage: 1

Surface: asphalt, concrete

Location: Black Hawk
Contact: Mark Ripplinger
Park Division Manager
Cedar Falls Parks Division
606 Union Road
Cedar Falls, IA 50613
(319) 273–8625
Mark_ripplinger@ci.cedar.falls.ia.us
www.ci.cedar.falls.ia.us

3 Cedar Valley Nature Trail

Endpoints: Hiawatha, Evansdale
Mileage: 53
Surface: asphalt, crushed stone

Location: Benton; Black Hawk; Buchanan; Linn
Contact: Steve Finegan
Executive Director
Black Hawk County Conservation Board
2410 West Lone Tree Road
Cedar Falls, IA 50613-1093
(319) 277–1536
conservation@co.
black-hawk.ia.us
www.co.linn.ia.us/conservation/
activities/trails.html

4 Chichaqua Valley Trail

Endpoints: Bondurant, Baxter
Mileage: 21
Surface: crushed stone, ballast

Location: Jasper; Polk
Contact: John Parsons
Parks Officer
Jasper County Conservation Board
115 North Second Avenue
Newton, IA 50208
(515) 792–9780

5 Cinder Path

Endpoints: Chariton, Humeston
Mileage: 16
Surface: crushed stone, ballast, concrete

Location: Lucas; Wayne

Contact: Dwayne Clanin
Supervisor
Lucas County Conservation
P.O. Box 78
Chariton, IA 50049-0078
(515) 774–2314
Lucasccb@lucasco.net

6 Comet Trail

Endpoints: Conrad, Wolf Creek Park
Mileage: 6
Surface: crushed stone, grass

Location: Grundy
Contact: Kevin Williams
Director
Grundy County Conservation Board
P.O. Box 36
Morrison, IA 50657-0036
(319) 345–2688
gccb@starroute.com

7 Fort Dodge Nature Trail

Endpoints: Fort Dodge
Mileage: 3
Surface: crushed stone, gravel

Location: Webster
Contact: Tony Salvatore
Parks and Recreation Supervisor
813 First Avenue South
Fort Dodge, IA 50501-4725
(515) 573–5791

8 Four Mile Creek Greenway Trail

Endpoints: Altoona, Des Moines
Mileage: 8
Surface: asphalt

Location: Polk
Contact: Ben Van Gundy
Polk County Conservation Board
Granger, IA 50109
(515) 323–5300
bvangun@co.polk.ia.us

9 Franklin Grove Heritage Trail

Endpoints: Belmond
Mileage: 1.8
Surface: asphalt

Location: Wright
Contact: Wayne Pals
City of Belmond
112 Second Ave. NE
Belmond, IA 50421-1111
(515) 444–3386

10 Grant Wood Sesquicentennial Rail-Trail

Endpoints: Martelle, Olin
Mileage: 14
Surface: crushed stone

Location: Jones
Contact: Tom Neenan
Iowa Trails Council

1201 Central Avenue
Center Point, IA 52213-0131
(319) 849–1844

11 Great Lakes Spine Trail

Endpoints: Milford, Spirit Lake
Mileage: 12
Surface: asphalt

Location: Dickinson
Contact: John Walters
Director
Dickinson County
Conservation Board
1924 240th Street
Milford, IA 51351-1376
(712) 338–4786

12 Great Western Trail

Endpoints: Des Moines
(Waterworks Park), Martinsdale
Mileage: 18
Surface: asphalt, crushed stone

Location: Warren; Polk
Contact: Ben Van Grundy
Director
Polk County Conservation Board
Jester Park
Granger, IA 50109
(515) 323–5300
PCCB_INFO@CO.POLK.IA.US
www.co.polk.ia.us

13 Harry Cook Nature Trail

Endpoints: Osage, Spring Park
Mileage: 2
Surface: crushed stone, gravel

Location: Mitchell
Contact: Ted Funk
Director
Parks and Recreation
Department
114 South Seventh Street
P.O. Box 29 City Hall
Osage, IA 50461-0029
(515) 732–3709

14 Heart of Iowa Nature Trail

Endpoints: Melbourne, Slater
Mileage: 32
Surface: crushed stone, dirt

Location: Marshall; Story
Contact: Steve Lekwa
Deputy Director
McFarland Park
56269 180th Street
Ames, IA 50010-9651
(515) 232–2516

15 Heritage Trail

Endpoints: Dubuque, Dyersville
Mileage: 27
Surface: crushed stone

Location: Dubuque
Contact: Robert Walton
Executive Director
Dubuque County Conservation
Board
13768 Swiss Valley Road
Peosta, IA 52068
(319) 556–6745

16 Hoover Nature Trail

Endpoints: Nichols, Conesville
Mileage: 7
Surface: crushed stone

Location: Muscatine
Contact: Charles Harper
President
Hoover Nature Trail
P.O. Box 531
Muscatine, IA 52761-0009
(319) 263–4043

17 Hoover Nature Trail– Burlington

Endpoints: Burlington
Mileage: 4
Surface: crushed stone

Location: Des Moines
Contact: Charles Harper
President
Hoover Nature Trail, Inc.
P.O. Box 531

Muscatine, IA 52761-0009
(319) 263–4043

18 Hoover Nature Trail– Cedar Rapids

Endpoints: Cedar Rapids
Mileage: 2
Surface: crushed stone

Location: Linn
Contact: Charles Harper
President
Hoover Nature Trail, Inc.
P.O. Box 531
Muscatine, IA 52761-0009
(319) 263–4043

19 Hoover Nature Trail– Columbus Junction

Endpoints: Columbus Junction
Mileage: 2
Surface: ballast

Location: Louisa
Contact: Charles Harper
President
Hoover Nature Trail
P.O. Box 531
Muscatine, IA 52761-0009
(319) 263–4043

20 Hoover Nature Trail– Morning Sun

Endpoints: Morning Sun
Mileage: 4
Surface: ballast

Location: Louisa

Contact: Charles Harper
President
Hoover Nature Trail
P.O. Box 531
Muscatine, IA 52761-0009
(319) 263–4043

21 Hoover Nature Trail– West Branch

Endpoints: West Branch
Mileage: 5
Surface: ballast

Location: Cedar; Johnson
Contact: Charles Harper
President
Hoover Nature Trail
P.O. Box 531
Muscatine, IA 52761-0009
(319) 263–4043

22 Hoover Nature Trail– West Liberty

Endpoints: West Liberty
Mileage: 5
Surface: crushed stone, ballast

Location: Cedar
Contact: Charles Harper
President
Hoover Nature Trail
P.O. Box 531
Muscatine, IA 52761-0009
(319) 263–4043

23 Jackson County Trail

Endpoints: Spragueville
Mileage: 3.3
Surface: crushed stone

Location: Jackson
Contact: Clark Schloz
County Road Engineer
201 West Platt
Maquoketa, IA 52060-2295
(319) 652–4782

24 Kewash Nature Trail

Endpoints: Keota, Washington
Mileage: 13
Surface: crushed stone

Location: Washington
Contact: Kathy Cuddeback
Washington County Conservation
Board
Courthouse
P.O. Box 889
Washington, IA 52353-0889
(319) 653–7765

25 Lamoni Recreational Trail

Endpoints: Lamoni (Cherry
Street), Interstate 35
Mileage: 3
Surface: grass, gravel

Location: Decatur
Contact: Louita Clothier
Friends of the Lamoni Rail-Trail
512 South Cherry
Lamoni, IA 50140
clothier@netins.net

26 Laurens Trail

Endpoints: Laurens
Mileage: 1.5
Surface: crushed stone, ballast,
grass

Location: Pocahontas
Contact: Tom Neenan
Executive Director
Iowa Trails Council
1201 Central Avenue
Center Point, IA 52213-9638
(319) 849–1844

27 Little River Nature Trail

Endpoints: Leon
Mileage: 2
Surface: concrete

Location: Decatur
Contact: Brent Carll
City Clerk
City Hall
104 First Street
Leon, IA 50144
(515) 446–1446

28 Maple Leaf Pathway

Endpoints: Diagonal
Mileage: 2.5
Surface: crushed stone, gravel,
grass, cinder

Location: Ringgold
Contact: Rick Hawkins
Director
Ringgold County Conservation
Board
Box 83A, RR 1
Mount Ayr, IA 50854
(515) 464–2787

29 McVay Trail

Endpoints: Indianola
Mileage: 1.6
Surface: asphalt, concrete

Location: Warren
Contact: Glenn Cowan
Director
Indianola Parks & Recreation
Department
110 North First Street
Indianola, IA 50125-2527
(515) 961–9420

30 Old Creamery Trail

Endpoints: Vinton, Dysart
Mileage: 15.3
Surface: crushed stone

Location: Benton, Tama
Contact: Tom Neenan
Iowa Trails Council
1201 Central Avenue
Center Point, IA 52213-0131
(319) 849–1844

31 Perry to Rippey Trail (Three County Trail)

Endpoints: Perry, Rippey
Mileage: 9
Surface: ballast, grass, dirt

Location: Greene; Boone; Dallas
Contact: Tom Foster
Director
Boone County Conservation
Board
610 H Avenue
Ogden, IA 50212-7453
(515) 353–4237

32 Pioneer Trail

Endpoints: Holland, Grundy
Center, Morrison, Reinbeck
Mileage: 11.5
Surface: crushed stone

Location: Grundy
Contact: Kevin Williams
Director
Grundy County Conservation
Board
P.O. Box 36
Morrison, IA 50657-0036
(319) 345–2688
gccb@stroute.com
www.grundycenter.com/
grundycountyconservation

33 Pony Hollow Trail

Endpoints: Elkader
Mileage: 4
Surface: grass, dirt

Location: Clayton
Contact: Tim Engelhardt
Clayton County Conservation
Board
29862 Osborne Road
Elkader, IA 52043-8247
(319) 245–1516
cccb@mwci.net

34 Praeri Rail Trail

Endpoints: Roland, Zearing
Mileage: 10.5
Surface: crushed stone, grass,
dirt

Location: Story
Contact: Steve Lekwa
Deputy Director
McFarland Park
56269 180th Street
Ames, IA 50010-9651
(515) 232–2516

35 Prairie Farmer Recreation Trail (Winneshiek County Trail)

Endpoints: Calmar, Cresco
Mileage: 18

Surface: crushed stone

Location: Winneshiek
Contact: David Oestmann
Director
Winneshiek County Conservation
Board
2546 Lake Meyer Road
Fort Atkinson, IA 52144-7435
(319) 534–7145

36 Puddle Jumper Trail

Endpoints: Orange City, Alton
Mileage: 2
Surface: crushed stone

Location: Sioux
Contact: Todd Larsen
Director
Orange City Parks & Recreation
Department
City Hall
Orange City, IA 51041
(712) 737–4885

37 Raccoon River Valley Trail

Endpoints: Jefferson, Waukee
Mileage: 51
Surface: asphalt, grass

Location: Greene, Guthrie,

Dallas
Contact: Tom Neenan
Executive Director
Iowa Trails Council
1201 Central Avenue
Center Point, IA 52213-9638
(319) 849–1844

38 Ringgold Trailway

Endpoints: Mt. Ayr
Mileage: 2
Surface: ballast

Location: Ringgold
Contact: Rick Hawkins
Director
Ringgold County Conservation
Board
Box 83A, RR 1
Mount Ayr, IA 50854
(515) 464–2787

39 Rock Island – Old Stone Arch Nature Trail

Endpoints: I-80 Exit 40, Shelby
Mileage: 4
Surface: asphalt

Location: Pottawattamie, Shelby
Contact: Mel Hursey
City of Shelby
419 East Street
Shelby, IA 51570
(712) 544–2638
smu@fmctc.com

40 Russell White Nature Trail

Endpoints: Lanesboro, Highway 286
Mileage: 3.8
Surface: ballast, grass

Location: Carroll
Contact: David Olson
Director
Carroll County Conservation
Board
22811 Swan Lake Drive
Carroll, IA 51401-9801
(712) 792–4614

41 Sauk Rail Trail

Endpoints: Carroll, Lake View
Mileage: 33.2
Surface: asphalt, crushed stone

Other use: hunting
Location: Carroll; Sac
Contact: Chris Bass
Director
Sac County Conservation Board
2970 280th Street
Sac City, IA 50583-7474
(712) 662–4530

42 Sergeant Road Trail

Endpoints: Waterloo, Hudson
Mileage: 6
Surface: asphalt

Location: Black Hawk
Contact: Kevin Blanshon
Transportation Director
INRCOG
501 Sycamore Street, Suite 333
Waterloo, IA 50703-4651
(319) 235–0311

43 Shell Rock River Trail (Butler County Trail)

Endpoints: Clarksville, Shell Rock
Mileage: 5.5
Surface: crushed stone

Location: Butler
Contact: Steve Brunsma
Director
Butler County Conservation
Board
28727 Timber Road
Clarksville, IA 50619
(319) 278–4237

44 Shimek State Forest Trail

Endpoints: Shimek State Forest
Mileage: 4.5
Surface: ballast, grass, dirt

Location: Van Buren; Lee
Contact: Wayne Fuhlbrugge
Area Forester
Iowa Department of Natural
Resources
Shimek State Forest
RR 1, Box 95
Farmington, IA 52626
(319) 878–3811

45 Solon–Lake Macbride Recreation Trail

Endpoints: Solon, Lake
Macbride State Park
Mileage: 5.3
Surface: crushed stone

Location: Johnson
Contact: Gwen Prentice
Park Ranger
Lake Macbride State Park
3525 Highway 382 NE
Solon, IA 52333-8911
(319) 644–2200
macbride@GTE.Net

46 South Riverside Trail

Endpoints: Cedar Falls Junction,
Waterloo
Mileage: 50 (2.6 miles are Rail-
Trail)
Surface: asphalt

Location: Black Hawk
Contact: Kevin Blanshon
Director of Transportation
501 Sycamore Street, Suite 333
Waterloo, IA 50703-5714
(319) 235–0311

47 Three Rivers Trail

Endpoints: Eagle Grove, Rolfe
Mileage: 36
Surface: crushed stone

Location: Humboldt;
Pocahontas; Wright
Contact: Jeanne Mae Ballgous
Director
Humboldt County Conservation
Board
Court House
Dakota City, IA 50529
(515) 332–4087

48 Upper Nish Habitat Trail

Endpoints: Irwin
Mileage: 6
Surface: crushed stone, ballast,
grass, dirt, concrete

Location: Shelby
Contact: Darby Sanders
Director
Shelby County Conservation
Board
514 Maple Road
Harlan, IA 51537-6600
(712) 744–3403

49 Volksweg Trail

Endpoints: Fifield Park, Lake Red
Rock
Mileage: 14
Surface: asphalt

Location: Marion
Contact: Marion County

Conservation Board
(515) 828–2213

50 Wabash Trace Nature Trail

Endpoints: Council Bluffs,
Blanchard
Mileage: 63
Surface: crushed stone

Location: Fremont; Mills; Page;
Pottawattamie
Contact: Lisa Hein
Trails and Greenways Coord.
Iowa Natural Heritage
Foundation
505 Fifth Avenue, Suite 444
Des Moines, IA 50309
(515) 288–1846
ihein@inhf.org
http://forum.heartland.net/
community/wabash-trace/

51 Wapsi–Great Western Trail

Endpoints: Riceville, Lake
Hendricks
Mileage: 10.5
Surface: crushed stone

Location: Howard; Mitchell
Contact: Elaine Govern
Chairman
Wapsi–Great Western Line
Committee
P.O. Box 116
Riceville, IA 50466-0116
(515) 985–4030

52 Waverly Rail-Trail

Endpoints: US 63, Waverly
Mileage: 7
Surface: asphalt

Location: Bremer
Contact: Tom Neenan
Executive Director
Iowa Trails Council
1201 Central Avenue
Center Point, IA 52213-9638
(319) 849–1844

53 Winkel Memorial Trail

Endpoints: Sibley to Allendorf,
spur to Willow Creek County
Recreation Area
Mileage: 10
Surface: gravel

Location: Osceola
Contact: Ron Spengler
Director
Osceola County Convervation
Board
5945 Highway 9
Ocheyedan, IA 51354-7517
(712) 758–3709

54 Winnebago River Trail

Endpoints: Forest City
Mileage: 2.5
Surface: crushed stone, ballast,
wood chips

Location: Winnebago
Contact: Robert Schwartz
Executive Director
Winnebago County Conservation
Board
33496 110th Avenue
Forest City, IA 50436-9205
(515) 565–3390

55 Yellow River Forest Trail

Endpoints: Yellow River State
Forest
Mileage: 30
Surface: gravel, grass, dirt

Location: Allamakee
Contact: Bob Honeywell
Area Forester
Yellow River State Forest
729 State Forest Road
Harpers Ferry, IA 52146-7539
(319) 586–2254
RHwell@means.net
www.state.ia.us-forestry

KANSAS

1 Lawrence Rail-Trail

Endpoints: Lawrence
Mileage: 1.1
Surface: crushed stone, ballast

Location: Douglas
Contact: Fred DeVictor
Director
Lawrence Parks & Recreation
Department
Box 708
Lawrence, KS 66044-0708
(785) 832–3450

2 Prairie Spirit Rail-Trail

Endpoints: Ottawa, Welda
Mileage: 33
Surface: asphalt, crushed stone

Location: Franklin; Anderson;
Allen

Contact: Trent McCown
Park Manager
Kansas Department of Wildlife &
Parks
419 South Oak
Garnett, KS 66032-1316
(785) 448–6767
www.ukans.edu/~hisite/
franklin/railtrail/

3 Short Grass Prairie Trail

Endpoints: Protection, Clark
County Line
Mileage: 2
Surface: dirt, ballast

Location: Comanche
Contact: Floretta Rogers
Short Grass Prairie Trail, Inc.
P.O. Box 902
Ashland, KS 67831
(316) 635–2227
rogers@ucom.net

4 Whistle Stop Park

Endpoints: Elkhart
Mileage: 1.8
Surface: asphalt

Location: Morton
Contact: Ed Johnson
Chairman Whistle Stop Park
Committee
Drawer 70
Elkhart, KS 67950-0070
(316) 697–2402

KENTUCKY

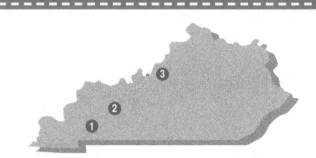

1 Cadiz Railroad Trail

Endpoints: Cadiz
Mileage: 1.5
Surface: asphalt

Location: Trigg
Contact: Jim Lancaster
City Clerk
City of Cadiz
P.O. Box 1464
Cadiz, KY 42211
(207) 522–8224
www.kyrailtrails.org

2 Paradise Trail

Endpoints: Central City,
Greenville
Mileage: 6
Surface: asphalt

Location: Muhlenberg
Contact: Rodney Kirtley
P.O. Box 137
Greenville, KY 42345
(270) 338–2529
cojudge@muhlen.com

3 River Walk Trail

Endpoints: Louisville
Mileage: 6.9
Surface: asphalt

Location: Jefferson
Contact: Sushil Gupta
Manager of Planning
City of Louisville Department of
Public Works
City Hall
601 West Jefferson
Louisville, KY 40202-2741
(502) 574–3102
www.kyrailtrail.org

Louisiana

1 Tammany Trace

Endpoints: Abita, Slidell
Mileage: 21
Surface: asphalt

Location: St. Tammany
Contact: Felicia Leonard
Transportation Planner
St. Tammany Parish Police Jury
428 East Boston Street
P.O. Box 628
Covington, LA 70433-2846
(504) 875–2601
For general information call
(504) 898–2529
www.stp.pa.sttammany.la.us/
departments/trace/trace.html

MAINE

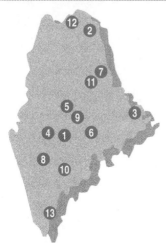

Other use: ATV
Location: Aroostook
Contact: Scott Ramsey
Supervisor, Off Road Vehicles
Bureau of Parks & Recreation
Department of Conservation
Station #22
Augusta, ME 04333-0022
(207) 287–3821

3 Calais Waterfront Walkway

Endpoints: Calais
Mileage: 1.5
Surface: crushed stone, gravel

Location: Washington
Contact: Jim Porter
Community Development
Director
City of Calais
P.O. Box 413
Calais, ME 04619-0413
(207) 454–2521

1 Anson to Bingham

Endpoints: Anson, Bingham
Mileage: 19
Surface: ballast

Location: Somerset
Contact: Roger Poulin
Kennebec Valley Trails
248 Madison Avenue
Skowhegan, ME 04976-1306
(207) 474–5151

2 Aroostook Valley Trail (Bargona and Aroostook Trail)

Endpoints: Washburn, Van Buren
Mileage: 71
Surface: gravel, ballast

4 Carrabassett River Trail (Woodabogan Trail)

Endpoints: Carrabassett,
Bigelow
Mileage: 19
Surface: grass, dirt

Location: Franklin
Contact: Susan Foster

Manager
Sugarloaf/USA Outdoor Center
RR 1, Box 5000
Kingfield, ME 04947-9799
(207) 237–6830
outdoor@somtel.com

5 Derby to Greenville

Endpoints: Derby, Greenville
Mileage: 60
Surface: gravel

Location: Piscataquis
Contact: Scott Ramsey
Supervisor, Off Road Vehicles
Bureau of Parks & Recreation
Department of Conservation
Station #22
Augusta, ME 04333-0022
(207) 287–3821

6 Downeast Trail (Sunrise Trail)

Endpoints: Brewer, Calais
Mileage: 126
Surface: crushed stone

Location: Hancock; Penobscot;
Washington
Contact: Sally Jacobs
Sunrise Trail Coalition
91 Bennoch Road
Orono, ME 04473-1409
(207) 581–2820

7 Houlton to Phair

Endpoints: Houlton, Phair
Mileage: 44
Surface: gravel, ballast

Other use: ATV, hunting
Location: Aroostook
Contact: Scott Ramsey
Supervisor, Off Road Vehicles
Bureau of Parks & Recreation
Department of Conservation
Station #22
Augusta, ME 04333-0022
(207) 287–3821

8 Jay to Farmington Trail

Endpoints: Jay, Farmington
Mileage: 15
Surface: gravel, ballast

Other use: ATV
Location: Franklin
Contact: Scott Ramsey
Supervisor, Off Road Vehicles
Bureau of Parks & Recreation
Department of Conservation
Station #22
Augusta, ME 04333-0022
(207) 287–3821

9 Lagrange Right-of-Way Trail

Endpoints: South Lagrange, Medford
Mileage: 15
Surface: gravel, ballast

Other use: ATV, hunting
Location: Piscataquis; Penobscot
Contact: Scott Ramsey
Supervisor, Off Road Vehicles
Bureau of Parks & Recreation
Department of Conservation
Station #22
Augusta, ME 04333-0022
(207) 287–3821

10 Old Narrow Gauge Volunteer Nature Trail

Endpoints: Randolph
Mileage: 2.4
Surface: ballast, dirt

Location: Kennebec
Contact: Wayne Libby
Town of Randolph
Code Enforcement & Public Works
P.O. Box 216
Randolph, ME 04345-0216
(207) 582–0335

11 Patten to Sherman

Endpoints: Patten, Sherman
Mileage: 7
Surface: gravel

Location: Aroostook; Penobsot
Contact: Scott Ramsey
Supervisor, Off Road Vehicles
Bureau of Parks & Recreation
Department of Conservation
Station #22
Augusta, ME 04333-0022
(207) 287–3821

12 Saint John Valley Heritage Trail

Endpoints: Fort Kent, St. Francis
Mileage: 18
Surface: crushed stone

Other use: dogsledding
Location: Aroostook
Contact: Charles Rudelitch
Economic Development Director
Town of Fort Kent
111 West Main Street
Fort Kent, ME 04743-1040
(207) 834–3507
charles.redulitch@fortkent.org

13 South Portland Greenbelt

Endpoints: South Portland
Mileage: 3.5
Surface: asphalt

Location: Cumberland
Contact: Charles (Tex) Haeuser
Planning Director
City Hall
25 Cottage Road
South Portland, ME 04106-3604
(207) 767–7602
tex@ime.net

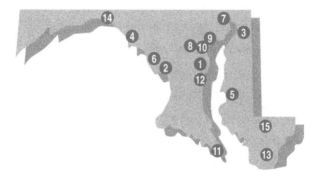

1 Baltimore and Annapolis Trail

Endpoints: Glen Burnie, Annapolis
Mileage: 13.3
Surface: asphalt

Location: Anne Arundel
Contact: David Dionne
Superintendent
Baltimore and Annapolis Trail
Park
P.O. Box 1007
Severna Park, MD 21146-8007
(410) 222–6244
trailman96@msn.com
www.his.com/~jmenzies/
urbanatb/rtrails/ba/ba.htm

2 Bethesda Trolley Trail

Endpoints: Bethesda, Rockville
Mileage: 1.3
Surface: asphalt

Location: Montgomery
Contact: Gail Tait-Nori
Montgomery County
Deptartment of Transportation
101 Monroe Street
10th Floor
Rockville, MD 20850-2540
(301) 217–2145

3 Chesapeake & Delaware Canal Trail

Endpoints: Chesapeake City, Delaware City
Mileage: 15
Surface: crushed stone, dirt

Location: Cecil; New Castle
Contact: David Hawley
Civil Engineer
U.S. Army Corps of Engineers
P.O. Box 77
Chesapeake City, MD 21915-0077
(410) 885–5621

4 Chesapeake & Ohio Canal National Historic Park

Endpoints: Cumberland,
Georgetown
Mileage: 184.5
Surface: crushed stone, gravel,
dirt

Location: Allegany; Frederick;
Montgomery; Washington
Contact: Douglas Faris
Superintendent
C&O National Historical Park
P.O. Box 4
Sharpsburg, MD 21782-0004
(301) 739–4200

5 Cross Island Trail

Endpoints: Kent Island
Mileage: 1
Surface: asphalt

Location: Queen Anne's County
Contact: Wes R. Johnson
Director

Department of Parks and
Recreation
Queen Anne's County
P.O. Box 37
Centreville, MD 21617
(410) 758–0835
wjohnson@qac.org

6 Goldmine Loop Trail

Endpoints: Potomac (Great Falls
Tavern)
Mileage: 3
Surface: dirt

Location: Montgomery
Contact: Faye Walmsley
Subdistrict Ranger
C&O Canal National Historic
Park
11710 MacArthur Boulevard
Potomac, MD 20854-1659
(301) 299–3613

7 Lower Susquehanna Heritage Greenway

Endpoints: Susquehanna State
Park, Conowingo Dam
Mileage: 50
Surface: crushed stone

Location: Harford
Contact: Rick Smith
Manager
Susquehanna State Park
3318 Rocks Chrome Hill Road
Jarrettsville, MD 21084-1741
(410) 836-6735

8 Mill Trail

Endpoints: Savage Park
Mileage: 8
Surface: crushed stone, gravel, ballast

Location: Howard
Contact: Clara Govin
Senior Park Planner
Howard County Recreation & Parks
7120 Oakland Mills Road
Columbia, MD 21046-1621
(410) 313–4687

9 Northern Central Railroad Trail

Endpoints: Ashland, Pennsylvania line
Mileage: 21
Surface: crushed stone

Location: Baltimore
Contact: Rob Marconi
Area Manager
Gunpowder Falls State Park
P.O. Box 480
Kingsville, MD 21087
(410) 592–2897
www.his.com/~jmenzies/
urbanatb/rtrails/ncr/ncr.htm

10 Number Nine Trolley Line

Endpoints: Ellicott City
Mileage: 2
Surface: asphalt

Location: Baltimore
Contact: John Mickanis
Western Region Supervisor
Baltimore County Department of Recreation & Parks
Banneker Center, Main & Wesley Avenues
Catonsville, MD 21228
(410) 887–0956

11 Point Lookout Railroad Trail

Endpoints: Point Lookout State Park
Mileage: 2
Surface: dirt

Location: Saint Mary's
Contact: Park Staff (Ranger)
Point Lookout State Park
P.O. Box 48
Scotland, MD 20687
(301) 872–5688

12 Poplar Park Trail

Endpoints: Annapolis
Mileage: 0.5
Surface: asphalt

Location: Anne Arundel
Contact: Stephen Carr
Pathways Coordinator
City of Annapolis
2009 Homewood Road
Annapolis, MD 21402
(410) 757–5916
stevecarr@toad.net

13 Snow Hill Rail-Trail

Endpoints: Snow Hill, Stockton
Mileage: 3
Surface: crushed stone

Location: Worcester
Contact: Lisa Challenger
Tourism Coordinator
Worcester County Department of
Economic Development
105 Pearl Street
Snow Hill, MD 21863-1051
(410) 632–3110

14 Western Maryland Rail Trail

Endpoints: Fort Frederick State
Park, Sidling Hill Wildlife
Management Area
Mileage: 10
Surface: asphalt

Location: Washington
Contact: Ralph Young
Park Manager
Fort Frederick State Park
Maryland Department of Natural
Resources
11100 Fort Frederick Road
Big Pool, MD 21711-1313
(301) 842–2155
www.hancockmd.com/visit/

15 Winterplace Park Trail

Endpoints: Salisbury, Walston
Switch
Mileage: 2
Surface: grass, crushed stone,
wood chips, gravel, dirt

Location: Wicomico
Contact: Aaron Levinthal
Greenways Coordinator
Wicomico County Parks,
Recreation, and Tourism
500 Glen Avenue
Salisbury, MD 21804
(410) 548–4900, x112
alevinthal@wicomicocounty.org

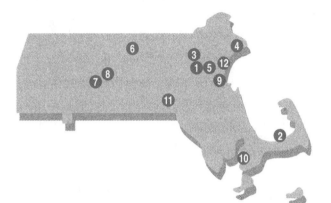

1 Bedford Narrow-Gauge Rail-Trail

Endpoints: Loomis Street (Bedford), Bedford-Billerica town line
Mileage: 3
Surface: crushed stone

Location: Middlesex
Contact: Jim Shea
Friends of Bedford Depot Park, Inc.
30 Independence Road
Bedford, MA 01730
(781) 275–3212

2 Cape Cod Rail Trail

Endpoints: Dennis, South Wellfleet
Mileage: 25
Surface: asphalt, grass, dirt, sand

Location: Barnstable
Contact: Daniel O'Brien
Bikeway & Rail Trail Planner
Department of Environmental Management
Division of Resource Conservation
100 Cambridge Street
Room 1404
Boston, MA 02202-0044
(617) 727–3160

3 Lowell Canal System Trails

Endpoints: Lowell
Mileage: 2.5
Surface: asphalt, concrete

Location: Middlesex
Contact: Christina Briggs
Planning Director
Lowell National Historical Park
67 Kirk Street
Lowell, MA 01852-5900
(508) 458–7653
www.nps.gov/lowe

4 Marblehead Rail-Trail (The Path)

Endpoints: Marblehead, Swampscott; with spur to Salem
Mileage: 5
Surface: gravel, ballast, grass, dirt

Location: Essex
Contact: Tom Hammond
Superintendent of Recreation
Marblehead Dept. of Recreation, Park and Forestry
10 Humphrey Street
Marblehead, MA 01945-1906
(781) 631–3350

5 Minuteman Bikeway

Endpoints: Arlington, Bedford
Mileage: 10.5
Surface: asphalt

Location: Middlesex
Contact: Alan McClennen, Jr.
Director
Planning and Community Development
Town of Arlington
730 Massachusetts Avenue

Arlington, MA 02174-4908
(781) 316–3091

6 North Central Pathway

Endpoints: Gardner
Mileage: 2.5
Surface: asphalt

Location: Worcester
Contact: Cynthia Boucher
North Central Pathway, Inc.
135 Gardner Road
Winchendon, MA 01475
(978) 297–2167
commwtr@banet.net

7 Northampton Bikeway

Endpoints: Northampton
Mileage: 2.6
Surface: asphalt

Location: Hampshire
Contact: Wayne Feiden
Principal Planner
Northampton Office of Planning & Development
210 Main Street, City Hall
Northampton, MA 01060-3110
(413) 586–6950
wfeiden@city.northampton.ma.us
www-unix.oit.umass.edu:-80/
~ditullio/Northamhome.html

8 Norwottuck Rail-Trail (Five Colleges Bikeway)

Endpoints: Amherst, Northampton
Mileage: 9
Surface: asphalt

Location: Hampshire
Contact: Daniel O'Brien
Bikeway & Rail Trail Planner
Department of Environmental
Management
Division of Resource
Conservation
100 Cambridge Street
Room 1404
Boston, MA 02202-0044
(617) 727–3160

9 Quarries Footpath

Endpoints: Quincy Quarries
Historic Site
Mileage: 1
Surface: dirt

Location: Norfolk
Contact: Maggie Brown
Chief Ranger
Blue Hills Reservation, South
Region
695 Hillside Street
Milton, MA 02186-5224
(617) 727–4573

10 Shining Sea Bikeway

Endpoints: Falmouth, Woods
Hole
Mileage: 4
Surface: asphalt

Location: Barnstable
Contact: Kevin Lynch
Chairman
Falmouth Bikeways Committee
52 Town Hall Square
Falmouth, MA 02540
(508) 968–5293
avnyd@aol.com
http://members.aol.com/fal-bike/bike/bike/index.html

11 Southern New England Trunkline Trail

Endpoints: Franklin, Douglas
Mileage: 21
Surface: crushed stone, ballast

Location: Norfolk; Worcester
Contact: Tom LaVoie
Assistant Regional Director
Department of Environmental
Management, Region III
P.O. Box 155
Jamaica Plain, MA 02130
(978) 368–0126

12 Southwest Corridor Park

Endpoints: Boston
Mileage: 5
Surface: asphalt

Location: Suffolk
Contact: Allan Morris
Parkland Manager
Southwest Corridor Park
38 New Heath Street
Jamaica Plain, MA 02130-1670
(617) 727–0057

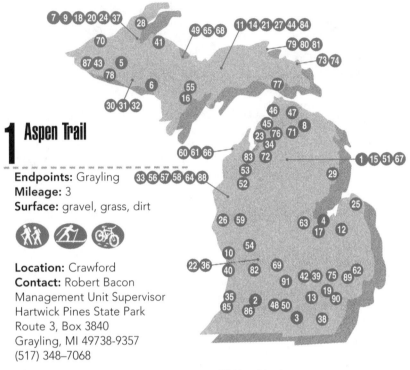

1 Aspen Trail

Endpoints: Grayling
Mileage: 3
Surface: gravel, grass, dirt

Location: Crawford
Contact: Robert Bacon
Management Unit Supervisor
Hartwick Pines State Park
Route 3, Box 3840
Grayling, MI 49738-9357
(517) 348–7068

2 Battle Creek Linear Park

Endpoints: Battle Creek
Mileage: 17
Surface: asphalt

Location: Calhoun
Contact: Linn Kracht
Recreation Superintendent
Battle Creek Department of
Parks & Recreation

35 Hambin Avenue
Battle Creek, MI 49017-4012
(616) 966–3431

3 Baw Beese Trail

Endpoints: Osseo, Hillsdale
Mileage: 6
Surface: asphalt, ballast

Location: Hillsdale
Contact: Mark Reynolds

Director
Hillsdale Recreation Department
43 McCollum Street
Hillsdale, MI 49242-1630
(517) 437–3579

4 Bay Hampton Rail Trail

Endpoints: Bay City, Hampton Township
Mileage: 6
Surface: asphalt

Location: Bay
Contact: Jim Bedell
Community Development
Planner
301 Washington Street
Bay City, MI 48708-5866
(517) 894–8154

5 Beaver Lodge Nature Trail

Endpoints: Ottawa National Forest
Mileage: 1.3
Surface: grass, wood chips, dirt

Location: Houghton
Contact: Dawn Buss
Forestry Technician
Ottawa National Forest
1209 Rockland Road
Ontonagon, MI 49953-1731
(906) 884–2411

6 Beaver Pete's Trail

Endpoints: Dickinson/
Menominee county line, Iron
Mountain
Mileage: 20
Surface: ballast

Location: Dickinson
Contact: Allan Keto
Assistant, Resource Protection
Copper Country State Forest
Norway Forest Area
US-2
Norway, MI 49870
(906) 563–9247

7 Bergland to Sidnaw Rail Trail

Endpoints: Sidnaw, Bergland
Mileage: 45
Surface: gravel, ballast, dirt

Other use: ATV
Location: Houghton; Ontonagon
Contact: Martin Nelson
Unit Manager
Michigan DNR
427 US Highway 41 North
Baraga, MI 49908-9627
(906) 353–6651

8 Big Bear Lake Nature Pathway

Endpoints: Mackinaw State
Forest

Mileage: 5
Surface: dirt

Location: Otsego
Contact: Bill O'Neill
Assistant Area Forester
Unit Manager
Michigan Department of Natural
Resources
Gaylord Forest Management
Division
P.O. Box 667
Gaylord, MI 49734
(517) 731–5806
oneillw@state.mi.us
www.dnr.state.mi.us

9 Bill Nicholls Trail

Endpoints: Houghton, McKeever
Mileage: 55
Surface: gravel, ballast, dirt, sand

Other use: ATV
Location: Ontonagon; Houghton
Contact: Martin Nelson
Unit Manager
Michigan DNR
427 US Highway 41 North
Baraga, MI 49908-9627
(906) 353–6651

10 Boardwalk of Grand Haven

Endpoints: Grand Haven
Mileage: 2.5
Surface: asphalt

Location: Ottawa
Contact: Laurel Nease
Visitors Bureau Coordinator
Grand Haven Visitors Bureau
1 South Harbor Drive
Grand Haven, MI 49417-1385
(616) 842–4499
inease@grandhavenchamber.org
www.grandhavenchamber.org

11 Bruno's Run Trail

Endpoints: Munising
Mileage: 7.3
Surface: dirt

Location: Alger
Contact: Dick Andersen
Recreation Supervisor
Hiawatha National Forest
Munising Ranger District
400 East Munising, RR #2 Box 400
Munising, MI 49862-1487
(906) 387–2512

12 Cass City Walking Trail

Endpoints: Cass City
Mileage: 1.4
Surface: gravel, ballast, grass,
wood chips, dirt

Location: Tuscola
Contact: Jane Downing
Village Manager
6505 Main Street
P.O. Box 123

Cass City, MI 48726-1524
(517) 872–2911
ccvillag@avci.net

13 Chelsea Hospital Fitness Trail

Endpoints: Chelsea
Mileage: 1
Surface: wood chips

Location: Washtenaw
Contact: Philip Boham
Vice President
Chelsea Community Hospital
775 S. Main Street
Chelsea, MI 48118-1370
(313) 475–3998

14 Coalwood Trail

Endpoints: Shingleton, Chatham
Mileage: 24
Surface: ballast

Other use: ATV
Location: Alger; Schoolcraft
Contact: Dick Andersen
Recreation Supervisor
Hiawatha National Forest
Munising Ranger District
400 East Munising, RR #2
Box 400
Munising, MI 49862-1487
(906) 387–2512

15 Cross Country Ski and Mountain Bike Trail

Endpoints: Hartwick Pines State Park
Mileage: 9
Surface: gravel, grass, dirt

Location: Crawford
Contact: Jon Gregorich
Supervisor
Hartwick Pines State Park
4216 Ranger Road
Grayling, MI 49738
(517) 348–7068

16 Felch Grade Trail

Endpoints: Narenta, Felch
Mileage: 45
Surface: gravel, dirt

Other use: ATV
Location: Delta; Menominee; Dickinson
Contact: Russ MacDonald
Asst. Area Forest Manager
Escanaba Forest Area Office
Escanaba River State Forest
6833 US 2-41 & M-35
Gladstone, MI 49837
(906) 786–2354

17 Frank N. Anderson Trail

Endpoints: Bay City State Park
Mileage: 1.4
Surface: asphalt

Location: Bay
Contact: Karen Gillespie
Park Secretary
Bay City State Recreation Area
3582 State Park Drive
Bay City, MI 48706
(517) 684–6282

18 Freda Trail

Endpoints: Freda, Bill Nicholls Trail
Mileage: 11.2
Surface: dirt

Other use: ATV
Location: Houghton
Contact: Dave Tuovila
Dist. Fire & Rec. Specialist
Michigan DNR
427 US Highway 41 North
Baraga, MI 49908-9627
(906) 353–6651

19 Gallup Park Trail

Endpoints: Ann Arbor, Parker Mill
Mileage: 4.3
Surface: asphalt

Location: Washtenaw
Contact: Thomas Raynes
Manager of Park Planning
Ann Arbor Department of Parks & Recreation
P.O. Box 8647

100 North Fifth Avenue
Ann Arbor, MI 48107-8647
(734) 994–2423
traynes@ci.ann-arbor.mi.us

20 Gay Trail

Endpoints: Gay Mohawk
Mileage: 27
Surface: dirt

Location: Houghton; Keweenaw
Contact: Martin Nelson
Area Forest Manager
Michigan DNR
427 US Highway 41 North
Baraga, MI 49908-9627
(906) 353–6651

21 Grand Marais Trail

Endpoints: Shingleton, Grand Marais
Mileage: 41.7
Surface: sand

Location: Alger; Schoolcraft
Contact: Jeff Stampfly
Area Forest Manager
Lake Superior State Forest
Shingleton Forest Area
M-28, P.O. Box 57
Shingleton, MI 49884
(906) 452–6227

22 Grand River Edges

Endpoints: Grand Rapids
Mileage: 0.5
Surface: asphalt

Location: Kent
Contact: Steve Pierpoint
Landscape Architect
Grand Rapids Planning
Department
300 Monroe Avenue, NW
Grand Rapids, MI 49503-2206
(616) 456–3031

23 Grass River Natural Area Nature Trail

Endpoints: Bellaire
Mileage: 8
Surface: crushed stone, ballast, dirt

Location: Antrim
Contact: Mark Randolph
Grass River Natural Area
P.O. Box 231
Bellaire, MI 49615-0231
(616) 533–8314
www.torchlake.com/grana

24 Hancock/Calumet Trail

Endpoints: Hancock, Calumet
Mileage: 13
Surface: asphalt, gravel, dirt

Other use: ATV
Location: Houghton
Contact: Martin Nelson
Unit Manager
Michigan DNR
427 US Highway 41 North
Baraga, MI 49908-9627
(906) 353–6651

25 Harbor Beach Bike-Pedestrian Path

Endpoints: Harbor Beach
Mileage: 1
Surface: asphalt

Location: Huron
Contact: Tom Youatt
City Administrator
City of Harbor Beach
766 State Street
Harbor Beach, MI 98441
(517) 479–3363

26 Hart-Montague Bicycle Trail State Park

Endpoints: Hart, Montague
Mileage: 22.5
Surface: asphalt

Location: Oceana; Muskegon
Contact: Peter LundBorg
Park Administrator
Silver Lake State Park
Management Unit
9679 West State Park Road
Mears, MI 49436-9667
(616) 873-3083

27 Haywire Trail

Endpoints: Manistique, Shingleton
Mileage: 33
Surface: ballast, cinder

Other use: ATV
Location: Alger; Schoolcraft
Contact: Dick Andersen
Recreation Supervisor
Hiawatha National Forest
Munising Ranger District
400 East Munising, RR #2
Box 400
Munising, MI 49862-1487
(906) 387–2512

28 Houghton Waterfront Trail

Endpoints: Houghton
Mileage: 4.5
Surface: asphalt

Location: Houghton
Contact: Scott MacInnes
Assistant City Manager
City of Houghton
P.O. Box 406
Houghton, MI 49931-0406
(906) 482–1700

29 Huron Forest Snowmobile Trails

Endpoints: Huron National Forest, Barton City
Mileage: 95
Surface: dirt

Other use: ATV
Location: Alcona; Oscoda
Contact: Nick Schmelter
Assistant Ranger
Huron National Forest
Huron Shores Ranger District
5761 Skeel Avenue
Oscoda, MI 48750
(517) 739–0728

30 Iron Range Trails— Beechwood to Sidnaw Trail

Endpoints: Beechwood, Gibbs City
Mileage: 48
Surface: ballast

Location: Iron
Contact: Dave Tuovila
Dist. Fire & Rec. Specialist
Michigan Department of Natural Resources
427 US Highway 41 North
Baraga, MI 49908-9627
(906) 353–6651

31 Iron Range Trails— Crystal Falls to Iron River Trail

Endpoints: Crystal Falls, Iron River
Mileage: 25
Surface: ballast

Location: Iron
Contact: Dave Tuovila
Dist. Fire & Rec. Specialist
Michigan DNR
427 US Highway 41 North
Baraga, MI 49908-9627
(906) 353–6651

32 Iron Range Trails— Crystal Falls to Stager Trail

Endpoints: Crystal Falls, Stager
Mileage: 11
Surface: ballast

Location: Iron
Contact: Dave Tuovila
Dist. Fire & Rec. Specialist
Michigan DNR
427 US Highway 41 North
Baraga, MI 49908-9627
(906) 353–6651

33 Iron's Area Tourist Association Snowmobile Trail

Endpoints: Manistee National Forest
Mileage: 22
Surface: ballast

Location: Lake; Manistee
Contact: John Hojnowski
Assistant Ranger
USDA Forest Service
Manistee Ranger District
412 Red Apple Road
Manistee, MI 49660
(616) 723–2211

34 Jordan River Pathway

Endpoints: Jordan River Valley
Mileage: 17.5
Surface: dirt

Location: Antrim
Contact: Bill O'Neill
Area Forest Manager
Michigan DNR, Gaylord Field Office
P.O. Box 667
Gaylord, MI 49735-0667
(517) 732–3541

35 Kal-Haven Trail Sesquicentennial State Park Trail

Endpoints: Kalamazoo, South Haven
Mileage: 33.5
Surface: crushed stone

Location: Kalamazoo; Van Buren
Contact: Kurt Maxwell
Trail Supervisor
Van Buren State Park 23960
Ruggles Road
South Haven, MI 49090-9492
(616) 637–4984

36 Kent Trails

Endpoints: Grand Rapids, Byron Center
Mileage: 15
Surface: asphalt

Location: Kent
Contact: Roger Sabine
Director of Parks
Kent County Parks Department
1500 Scribner NW
Grand Rapids, MI 49504-3299
(616) 336–3697

37 Keweenaw Trail

Endpoints: Houghton, Calumet
Mileage: 58

Surface: grass, dirt

Location: Houghton; Keweenaw
Contact: Martin Nelson
Unit Manager
Michigan DNR
427 US Highway 41 North
Baraga, MI 49908-9627
(906) 353–6651

38 Kiwanis Trail

Endpoints: Adrian, Tecumseh
Mileage: 7
Surface: asphalt, ballast

Location: Lenawee
Contact: Mark Gasche
Community Services Director
Adrian City Hall
100 East Church Street
Adrian, MI 49221-2773
(517) 263–2161

39 Lakelands Trail State Park

Endpoints: Pinckney, Stockbridge
Mileage: 12.5
Surface: crushed stone

Location: Jackson; Livingston; Oakland
Contact: Jon LaBossiere
Pinckney Recreation Area

8555 Silver Hill
Pinckney, MI 48169-8901
(313) 426–4913

40 Lakeside Trail

Endpoints: Spring Lake
Mileage: 1.8
Surface: asphalt

Location: Ottawa
Contact: Andy Lukasik
Village Manager
Village of Spring Lake
102 W. Savidge Street
Spring Lake, MI 49456-1603
(616) 842–1393

41 L'Anse to Big Bay Trail

Endpoints: L'Anse, Big Bay
Mileage: 54
Surface: dirt

Location: Baraga; Marquette
Contact: Martin Nelson
Area Forest Manager
Michigan DNR
427 US Highway 41 North
Baraga, MI 49908-9627
(906) 353–6651

42 Lansing River Trail

Endpoints: Lansing
Mileage: 6
Surface: asphalt

Location: Ingham
Contact: Dick Schaefer
Landscape Architect
Parks & Recreation
318 North Capital Avenue
Lansing, MI 48933-1605
(517) 483–4277

43 Little Falls Trail

Endpoints: Ottawa National
Forest
Mileage: 6.5
Surface: ballast, grass

Location: Gogebic; Ontonagon
Contact: Wayne Petterson
Forestry Technician
Ottawa National Forest
P.O. Box 276
Watersmeet, MI 49969-0276
(906) 358–4551

44 Little Lake–Chatham Snowmobile Trail

Endpoints: Chatham, Little Lake
Mileage: 26
Surface: ballast, dirt, cinder

Location: Marquette; Alger
Contact: Bill Brondyke
Area Forest Manager
Gwinn Forest Area
410 West M-35

Gwinn, MI 49841
(906) 346–9201

45 Little Traverse Wheelway

Endpoints: Petoskey
Mileage: 2.3
Surface: asphalt

Location: Emmet
Contact: Melanie Chiodini
Top of Michigan Trails Council
445 East Mitchell Street
Petoskey, MI 49770
(616) 348–8280

46 Mackinaw/Alanson Trail

Endpoints: Mackinaw Alanson
Mileage: 24
Surface: gravel, ballast, dirt, grass

Location: Emmet
Contact: Bill O'Neill
Unit Manager
Michigan Department of Natural Resources
Forest Management Unit
P.O. Box 667
Gaylord, MI 49734
(517) 731–5806
oneillw@state.mi.us
www.dnr.state.mi.us

47 Mackinaw to Hawks Trail

Endpoints: Hawks, Mackinaw City
Mileage: 59
Surface: ballast

Location: Cheboygan; Presque Isle
Contact: Philip Wells
Trailways Program Leader
Michigan Department of Natural Resources
Forest Management Division
P.O. Box 30452
Lansing, MI 48909-7952
(517) 335 3038
wellsp@state.mi.us

48 Main Trail

Endpoints: Whitehouse Nature Center, Albion College
Mileage: 0.5
Surface: gravel, grass, wood chips, dirt

Location: Calhoun
Contact: Tamara Crupi
Director
Albion College
Whitehouse Nature Center
KC 4868
Albion, MI 49224
(517) 629–0582
tcrupi@albion.edu

49 Mattson Lower Harbor Park Trail

Endpoints: Harvey, Marquette
Mileage: 8
Surface: asphalt

Location: Marquette
Contact: Leslie Hugh
Director
City of Marquette Parks and
Recreation Department
401 East Fair Avenue
Marquette, MI 49855
(906) 228–0460

50 McClure Riverfront Park

Endpoints: Albion
Mileage: 0.2
Surface: grass, wood chips

Location: Calhoun
Contact: Joe Domingo
Superintendent
Albion Department of Parks and
Recreation
112 West Street Cass
Albion, MI 49224
(517) 629–5535

51 Mertz Grade Trail

Endpoints: Grayling
Mileage: 2
Surface: gravel, grass, dirt

Location: Crawford
Contact: John Gregorich
Department of Natural Resources
Unit Supervisor
Hartwick Pines State Park
4216 Ranger Road
Grayling, MI 49738
(517) 348–7068

52 Michigan Shore to Shore Riding-Hiking Trail— Cadillac Spur

Endpoints: Cadillac
Mileage: 35
Surface: sand

Location: Wexford; Missaukee;
Grand Traverse
Contact: Steve Cross
Forest Management Specialist
Forest Management Division
8015 Mackinaw Trail
Cadillac, MI 49601-9746
(616) 775–9727

53 Michigan Shore to Shore Riding-Hiking Trail— Scheck's Place

Endpoints: Empire, Sheck's Place
Mileage: 40
Surface: sand

Location: Grand Traverse; Benzie
Contact: Steve Cross
Forest Management Specialist
Forest Management Division
8015 Mackinaw Trail
Cadillac, MI 49601-9746
(616) 775–9727

54 Musketawa Trail

Endpoints: Marne, Muskegon
Mileage: 26
Surface: asphalt

Location: Muskegon; Ottawa
Contact: Harold Drake
President
Village of Ravenna
12090 Crockery Creek Drive
Ravenna, MI 49451-9460
(616) 853–2360

55 Nahma Grade Trail

Endpoints: Rapid River, Alger
county line
Mileage: 32
Surface: dirt

Location: Delta
Contact: Anne Okonek
Assistant District Ranger
Hiawatha National Forest
Rapid River Ranger District
8181 US Hwy. 2
Rapid River, MI 49878-9501
(906) 474–6442

56 Nordhouse Dunes Trail System

Endpoints: Manistee National
Forest
Mileage: 14
Surface: grass, dirt

Location: Mason
Contact: Teresa Maday
Outdoor Recreation Planner
Manistee National Forest
Manistee/Cadillac Ranger District
412 Red Apple Road
Manistee, MI 49660-9616
(616) 723–2211

57 North Country National Scenic Trail—Baldwin

Endpoints: Baldwin
Mileage: 1.5
Surface: dirt

Other use: Snowshoeing
Location: Lake
Contact: Executive Director
North Country Trail Association
3777 Sparks Drive SE, Suite 105
Grand Rapids, MI 49546-6186
(616) 454–5506

58 North Country National Scenic Trail—Manistee Ranger District

Endpoints: Red Bridge, Marilla
Trailhead
Mileage: 43
Surface: dirt

Location: Manistee; Mason; Lake
Contact: Ramona Venegas
Wilderness Ranger
Manistee Ranger District
USDA Forest Service
412 Red Apple Road
Manistee, MI 49660-9616
(616) 723–2211

59 North Country National Scenic Trail—White Cloud

Endpoints: White Cloud
Mileage: 0.3
Surface: dirt

Other use: snowshoeing
Location: Newaygo
Contact: Executive Director
North Country Trail Association
3777 Sparks Drive SE
Suite 105
Grand Rapids, MI 49546-6186
(616) 454–5506

60 Old Grade Nature Trail

Endpoints: Glen Lake
Mileage: 1
Surface: grass

Location: Leelanau
Contact: William Herd
Park Ranger
Sleeping Bear Dunes National
Lakeshore
9922 Front Street
Empire, MI 49630-0277
(616) 326–5134

61 Old Grade Trail

Endpoints: North Manitou Island
Mileage: 8
Surface: grass, dirt

Location: Leelanau
Contact: William Herd
Park Ranger
Sleeping Bear Dunes National
Lakeshore
9922 Front Street
Empire, MI 49630-0277
(616) 326–5134

62 Paint Creek Trailway

Endpoints: Rochester, Rochester
Hills, Oakland, Orion
Mileage: 8.5
Surface: crushed stone, ballast,
dirt

Location: Oakland
Contact: William Stark
Trailways Coordinator
Paint Creek Trailways
Commission
4349 Collins Road
Rochester, MI 48306-1619
(248) 651–9260
www.orion.lib.mi.us/lacin/pctc

63 Pere Marquette Rail-Trail of Mid-Michigan

Endpoints: Midland, Clare
Mileage: 22
Surface: asphalt

Location: Midland
Contact: William Gibson
Director
Midland County Parks &

Recreation Dept.
220 W. Ellsworth Street
Midland, MI 48640-5194
(517) 832–6876
www.users.mdn.net/fopmrt/
friends.html

64 Pere-Marquette State Trail

Endpoints: Baldwin, Clare
Mileage: 54.7
Surface: asphalt, ballast, sand

Location: Clare; Lake; Osceola
Contact: Philip Wells
Trailways Program Leader
Michigan Department of Natural
Resources
Forest Management Division
P.O. Box 30452
Lansing, MI 48909-7952
(517) 335–3038
WELLSP@STATE.MI.US

65 Peshekee to Clowry ORV Trail

Endpoints: Near Champion
Mileage: 6.1
Surface: gravel, ballast, dirt

Location: Marquette
Contact: Al Keto
Recreation Specialist
1990 US-41 South
Marquette, MI 49855
(906) 228–6561

66 Platte Plains Trail

Endpoints: Sleepy Bear Dunes
National Lake Shore
Mileage: 14.7
Surface: grass, dirt, sand

Location: Benzie
Contact: William Herd
Park Ranger
Sleeping Bear Dunes National
Lakeshore
9922 Front Street
Empire, MI 49630-0277
(616) 326–5134

67 Railroad Trail

Endpoints: Gaylord, Indian River,
Frederick
Mileage: 68 (22 are Rail-Trail)
Surface: grass, dirt

Location: Crawford; Otsego
Contact: Phil Silverio-Mazzela
Trail Coordinator
Alpine Snowmobile Trails, Inc.
2583 Old 27 South
Gaylord, MI 49735
(517) 732–7171

68 Republic/Champion Grade Trail

Endpoints: Champion, Republic
Mileage: 8.1
Surface: ballast

Other use: ATV

Location: Marquette
Contact: Dennis Nezich
Area Forest Manager
Ishpeming Forest Area
Escanaba River State Forest
1985 US-41
Ishpeming, MI 49849
(906) 485–1031

69 Rivertrail Park

Endpoints: Portland
Mileage: 3.7
Surface: asphalt

Location: Ionia
Contact: Mary Scheurer
Parks and Recreation
Department
City of Portland
259 Kent Street
Portland, MI 48875-1458
(517) 647–7985

70 Rockland to Mass Trail

Endpoints: Rockland
Mileage: 7
Surface: ballast

Location: Ontonagon
Contact: Martin Nelson
Area Forest Manager
Michigan DNR
427 US Highway 41 North
Baraga, MI 49908-9627
(906) 353–6651

71 Shingle Mill Pathway

Endpoints: Pigeon River Country
Forest Management Unit
Mileage: 11
Surface: dirt

Location: Otsego
Contact: Joe Jarecki
Area Forest Manager
Pigeon River Country Forest Area
9966 Twin Lakes Road
Vanderbilt, MI 49795-9767
(517) 983–4101

72 Skegemog Lake Pathway

Endpoints: Skegemog Lake
Wildlife Area
Mileage: 0.8
Surface: ballast

Location: Kalkaska
Contact: Jerry Grieve
Assistant Area Forest Manager
Tranerce City Unit
2089 North Birch
Kalkaska, MI 49646-9448
(616) 258–2711
grieveg@state.mi.us

73 Soo/Strongs Trail— Raco to Strongs

Endpoints: Raco, Strongs
Mileage: 12
Surface: ballast

Location: Chippewa
Contact: William Rhoe
District Ranger
Hiawatha National Forest
Sault Ste. Marie Ranger District
4000 I-75, Business Spur
Sault Ste. Marie, MI 49783
(906) 635–5511

74 Soo/Strongs Trail— Sault Ste. Marie to Raco

Endpoints: Sault Ste. Marie, Raco
Mileage: 20
Surface: ballast, dirt, sand

Other use: ATV
Location: Chippewa
Contact: Patrick Halfrisch
Assistant Unit Land Manager
Sault Ste. Marie Forest Area
Lake Superior State Forest
P.O. Box 798
Sault Ste. Marie, MI 49783-0798
(906) 635–5281

75 South Lyon Rail-Trail

Endpoints: South Lyon
Mileage: 33
Surface: asphalt

Location: Oakland
Contact: Rodney Cook
City Manager
City of South Lyon
335 South Warren

South Lyon, MI 48178-1377
(248) 437–1735

76 Spring Brook Pathway

Endpoints: Mackinaw State Forest
Mileage: 6.3
Surface: ballast, dirt

Location: Charlevoix
Contact: Bill O'Neill
Area Forest Manager
Michigan DNR, Gaylord Field Office
P.O. Box 667
Gaylord, MI 49735-0667
(517) 732–3541

77 St. Ignace to Trout Lake

Endpoints: St. Ignace, Trout Lake
Mileage: 26
Surface: crushed stone

Location: Mackinac
Contact: Joe Hart
Assistant District Manager
Hiawatha National Forest
1498 W. US-2
St. Ignace, MI 49781
(906) 643–7900

78 State Line Trail

Endpoints: Wakefield, Stager
Mileage: 107
Surface: ballast

Other use: ATV
Location: Iron; Gogebic
Contact: Martin Nelson
Unit Manager
Michigan DNR
427 US Highway 41 North
Baraga, MI 49908-9627
(906) 353-6651

79 Tahquamenon Falls State Park–Clark Lake Loop

Endpoints: Tahquamenon Falls
State Park
Mileage: 5
Surface: grass, dirt

Location: Chippewa; Luce
Contact: Jon Spieles
Park Interpreter
Tahquamenon Falls State Park
41382 West M-123
Paradise, MI 49768
(906) 492-3415
J.spieles@up.net

80 Tahquamenon Falls State Park–North Country Loop

Endpoints: Tahquamenon Falls
State Park
Mileage: 23
Surface: grass, dirt

Location: Chippewa; Luce
Contact: Jon Spieles
Park Interpreter
Tahquamenon Falls State Park
Route 48, Box 225

41382 West M-123
Paradise, MI 49768
(906) 492-3415

81 Tahquamenon Falls State Park–Wilderness Loop

Endpoints: Tahquamenon Falls
State Park
Mileage: 7.4
Surface: grass, dirt

Location: Chippewa; Luce
Contact: Jon Spieles
Park Interpreter
Tahquamenon Falls State Park
Route 48, Box 225
Paradise, MI 49768
(906) 492-3415

82 Thornapple Trail/Paul Henry Trail

Endpoints: Kentwood
Mileage: 2.5
Surface: asphalt

Location: Kent
Contact: Charles Ziesemer
Director
Kentwood Parks and Recreation
355 Forty-eighth Street
Kentwood, MI 49548
(616) 531-3398
ziesemerc@ci.kentwood.mi.us

83 Traverse Area Recreation Trail (TART)

Endpoints: Traverse City, Acme
Mileage: 5.6

Surface: asphalt

Location: Grand Traverse
Contact: Mike Dillenbeck
Manager
Grand Traverse County Road
Commission
3949 Silver Lake Road
Traverse City, MI 49684-8946
(616) 922–4848

84 Tyoga Historical Pathway

Endpoints: Deerton
Mileage: 1.4
Surface: ballast

Location: Alger
Contact: Dennis Nezich
Area Forest Manager
Ishpeming Forest Area
Escanaba River State Forest
1985 US-41
Ishpeming, MI 49849
(906) 485–1031

85 Van Buren Trail State Park

Endpoints: Hartford, South
Haven
Mileage: 14
Surface: gravel, ballast, dirt

Location: Van Buren
Contact: Kurt Maxwell

Trail Supervisor
Van Buren State Park
23960 Ruggles Rd.
South Haven, MI 49090-9492
(616) 637–2788

86 Vicksburg Recreation Area Trailway

Endpoints: Vicksburg
Mileage: 1.8
Surface: asphalt

Location: Kalamazoo
Contact: Matthew L. Crawford
Village Manager
Village of Vicksburg
126 N. Kalamazoo Avenue
Vicksburg, MI 49097
(646) 649–1919
mcrawford000@ameritech.net

87 Watersmeet/Land O'Lakes Trail

Endpoints: Watersmeet, Land
O'Lakes
Mileage: 8.8
Surface: ballast

Other use: ATV
Location: Gogebic
Contact: Wayne Petterson
Forestry Technician
Ottawa National Forest
P.O. Box 276
Watersmeet, MI 49969-0276
(906) 358–4551

88 Wellston Area Tourist Association Snowmobile Trail

Endpoints: Manistee National Forest
Mileage: 51.5
Surface: ballast

Location: Manistee; Lake
Contact: Teresa Maday
Outdoor Recreation Planner
Manistee National Forest
Manistee/Cadillac Ranger District
412 Red Apple Road
Manistee, MI 49660-9616
(616) 723–2211

89 West Bloomfield Trail Network

Endpoints: West Bloomfield Township
Mileage: 5.3
Surface: crushed stone

Location: Oakland
Contact: Dan Navarre
Director
West Bloomfield Parks & Recreation Commission
4640 Walnut Lake Road
West Bloomfield, MI 48323-1940
(810) 738–2500
Trailnet88@aol.com

90 West Campus Bicycle Path

Endpoints: Eastern Michigan University
Mileage: 1
Surface: asphalt

Location: Washtenaw
Contact: Daniel Klenczar
Project Manager
Eastern Michigan University
Physical Plant
Ypsilanti, MI 48197
(734) 487–1337

91 White Pine Trail State Park

Endpoints: Cadillac, Howard City
Mileage: 92
Surface: asphalt, crushed stone, gravel, ballast

Location: Kent; Mecosta; Montcalm; Osceola; Wexford
Contact: Paul Yauk
Staff Specialist
Michigan Department of Natural Resources
Parks and Recreation Division
P.O. Box 30257
Lansing, MI 48909-7757
(517) 335–4824
http://multimag.com/city/mi/reedcity/white.html

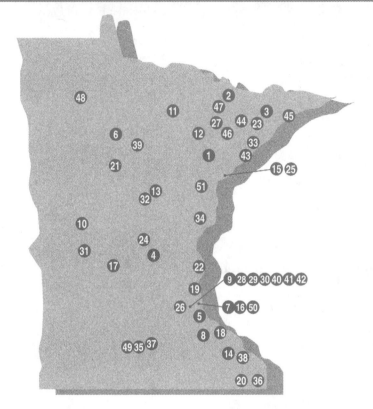

1 Alburn-Pengilly Greenway Trail

Endpoints: Albert, Grand Rapids
Mileage: 40
Surface: gravel, ballast

Location: Itaska; St. Louis
Contact: Jack Klassen
Trail Coordinator
Alburn Snow Devils
6697 Highway 47

Alborn, MN 55702-8234
(218) 345-6304

2 Arrowhead State Trail

Endpoints: Ericsburg, Tower
Mileage: 143
Surface: ballast, grass, dirt

Location: St. Louis; Koochiching
Contact: Ann Bjorgo

Area Supervisor
Minnesota DNR, Trails and
Waterways Unit
P.O. Box 388
406 Main Street
Tower, MN 55790-0388
(218) 753–6256
ann.bjorgo@dnr.state.mn.us
www.dnr.state.mn.us

3 Bear Island—Lake Trail

Endpoints: Bear Island State
Forest
Mileage: 13
Surface: ballast

Location: St. Louis
Contact: Mike Magnuson
Area Forester
Tower Area Forestry Office
609 North Second Street
P.O. Box 432
Tower, MN 55790
(218) 753–4500

4 Beaver Island Trail (Tileston Mill Spur)

Endpoints: St. Cloud
Mileage: 2.7
Surface: asphalt

Location: Stearns
Contact: Prentiss Foster
Director
St. Cloud Parks Department
400 Second Street South
St. Cloud, MN 56301-3699
(612) 255–7216
pfoster@ci.st.cloud.mn.us

5 Big Rivers Regional Trail

Endpoints: Mendota Heights
(near Minneapolis), Lillydale
Mileage: 4.2
Surface: asphalt

Other use: Winter hiking
Location: Dakota
Contact: Parks Director
Dakota County Parks Department
Spring Lake Park
Hastings, MN 55033
(651) 438–4660
parks@gsc.co.dakota.mn.us

6 Blue Ox Trail (Voyageur Trail)

Endpoints: Bemidji, International
Falls
Mileage: 107
Surface: ballast

Location: Beltrami; Itasca;
Koochiching
Contact: Ardon Belcher
Regional Supervisor
Minnesota DNR, Trails &
Waterways Unit
2115 Birchmount Beech Road NE
Bemidji, MN 56601-8571
(612) 296–6048

7 Burlington Northern Regional Trailway

Endpoints: St. Paul, Maplewood
Mileage: 5
Surface: asphalt

Location: Ramsey
Contact: Don Ganje
Landscape Architect
City of St. Paul/Divison of Parks &
Recreation
300 City Hall Annex
25 West Fourth Street
St. Paul, MN 55102
(651) 266–6425
don.ganje@ci.stpaul.mn.us

8 Cannon Valley Trail

Endpoints: Cannon Falls, Red
Wing
Mileage: 19.7
Surface: asphalt

Location: Goodhue
Contact: Scott Roepke
Cannon Valley Trail
306 West Mill Street
Cannon Falls, MN 55009
(507) 263–0508
www.cannonfalls.org

9 Cedar Lake Trail

Endpoints: Minneapolis
Mileage: 3.6
Surface: asphalt

Location: Hennepin
Contact: Jon Wertjes
Minneapolis Transportation
Department

City Hall
350 South Fifth Street, Room 233
Minneapolis, MN 55415-1316
(612) 673–2411

10 Central Lakes Trail

Endpoints: Osakis, Furgus Falls
Mileage: 63
Surface: gravel

Location: Douglas; Grant; Otter
Tail
Contact: Donald Lieffort
Park Superintendent
Douglas County Public Works
Department
P.O. Box 3
Alexandria, MN 56308
(320) 763–6001
al.lieffort@mail.co.douglas.mn.us

11 Circle L Trail

Endpoints: Big Fork, George
Washington State Forest
Mileage: 24.8
Surface: grass, dirt

Other use: ATV
Location: Itasca
Contact: Ben Anderson
Program Forester
Minnesota DNR, Division of
Forestry
P.O. Box 95
Effie, MN 56639-0095
(218) 743–3694

12 Circle T Trail

Endpoints: Nashwauk, George Washington State Forest
Mileage: 39.5
Surface: grass, dirt

Location: Itasca
Contact: Trail Manager
Minnesota DNR, Division of
Forestry
1208 East Howard Street
Hibbing, MN 55746
(218) 262–6760

13 Cuyuna Trail

Endpoints: Aitkin to Crosby,
spurs to Deerwood, Riverton,
and Trommald
Mileage: 18.8
Surface: grass, dirt

Location: Crow Wing
Contact: Crosby Chamber of
Commerce
P.O. Box 23
Crosby, MN 56441-0023
(218) 546–8131

14 Douglas State Trail

Endpoints: Rochester, Pine
Island
Mileage: 12.5
Surface: asphalt, ballast

Location: Goodhue; Olmsted
Contact: Joel Wagar
Area Manager
Minnesota DNR, Trails and
Waterways Unit
2300 Silver Creek Road NE
Rochester, MN 55906-4505
(507) 285–7176
www.dnr.state.mn.us

15 DWP Trail

Endpoints: Carlton, West Duluth
Mileage: 5
Surface: gravel

Location: St. Louis
Contact: Kelly Fleissner
City Forester
City of Duluth
Department of Public Works
110 N. Forty-second Avenue
West
City Hall Room 208
Duluth, MN 55802
(218) 723–3586

16 Gateway Segment of the Willard Munger Trail

Endpoints: St. Paul, Pine Point
Regional Park
Mileage: 19
Surface: asphalt

Location: Washington; Ramsey
Contact: Scott Kelling
Area Supervisor
Minnesota Department of
Natural Resources
1200 Warner Road

St. Paul, MN 55106-6793
(612) 297–2911

17 Glacial Lakes State Trail

Endpoints: Willmar, Stearns
County Line near Hawick
Mileage: 22
Surface: asphalt, crushed stone,
grass

Other use: dogsledding
Location: Kandiyohi; Stearns
Contact: Jeff Brown
Trail Manager
Minnesota DNR
P.O. Box 508
New London, MN 56273-0508
(612) 354–4940
www.dnr.state.mn.us/compass
trails/glacial/glacial.html

18 Goodhue Pioneer Trail (R. J. Dorer Memorial Trail)

Endpoints: R. J. Dorer Hardwood
State Forest, Hay Creek
Mileage: 8.9
Surface: grass, dirt

Other use: Hunting
Location: Goodhue
Contact: Kyle Klatt
Planning Technician
City of Red Wing
P.O. Box 34
Red Wing, MN 55066-0034
(612) 385–3622
kyle.wklatt@ci.red-wing.mn.us

19 Hardwood Creek Trail

Endpoints: Forest Lake, Hugo
Mileage: 9.5
Surface: asphalt, grass

Location: Washington
Contact: John Elholm
Operations Coordinator/Parks
Planner
Washington County Parks
11660 Myeron Road North
Stillwater, MN 55082
(651) 460–4303
john.elholm@co.washington.mn.us
www.co.washington.mn.us

20 Harmony—Preston Valley Trail (Root River Trail)

Endpoints: Fountain, Harmony
Mileage: 18
Surface: asphalt

Location: Fillmore
Contact: Craig Blommer
Area Supervisor
Minnesota DNR, Trails and
Waterways Unit
2300 Silver Creek Road NE
Rochester, MN 55906-4505
(507) 280–5061
www.dnr.state.mn.us

21 Heartland State Trail

Endpoints: Park Rapids, Cass Lake
Mileage: 51
Surface: asphalt, gravel

Location: Cass; Hubbard
Contact: Pat Tangeman
Trails & Waterways Technician
Heartland State Trail
P.O. Box 112
Nevis, MN 56467-0112
(218) 652–4054

22 Interstate State Park to Taylor Falls Trail

Endpoints: Interstate State Park, Taylor Falls
Mileage: 1
Surface: grass

Location: Chisago
Contact: Steve Anderson
Park Manager
Interstate State Park
P.O. Box 254
Taylor Falls, MN 55084-0254
(612) 465–5711

23 Iron Ore Trail

Endpoints: Tower, Embarass
Mileage: 15
Surface: ballast

Location: St. Louis
Contact: Thomas Peterson
Area Supervisor
Minnesota DNR, Trails and Waterways Unit
500 Lafayette Road
St. Paul, MN 55155-4052
(218) 753–6256

24 Lake Wobegon Trail

Endpoints: Avon, Sauk Centre
Mileage: 27.7
Surface: asphalt

Location: Stearns
Contact: Pete Theismann
Park Technician
Stearns County Parks
1802 County Road 137
Waite Park, MN 56387
(320) 255–6172
pete.theismann@co.stearns.mn.us
www.lakewobegontrails.com

25 Lakewalk Trail—Duluth

Endpoints: Canal Park Museum, Twenty-sixth Ave. East & London Rd.
Mileage: 3.8
Surface: asphalt

Location: St. Louis
Contact: Sue Moyer
Director
Duluth Parks and Recreation Dept.

City Hall, Room 330
411 W. First Street
Duluth, MN 55802-1102
(218) 723–3337
www.ci.duluth.mn.us

26 Luce Line State Trail

Endpoints: Plymouth, Cosmos
Mileage: 65
Surface: crushed stone, grass

Location: Hennepin; Carver;
McLeod; Meeker
Contact: Richard Schmidt
Trails & Waterways Technician
Minnesota DNR, Trails and
Waterways Unit
3980 Watertown Road
Maple Plain, MN 55359-9615
(612) 475–0371

27 Mesabi Trail (Hibbing to Chisholm Segment)

Endpoints: Hibbing, Chisholm
Mileage: 7.5
Surface: asphalt

Location: St. Louis
Contact: Bon Manzaline
Director
St. Louis and Lake Countries
Regional RR Authority
Suite 6B, US Bank Place
230 First St. South
Virginia, MN 55792
(218) 749–0697

28 Minnehaha Trail

Endpoints: Fort Snelling State
Park, Minneapolis
Mileage: 5
Surface: asphalt

Location: Hennepin
Contact: David Berg
Park Specialist
Fort Snelling State Park
1 Post Road
St. Paul, MN 55111
(612) 725–2389

29 Minnesota Valley State Trail

Endpoints: Minneapolis, Le
Sueur
Mileage: 75
Surface: asphalt, crushed stone

Location: Dakota; Hennepin;
Scott
Contact: Bill Weir
Trails Coordinator
Minnesota Department of
Natural Resources
1200 Warner Road
St. Paul, MN 55106
(612) 722–7994

30 Minnetonka Loop Trail System

Endpoints: Minnetonka
Mileage: 32

Surface: crushed stone

Location: Hennepin; Carver
Contact: Dean Elstad
Loop Trail Coordinator
City of Minnetonka
14600 Minnetonka Blvd.
Minnetonka, MN 55345-1597
(612) 938–7245
delstad@ci.minnentonka.mn.us

31 Minnewaska Snowmobile Trail (D.A.T.A. Trail System)

Endpoints: Starbuck, Villard
Mileage: 25
Surface: gravel, dirt

Location: Pope
Contact: Bill Anderson
Trail Manager
Douglas Area Trails Association
P.O. Box 112
Alexandria, MN 56308-0112
(612) 834–2033

32 Paul Bunyan State Trail

Endpoints: Brainerd-Baxter,
Bemidji and Hackensack
Mileage: 100
Surface: asphalt, ballast

Location: Beltrami; Cass; Crow
Wing; Hubbard
Contact: Terry McGaughey

Volunteer Coordinator
Paul Bunyan Trail
P.O. Box 356
124 North Sixth Street
Brainerd, MN 56401-0356
(218) 829–2838
terry@paulbunyantrail.com
www.brainerd.com/pbtrail/
pbtrail.html

33 Pequaywam Lake Snowmobile Trail (Cloquet Valley Trail)

Endpoints: Cloquet Valley State
Forest, Aurora
Mileage: 50
Surface: ballast, dirt

Location: St. Louis
Contact: Tom Peterson
Area Supervisor
Two Harbors Division of Trails
and Waterways
1568 Highway 2
Two Harbors, MN 55616
(218) 834–6622
www.dnr.state.mn.us

34 Quarry Loop Trail

Endpoints: Banning State Park
Mileage: 2
Surface: gravel, ballast

Location: Pine
Contact: Randy Gordon
Park Manager
Banning State Park
P.O. Box 643
Sandstone, MN 55072
(320) 245–2668

35 Red Jacket Trail

Endpoints: Mankato, Rapidan
Mileage: 5.6
Surface: asphalt, crushed stone

Location: Blue Earth
Contact: Dean Ehlers
Park Superintendent
Parks Department
P.O. Box 3083
Mankato, MN 56002-3083
(507) 625–3282

36 Root River State Trail

Endpoints: Fountain, Rushford
Mileage: 37.4
Surface: asphalt, grass

Location: Fillmore; Houston
Contact: Craig Blommer
Area Supervisor
Minnesota DNR, Trails and
Waterways Unit
2300 Silver Creek Road, NE
Rochester, MN 55906-4505
(507) 280–5061
www.dnr.state.mn.us

37 Sakatah Singing Hills State Trail

Endpoints: Faribault, Mankato
Mileage: 39
Surface: asphalt, grass

Location: Blue Earth; Le Sueur;
Rice
Contact: Randy Schoeneck
Trail Technician
Minnesota DNR
Sakatah State Park
P.O. Box 11
Elysian, MN 56028-0011
(507) 267–4772
www.dnr.mn.state.us

38 Silver Creek Bike Trail

Endpoints: Rochester
Mileage: 1.31
Surface: asphalt

Location: Olmsted
Contact: David Rossman
Transportation Engineer
Rochester Public Works
Department
201 Fourth Street SE, Rm 108
Rochester, MN 55904-3740
(507) 281–6194

39 Soo Line Trail

Endpoints: Cass Lake, Moose
Lake State Park
Mileage: 114
Surface: gravel, ballast

Other use: ATV
Location: Aitkin; Carlton; Cass
Contact: Bill Stocker
District Ranger
Chippewa National Forest
Route 3, Box 244
Cass Lake, MN 56633-8929
(218) 335–2283

40 Southwest Regional LRT Trail—North Corridor

Endpoints: Hopkins, Minnetonka
Mileage: 15
Surface: asphalt, crushed stone

Location: Carver; Hennepin
Contact: Delbert Miller
Trails Coordinator
Hennepin County Parks
12615 County Road 9
Plymouth, MN 55441-1299
(612) 559–6754
Dmiller@hennepinparks.org
www.hennepinparks.org/

41 Southwest Regional LRT Trail—South Corridor

Endpoints: Chanhassen, Hopkins
Mileage: 11.5
Surface: crushed stone

Location: Carver; Hennepin
Contact: Delbert Miller
Trails Coordinator
Hennepin County Parks
12615 County Road 9
Plymouth, MN 55441-1248

(612) 559–6754
Dmiller@hennepinparks.org/
www.hennepinparks.org/

42 St. Anthony Falls Heritage Trail (Stone Arch Bridge)

Endpoints: Minneapolis
Mileage: 1.5
Surface: concrete

Location: Hennepin
Contact: David Wiggins
Program Manager
Minnesota Historical Society
125 Main Street SE
Minneapolis, MN 55414-2143
(612) 627–5433

43 Superior Hiking Trail

Endpoints: Canadian Border, Two Harbors
Mileage: 220 (3 are Rail-Trail)
Surface: ballast, dirt

Other use: Snowshoeing
Location: St. Louis; Lake; Cook
Contact: Nancy Odden
Executive Director
Superior Hiking Trail Association
P.O. Box 4
Two Harbors, MN 55616-0004
(218) 834–4436
suphike@mn.net
www.shta.org

44 Taconite State Trail

Endpoints: Ely, Grand Rapids
Mileage: 165

Surface: gravel, ballast, grass, dirt

Location: St. Louis
Contact: Ann Bjorgo
Area Supervisor
Minnesota Department of
Natural Resources
406 Main Street
P.O. Box 388
Tower, MN 55790
(218) 753–6256
www.dnr.state.mn.us

45 Tomahawk Trail

Endpoints: Ely, Little Marais
Mileage: 65
Surface: ballast, grass

Location: Lake; St. Louis
Contact: Minnesota DNR
1568 HWYZ
Two Harbors, MN 55616
(218) 834–6626

46 Trailblazers Path (part of Mesabi Trail)

Endpoints: Hibbing, Lake Swan
Mileage: 10
Surface: asphalt, gravel, ballast

Location: Itaska; St. Louis
Contact: Douglas Swenson
Hibbing Trailblazers

P.O. Box 432
Hibbing, MN 55746-0432
(218) 262–5595
senbay@uslink.net

47 Virginia Trails

Endpoints: Virginia
Mileage: 1
Surface: crushed stone, gravel

Location: St. Louis
Contact: John Bachman
Director
City of Virginia Park & Recreation
Department
Virginia, MN 55792
(218) 741–3583

48 Wapiti Trail

Endpoints: Thief/River Falls, Grygla
Mileage: 50.2 (17 are Rail-Trail)
Surface: ballast, grass, dirt

Location: Marshall; Pennington
Contact: Alan Swanson
Goodrich Trailblazers
Snowmobile Club
Route 2, Box 28A
Goodridge, MN 56725-9724
(218) 378-4570
www.dnr.state.mn.us

49 West Mankato Trail

Endpoints: Mankato City
Mileage: 1.5
Surface: asphalt

Location: Blue Earth
Contact: Floyd Roberts
Parks Superintendent
City of Mankato Parks and
Forestry
P.O. Box 3368
Mankato, MN 56002-3368
(507) 387-8650
Trailnet88@aol.com

50 West River Parkway

Endpoints: Saint Paul, Brooklyn Center
Mileage: 4.84
Surface: asphalt, concrete

Location: Anoka; Ramsey
Contact: Bob Mattson
Park & Recreation Planner
Minneapolis Park and Recreation Board
200 Grain Exchange
400 South Fourth Street
Minneapolis, MN 55415-1400
(612) 661-4824

51 Willard Munger State Trail (Alex Laveau Memorial Trail)

Endpoints: Hinckley, Duluth
Mileage: 72
Surface: asphalt

Location: Carlton; Pine
Contact: Kevin Arends
Area Supervisor
Minnesota DNR, Trails and
Waterways Unit
Route 2, 701 South Kenwood
Moose Lake, MN 55767
(218) 485-5410

MISSISSIPPI

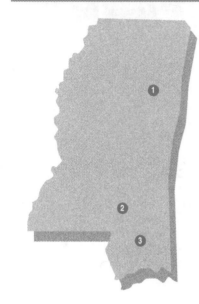

2 Longleaf Trace Trail

Endpoints: Hattiesburg, Prentiss
Mileage: 39
Surface: asphalt

Location: Forrest, Jefferson Davis, Lamar
Contact: Jim Moore
707 Hutchinson Avenue
Hattiesburg, MS 39401-4138
(601) 544–1978

3 Tuxachanie National Recreation Trail

Endpoints: DeSoto National Forest
Mileage: 22.8
Surface: dirt

Location: Harrison; Stone
Contact: Diane Tyrone
Forester
Desoto Ranger District
P.O. Box 248
654 West Frontage Road
Wiggins, MS 39577-0248
(601) 928–5291

1 Catherine "Kitty" Bryan Dill Memorial Parkway

Endpoints: West Point
Mileage: 1.2
Surface: concrete

Location: Clay
Contact: Dewel Brasher, Jr.
City Manager
City of West Point
P.O. Box 1117
West Point, MS 39773-1117
(601) 494–2573

MISSOURI

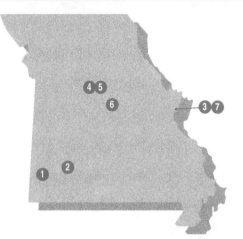

1 Frisco Greenway

Endpoints: Joplin, Webb City
Mileage: 4
Surface: crushed stone, ballast

Location: Jasper
Contact: Paul Teverow
President
Joplin Trails Coalition
P.O. Box 2102
Joplin, MO 64803-2102
(417) 625–3114

2 Frisco Highline Trail

Endpoints: Walnut Grove, Willard
Mileage: 11.2
Surface: crushed stone, ballast

Location: Greene; Polk
Contact: Terry Whaley
Executive Director
Ozark Greenways
P.O. Box 50733
Springfield, MO 65805-0733
(417) 864–2014
Terry_whaley@ci.springfield.
mo.us
www.springfield.missouri.org/
gov/ozarkgreenways/

3 Grant's Trail

Endpoints: St. Louis
Mileage: 4.2
Surface: asphalt, crushed stone, ballast

Location: St. Louis
Contact: Fred Earnie
Executive Director
Trailnet, Inc.

3900 Reavis Barracks Road
St. Louis, MO 63125-2308
(314) 416–9930
granttrail@stlnot.com
www.trailnet.org

4 Katy Spur Trail

Endpoints: Jefferson City, North
Jefferson
Mileage: 1
Location: Cole
Contact: Jefferson City
P.O. Box 166
Booneville, MO 65233-0166
(816) 882–8196

5 Katy Trail State Park

Endpoints: St. Charles, Sedalia
Mileage: 185
Surface: crushed stone

Location: Boone; Callaway;
Cooper; Henry; Howard;
Montgomery; Pettis; St. Charles;
Warren
Contact: Larry Larson
District Manager
Missouri River District
P.O. Box 166
Booneville, MO 65233-0166
(660) 882–8196
www.global-image.com/
katytrail/intro.html

6 M.K.T. Nature/Fitness Trail

Endpoints: Columbia, McBain
Mileage: 8.5
Surface: crushed stone

Location: Boone
Contact: Steve Saitta
Parks Development
Superintendent
Columbia Parks and Recreation
Department
P.O. Box N
Columbia, MO 65205-5013
(573) 874–7203

7 West Alton Trail

Endpoints: West Alton, Missouri
River
Mileage: 1.3
Surface: crushed stone

Location: St. Charles
Contact: Ted Curtis
Executive Director
Trailnet, Inc.
3900 Reavis Barracks Rd.
St. Louis, MO 63125-2308
(314) 416–9930
trailnet@trailnet.org

MONTANA

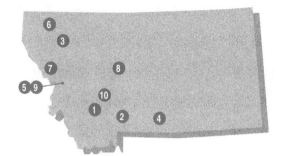

1 Butte to Toll Mountain Cross-Country Ski Trail

Endpoints: Deerlodge National Forest
Mileage: 7
Surface: ballast

Location: Jefferson
Contact: Wendell Beardsley
Trails Program Coordinator
USDAFS, Region 1
200 East Broadway
P.O. Box 7669
Missoula, MT 59802-4598
(406) 329–3150

2 Gallagator Linear Trail

Endpoints: Bozeman
Mileage: 1.5
Surface: gravel, ballast

Location: Gallatin
Contact: Sue Harkin
Recreation Superintendent
Bozeman Recreation Department
P.O. Box 640
1211 West Main Street
Bozeman, MT 59771-0640
(406) 587–4724
sharkin@gomontana.com

3 Great Northern Historical Trail

Endpoints: Kalispell, Marion
Mileage: 2.5
Surface: gravel

Location: Flathead
Contact: John Hale
Board Member
Rails-to-Trails of Northwest Montana
P.O. Box 1103
Kalispell, MT 59903-1103
(406) 752–8383

4 Heights Bike Trail (Kiwanis Bike Trail)

Endpoints: Billings
Mileage: 5
Surface: concrete

Location: Yellowstone
Contact: Mike Hink
Director
Department of Parks, Recreation and Public Lands
510 North Broadway
4th Floor Library
Billings, MT 59101-1156
(406) 657-8369

5 Kim Williams Nature Trail

Endpoints: Missoula
Mileage: 2.5
Surface: ballast

Location: Missoula
Contact: Jim Van Fossen
Director
Missoula Parks & Recreation Department
100 Hickory Street
Missoula, MT 59801-1859
(406) 721-7275
www.marsweb.com/~missoula/feetfrst.html

6 Kootenai Trail

Endpoints: Kootenai National Forest
Mileage: 6
Surface: gravel

Location: Lincoln
Contact: Eric Heyn
Resource Forester
Kootenai National Forest
1299 Highway 93 North
Eureka, MT 59917
(406) 296-2536

7 NorPac Trail

Endpoints: Lolo National Forest, Idaho State Line
Mileage: 12.1
Surface: ballast

Location: Mineral
Contact: Carol Johnson
Lolo National Forest
Superior Ranger District
P.O. Box 460
Superior, MT 59872
(406) 822-4233

8 River's Edge Trail

Endpoints: Great Falls
Mileage: 13
Surface: asphalt, gravel, dirt, concrete

Location: Cascade
Contact: Doug Wicks
Vice President
Recreational Trails, Inc.
P.O. Box 553
Great Falls, MT 59403-0553
(406) 761–4966
trailsrus@in-tch.com

9 Southside Trail

Endpoints: Missoula
Mileage: 1.5
Surface: asphalt, gravel, ballast

Location: Missoula
Contact: Jim Van Fossen
Director
Missoula Parks & Recreation
Department
100 Hickory Street
Missoula, MT 59801-1859
(406) 721–7275

10 Spring Meadows Lake and Centennial Park Trail

Endpoints: Helena
Mileage: 2
Surface: crushed stone

Location: Lewis and Clark
Contact: Randy Lilje
Park Manager
Helena Area Resource Office of
Fish, Wildlife and Parks
930 Custer West
Helena, MT 59620
(405) 447–8463

NEBRASKA

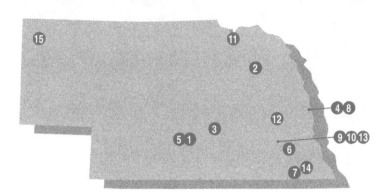

1 Cottonmill—Fort Kearny Trail

Endpoints: Kearney, Fort Kearny
Mileage: 3.1
Surface: asphalt, crushed stone, concrete

Location: Buffalo
Contact: Neil Lewis
Kearney Parks & Recreation Department
P.O. Box 1180
Kearney, NE 68848-1180
(308) 233–3230

2 Cowboy Trail

Endpoints: Neligh, O'Neill, Valentine
Mileage: 47 (in 3 sections)
Surface: crushed stone, concrete

Location: Antelope; Cherry; Holt
Contact: Larry Voecks
State Trail Coordinator
Nebraska Games and Parks Commission
2201 North Thirteenth Street
Norfolk, NE 68701-2267
(402) 370–3374
netrails@ngpc.state.ne.us
www.ngpc.state.ne.us

3 Dannebrog Rail-Trail

Endpoints: Dannebrog
Mileage: 3
Surface: wood chips, concrete

Location: Howard
Contact: Shirley Johnson
Treasurer and Public Relations
Dannenbrog Trail Association
P.O. Box 216
522 East Roger Welsch Avenue
Dannenbrog, NE 68831-0216
(308) 226–2237

4 Field Club Trail

Endpoints: Omaha
Mileage: 1.5
Surface: concrete

Location: Douglas
Contact: Jerry Leahy
Assistant Director
Douglas County Environmental
Services
3015 Menke Circle
Omaha, NE 68134-4638
(402) 444–7775

5 Fort Kearny Hike-Bike Trail

Endpoints: Basswood Strip State
Wildlife Area, Fort Kearny State
Recreation Area
Mileage: 1.8
Surface: ballast, cinder

Location: Kearney; Buffalo
Contact: Eugene Hunt
Superintendent
Fort Kearny State
Recreation Area
Route 4
1020 V. Road
Kearney, NE 68847-9804
(308) 865–5305
www.ngpc.state.ne.us

6 Hickman Linear Bike Trail

Endpoints: Hickman
Mileage: 0.8
Surface: asphalt

Location: Lancaster
Contact: Jim Plouzek
Mayor
City of Hickman
P.O. Box 127
Hickman, NE 68372-0127
(402) 792–2212

7 Iron Horse Trail Lake Park

Endpoints: Nemaha Natural
Resources District
Mileage: 2.9
Surface: ballast

Other use: Hunting
Location: Pawnee
Contact: Pat Foote
SCORP
Nebraska Game & Parks
Commission
220 North Thirty-third Street
Lincoln, NE 68503-3303
(402) 471–0641

8 Keystone Trail

Endpoints: Omaha
Mileage: 12
Surface: concrete

Location: Douglas; Sarpy
Contact: Dolores Silkworth
Park and Recreation Planner
Parks, Recreation and Public
Property
Omaha/Douglas Civic Center
1819 Farnam Street , Suite 1111
Omaha, NE 68183-0111
(402) 444–4985

9 MoPac East Trail

Endpoints: Lincoln
Mileage: 24
Surface: crushed stone

Location: Lancaster; Cass
Contact: Dan Schulz
Resources Coordinator
Lower Platte South Natural
Resource District
3125 Portig Street
P.O. Box 83581
Lincoln, NE 68501-3581
(402) 476–2729
dan@lpsnrd.org
www.lpsnrd.org

10 MoPac Trail

Endpoints: Lincoln
Mileage: 4
Surface: concrete

Location: Lancaster; Cass
Contact: Lynn Johnson

Planning and Construction
Manager
City of Lincoln Parks and
Recreation Department
2740 A Street
Lincoln, NE 68502
(402) 441–8255

11 Niobrara Trail

Endpoints: Niobrara State Park
Mileage: 2.1
Surface: crushed stone

Location: Knox
Contact: Tom Motacek
Superintendent
Niobrara State Park
P.O. Box 226
Niobrara, NE 68760-0226
(402) 857–3373

12 Oak Creek Trail

Endpoints: Brainard, Valparaiso
Mileage: 12
Surface: crushed stone

Location: Saunders; Butler
Contact: Dan Schulz
Resources Coordinator
Lower Platte South Natural
Resources District
3125 Portia Street
P.O. Box 83581
Lincoln, NE 68501-3581
(402) 476–2729
dan@lpsnrd.org
www.lpsnrd.org

13 Rock Island Trail

Endpoints: Lincoln
Mileage: 5
Surface: concrete

Location: Lancaster
Contact: Lynn Johnson
Planning and Construction
Manager
Lincoln Department of Parks and
Recreation
2740 A Street
Lincoln, NE 68502-3113
(402) 441-7847

14 Steamboat-Trace Trail

Endpoints: Brownville, Peru
Mileage: 9.5
Surface: crushed stone

Location: Otoe; Nemaha
Contact: Paul Rohrbaugh
Nemaha Natural Resources
District
125 Jackson Street
Tecumseh, NE 68450-2133
(402) 335-3325

15 White River Trail

Endpoints: Andrews, Harrison
Mileage: 10
Surface: ballast

Location: Dawes; Sioux
Contact: Jim Lemmon
Fort Robinson State Park
P.O. Box 392
Crawford, NE 69339
(308) 665-2900

1 Historic Railroad Hiking Trail

Endpoints: Lake Mead National
Recreation Area
Mileage: 6
Surface: gravel, dirt

Location: Clark
Contact: Karen Whitney
Public Affairs Officer
Lake Mead National Recreation
Area
601 Nevada Highway
Boulder City, NV 89005-2426
(702) 293–8907

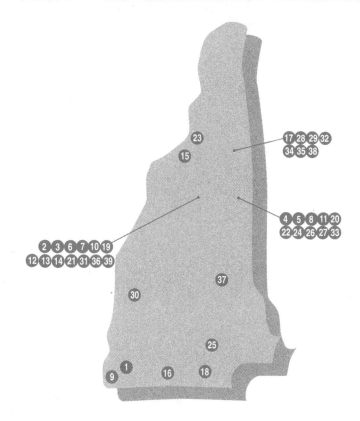

1 Ashuelot Rail Trail

Recreation, Trails Bureau
172 Pembroke Road
P.O. Box 856
Concord, NH 03302-1856
(603) 271–3254

Endpoints: Hinsdale, Keene
Mileage: 23
Surface: gravel, ballast

Location: Cheshire
Contact: Bob Spoerl
Program Specialist
N.H. Division of Parks &

2 Black Pond Trail

Endpoints: White Mountain
National Forest
Mileage: 0.8
Surface: dirt

Location: Grafton
Contact: Dave Hrdlicka
Trails Coordinator
White Mountain National Forest
Pemigewassett Ranger District
RFD 3, Route 175, Box 15
Plymouth, NH 03264
(603) 536–1310

3 Cedar Brook Trail

Endpoints: White Mountain
National Forest
Mileage: 5.7
Surface: ballast

Location: Grafton
Contact: Dave Hrdlicka
Trails Coordinator
White Mountain National Forest
Pemigewassett Ranger District
RFD 3, Route 175, Box 15
Plymouth, NH 03264
(603) 536–1310

4 Dry River Trail

Endpoints: White Mountain
National Forest
Mileage: 10.5
Surface: ballast

Location: Carroll
Contact: Eric Swett
Forest Technician
White Mountain National Forest
Saco Ranger District
33 Kancamagus Highway
Conway, NH 03818-6019
(603) 447–5448

5 East Branch Trail

Endpoints: White Mountain
National Forest
Mileage: 8
Surface: ballast

Location: Carroll
Contact: Eric Swett
Forest Technician
White Mountain National Forest
Saco Ranger District
33 Kancamagus Highway
Conway, NH 03818-6019
(603) 447–5448

6 East Pond Trail

Endpoints: White Mountain
National Forest
Mileage: 5
Surface: gravel, grass, dirt

Location: Grafton
Contact: Dave Hrdlicka
Trails Coordinator
White Mountain National Forest
Pemigewassett Ranger District
RFD 3, Route 175, Box 15
Plymouth, NH 03264
(603) 536–1310

7 Ethan Pond Trail

Endpoints: White Mountain
National Forest
Mileage: 5.6
Surface: ballast, grass, dirt

Location: Grafton
Contact: Dave Hrdlicka
Trails Coordinator
White Mountain National Forest
Pemigewassett Ranger District
RFD 3, Route 175, Box 15
Plymouth, NH 03264
(603) 536–1310

8 Flat Mountain Pond Trail

Endpoints: White Mountain
National Forest
Mileage: 9
Surface: ballast

Location: Carroll
Contact: Eric Swett
Forest Technician
White Mountain National Forest
Saco Ranger District
33 Kancamagus Highway
Conway, NH 03818-6019
(603) 447–5448

9 Fort Hill Branch

Endpoints: Hinsdale
Mileage: 9
Surface: gravel, ballast

Location: Cheshire
Contact: Bob Spoerl
Program Specialist
N.H. Division of Parks &

Recreation, Trails Bureau
172 Pembroke Road
P.O. Box 856
Concord, NH 03302-1856
(603) 271–3254
b_spoerl@gwsmtp.dred.state.
nh.us

10 Franconia Brook Trail

Endpoints: White Mountain
National Forest
Mileage: 7.2
Surface: ballast

Location: Grafton
Contact: Dave Hrdlicka
Trails Coordinator
White Mountain National Forest
Pemigewassett Ranger District
RFD 3, Route175, Box 15
Plymouth, NH 03264
(603) 536–1310

11 Guinea Pond Trail

Endpoints: White Mountain
National Forest
Mileage: 4
Surface: ballast

Location: Carroll
Contact: Dave Hrdlicka
Trails Coordinator
White Mountain National Forest
Pemigewassett Ranger District
RFD 3, Route 175, Box 15
Plymouth, NH 03264
(603) 536–1310

12 Lincoln Brook Trail

Endpoints: White Mountain National Forest
Mileage: 6.7
Surface: gravel, dirt

Location: Grafton
Contact: Dave Hrdlicka
Trails Coordinator
White Mountain National Forest
Pemigewassett Ranger District
RFD 3, Route 175, Box 15
Plymouth, NH 03264
(603) 536–1310

13 Lincoln Woods Trail

Endpoints: White Mountain National Forest
Mileage: 2.7
Surface: ballast

Location: Grafton
Contact: Dave Hrdlicka
Trails Coordinator
White Mountain National Forest
Pemigewassett Ranger District
RFD 3, Route 175, Box 15
Plymouth, NH 03264
(603) 536–1310

14 Little East Pond Trail

Endpoints: White Mountain National Forest
Mileage: 1.7
Surface: ballast

Location: Grafton
Contact: Dave Hrdlicka
Trails Coordinator
White Mountain National Forest
Pemigewassett Ranger District
RFD 3, Route 175, Box 15
Plymouth, NH 03264
(603) 536–1310

15 Littleton to Woodsville

Endpoints: Littleton, Woodsville
Mileage: 19
Surface: ballast

Location: Grafton
Contact: Paul Gray
Bureau Chief
New Hampshire Bureau of Trails
P.O. Box 1856
Concord, NH 03302-1856
(603) 271–3254

16 Mason Railroad Trail

Endpoints: Wilton, Townsend, MA
Mileage: 6.7
Surface: ballast

Location: Hillsborough
Contact: Liz Fletcher
Commissioner
Mason Conservation Commission
Mann House
Darling Hill Road
Mason, NH 03048
(603) 878–2070

17 Moriah Brook Trail

Endpoints: White Mountain National Forest
Mileage: 5.3
Surface: gravel, dirt

Location: Coos
Contact: Terri Marceron
Assistant Ranger
White Mountain National Forest
Androscoggin Ranger District
80 Glen Road
Gorham, NH 03581-1322
(603) 466–2713

18 Nashua-Worcester Rail Trail

Endpoints: Nashua
Mileage: 1.3
Surface: asphalt, grass

Location: Hillsborough
Contact: Mark Archambault
Long Range Planner
Community Development
Divison of the City of Nashua
229 Main Street
Nashua, NH 03060
(603) 594–3360
archambaultm@nashuanh.org

19 North Twin Trail

Endpoints: White Mountain National Forest
Mileage: 4.3
Surface: dirt

Location: Grafton
Contact: Roger Collins
Forest Technician
White Mountain National Forest
Ammonusac Ranger District
P.O. Box 239
Bethlehem, NH 03574-0239
(603) 869–2626

20 Oliverian Trail

Endpoints: White Mountain National Forest
Mileage: 3.5
Surface: dirt

Location: Carroll
Contact: Eric Swett
Forest Technician
White Mountain National Forest
Saco Ranger District
33 Kancamagus Highway
Conway, NH 03818-6019
(603) 447–5448

21 Osseo Trail

Endpoints: White Mountain National Forest
Mileage: 5.8
Surface: gravel, dirt

Location: Grafton
Contact: Dave Hrdlicka
Trails Coordinator

White Mountain National Forest
Pemigewassett Ranger District
RFD 3, Route 175, Box 15
Plymouth, NH 03264
(603) 536–1310

22 Pine Bend Brook Trail

Endpoints: White Mountain
National Forest
Mileage: 4.3
Surface: gravel

Location: Carroll
Contact: Eric Swett
Forest Technician
White Mountain National Forest
Saco Ranger District
33 Kancamagus Highway
Conway, NH 03818-6019
(603) 447–5448

23 Pondicherry Trail

Endpoints: Whitefield, Jefferson
Mileage: 2
Surface: gravel, grass, dirt,
crushed stone

Location: Coos
Contact: David Govatski
Jefferson Conservation
Commission
Route 115, Box 157-A
Jefferson, NH 03583
(603) 869–2626
dgovatski@fs.fed.us

24 Rob Brook Trail

Endpoints: White Mountain
National Forest
Mileage: 2
Surface: ballast

Location: Carroll
Contact: Eric Swett
Forest Technician
White Mountain National Forest
Saco Ranger District
33 Kancamagus Highway
Conway, NH 03818-6019
(603) 447–5448

25 Rockingham Recreational Trail

Endpoints: Manchester,
Newfields
Mileage: 28
Surface: gravel, ballast

Other use: dogsledding
Location: Hillsborough;
Rockingham
Contact: Paul Gray
Chief, Bureau of Trails
Division of Parks and Recreation
172 Pembroke Road
P.O. Box 1865
Concord, NH 03302-1856
(603) 271–3254

26 Rocky Branch Trail

Endpoints: White Mountain National Forest
Mileage: 9
Surface: ballast

Location: Carroll
Contact: Eric Swett
Forest Technician
White Mountain National Forest
Saco Ranger District
33 Kancamagus Highway
Conway, NH 03818-6019
(603) 447–5448

27 Sawyer River Trail

Endpoints: White Mountain National Forest
Mileage: 4
Surface: ballast

Location: Carroll
Contact: Eric Swett
Forest Technician
White Mountain National Forest
Saco Ranger District
33 Kancamagus Highway
Conway, NH 03818-6019
(603) 447–5448

28 Shelburne Trail

Endpoints: White Mountain National Forest

Mileage: 7.2
Surface: dirt

Location: Coos
Contact: Terri Marceron
Assistant Ranger
White Mountain National Forest
Androscoggin Ranger District
80 Glen Road
Gorham, NH 03581-1322
(603) 466–2713

29 Spider Bridge Loop Trail

Endpoints: White Mountain National Forest
Mileage: 4.5
Surface: gravel

Location: Coos
Contact: George Pozzuto
District Ranger
White Mountain National Forest
Androscoggin Ranger District
300 Glen Road
Gorham, NH 03581-1322
(603)466–2713

30 Sugar River Recreation Trail

Endpoints: Newport, Claremont
Mileage: 8
Surface: gravel, ballast

Location: Sullivan
Contact: Bob Spoerl
Program Specialist

N.H. Division of Parks &
Recreation, Trails Bureau
172 Pembroke Road
P.O. Box 856
Concord, NH 03302-1856
(603) 271–3254

31 Thoreau Falls Trail

Endpoints: White Mountain
National Forest
Mileage: 5.1
Surface: ballast, dirt

Location: Grafton
Contact: Dave Hrdlicka
Trails Coordinator
White Mountain National Forest
Pemigewassett Ranger District
RFD 3, Route 175, Box 15
Plymouth, NH 03264
(603) 536–1310

32 Trestle Trail

Endpoints: White Mountain
National Forest
Mileage: 1
Surface: dirt

Location: Coos
Contact: Roger Collins
Forest Technician
White Mountain National Forest
Ammonusac Ranger Distict
P.O. Box 239
Bethlehem, NH 03574-0239
(603) 869–2626

33 Upper Nanamocomuck Trail

Endpoints: White Mountain
National Forest
Mileage: 9.3
Surface: ballast

Location: Carroll
Contact: Eric Swett
Forest Technician
White Mountain National Forest
Saco Ranger District
33 Kancamagus Highway
Conway, NH 03818-6019
(603) 447–5448

34 West Milan Trail

Endpoints: White Mountain
National Forest
Mileage: 4.5
Surface: gravel

Location: Coos
Contact: George Pozzuto
District Ranger
White Mountain National Forest
Androscoggin Ranger District
300 Glen Road
Gorham, NH 03581-1322
(603) 466–2713

35 Wild River Trail

Endpoints: White Mountain
National Forest
Mileage: 4.5
Surface: gravel, dirt

Location: Coos
Contact: Terri Marceron
Assistant Ranger
White Mountain National Forest
Androscoggin Ranger District
80 Glen Road
Gorham, NH 03581-1322
(603) 466–2713

36 Wilderness Trail

Endpoints: White Mountain
National Forest
Mileage: 8.9
Surface: ballast, dirt

Location: Grafton
Contact: Dave Hrdlicka
Trails Coordinator
White Mountain National Forest
Pemigewassett Ranger District
RFD 3, Route 175, Box 15
Plymouth, NH 03264
(603) 536–1310

37 Wolfeboro/Sanbornville Recreational Trail— Russell Chase Path

Endpoints: Wolfeboro Falls,
Sanbornville
Mileage: 12
Surface: crushed stone, gravel,
dirt

Location: Carroll
Contact: Sue Glenn

Director of Parks & Recreation
Town of Wolfeboro
P.O. Box 629
Wolfeboro, NH 03894-0629
(603) 271–3254

38 York Pond Trail

Endpoints: White Mountain
National Forest
Mileage: 6.5
Surface: dirt

Location: Coos
Contact: George Pozzuto
District Ranger
White Mountain National Forest
Androscoggin Ranger District
300 Glen Road
Gorham, NH 03581-1322
(603) 466–2713

39 Zealand Trail

Endpoints: White Mountain
National Forest, Bethlehem
Mileage: 2.5
Surface: dirt

Location: Grafton
Contact: Roger Collins
Forest Technician
White Mountain National Forest
660 Trudeau Road
P.O. Box 239
Bethlehem, NH 03574-0239
(603) 869–2626
rcollins/R9_whiteMTN@fed.us

NEW JERSEY

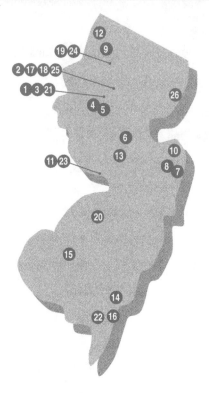

1 Berkshire Valley Management Area Trail

Endpoints: Lake Hopatcong
Mileage: 3
Surface: ballast

Location: Morris
Contact: John Piccolo
Black River Wildlife
Management Area
275 North Road

Chester, NJ 07930-2332
(908) 879–6252

2 Black River County Park Trail

Endpoints: Chester
Mileage: 1.6
Surface: dirt

Location: Morris
Contact: Al Kent
Commissioner
Morris County Park Commission

P.O. Box 1295
Morristown, NJ 07962-1295
(201) 326–7600

3 Black River Wildlife Management Area Trail

Endpoints: Chester
Mileage: 4
Surface: ballast

Location: Morris
Contact: John Piccolo
Black River Wildlife Management
Area
275 North Road
Chester, NJ 07930-2332
(908) 879–6252

4 Capoolong Creek Wildlife Management Area

Endpoints: Pittstown,
Landsdown
Mileage: 2.8
Surface: grass, dirt, cinder

Location: Hunterdon
Contact: Steve Smysler
Land Management Supervisor
Clinton Wildlife Management
Area
7 Van Syckel's Road
Hampton, NJ 08827
(908) 735–8793

5 Columbia Trail

Endpoints: High Bridge,
Hunterdon/Morris county line

Mileage: 8
Surface: asphalt, crushed stone,
ballast

Location: Hunterdon
Contact: Pam Thier
Director
Hunterdon County Parks System
1020 Highway 13
Lebanon, NJ 08833
(908) 782–1158

6 Delaware and Raritan Canal State Park Trail

Endpoints: Frenchtown to
Trenton, Trenton to New
Brunswick
Mileage: 68
Surface: crushed stone, gravel

Location: Hunterdon; Mercer;
Somerset
Contact: Susan Herron
Superintendent
Delaware and Raritan Canal State
Park Trail
625 Canal Road
Somerset, NJ 08873-7309
(732) 873–3050

7 Edgar Felix Memorial Bikeway

Endpoints: Manasquan, Allaire
State Park
Mileage: 3.6
Surface: asphalt

Location: Monmouth
Contact: Thomas White
Director
Wall Township Parks and
Recreation
2700 Allaire Road
Wall, NJ 07719-9570
(908) 449–8444

8 Freehold and Jamesburg Railroad Trail

Endpoints: Allaire State Park
Mileage: 4.5
Surface: gravel, dirt

Location: Monmouth
Contact: Nicholas DeMicco
Superintendent
Allaire State Park
P.O. Box 220
Farmingdale, NJ 07727-0220
(908) 938–2371

9 Hamburg Mountain Wildlife Management Area

Endpoints: Ogdensburg,
Franklin
Mileage: 3
Surface: ballast, dirt, cinder

Location: Sussex
Contact: Vincent Mercurio
Supervisor WMA
N.J. Division of Fish, Game &
Wildlife
150 Fradon-Springdale Road

Newton, NJ 07860-5217
(201) 383–0918

10 Henry Hudson Trail

Endpoints: Atlantic Highlands,
Aberdeen
Mileage: 9
Surface: asphalt

Location: Monmouth
Contact: Laura Kirkpatrick
Public Information Officer
Monmouth County Park System
850 Newman Springs Road
Lincroft, NJ 07738
(732) 842–4000

11 Johnson Trolley Line Trail

Endpoints: Lawrence Township
Mileage: 2.5
Surface: asphalt, gravel, grass,
dirt

Location: Mercer
Contact: Celeste Tracy
Supervising Planner
N.J. Division of Parks and
Forestry
22 South Clinton Street
CN 404
P.O. Box 404
Trenton, NJ 08625-0404
(609) 984–1173
ctracy@dep.state.nj.us

12 Karamac Trail

Endpoints: Delaware Water Gap National Recreation Area
Mileage: 2
Surface: dirt, cinder

Location: Warren
Contact: Wayne Valentine
New Jersey District Ranger
Delaware Watergap National Recreation Area
2 Walpack-Flatbrookville Road
Layton, NJ 07851
(973) 948–6500
wayne-valentine@nps.gov

13 Kingston Branch Loop Trail

Endpoints: Kingston, Rocky Hill
Mileage: 3.7
Surface: crushed stone, gravel

Location: Somerset
Contact: D&R Canal State Park
625 Canal Road
Somerset, NJ 08873-7309
(732) 873–3050

14 Linwood Bikepath (George K. Francis Bikepath)

Endpoints: Linwood, Somers Point
Mileage: 3.8
Surface: asphalt

Location: Atlantic
Contact: Gary Gardner
City Clerk

Linwood City Hall
400 Poplar Avenue
Linwood, NJ 08221-1899
(609) 927–4108

15 Monroe Township Bikepath

Endpoints: Monroe
Mileage: 4
Surface: asphalt

Location: Gloucester
Contact: Frank Campisi
Community Affairs Director
Monroe Township Parks and Recreation
301 Bluebell Road
Williamstown, NJ 08094
(609) 728–9840
mtdca@buyrite.com

16 Ocean City Trail

Endpoints: Ocean City
Mileage: 0.9
Surface: asphalt

Location: Cape May
Contact: George Savastano
Director of Public Works
Ocean City Public Works Dept.
1040 Haven Avenue
Ocean City, NJ 08226
(609) 525–9261

17 Ogden Mine Railroad Path

Endpoints: Hurdtown
Mileage: 2.5
Surface: crushed stone, ballast, dirt, cinder

Location: Morris; Sussex
Contact: Al Kent
Commissioner
Morris County Park Commission
P.O. Box 1295
Morristown, NJ 07962-1295
(201) 326–7600

18 Patriots' Path

Endpoints: East Hanover,
Washington
Mileage: 12
Surface: asphalt, gravel, dirt

Location: Morris
Contact: Al Kent
Trail Coodinator
Morris County Park Commission
P.O. Box 1295
Morristown, NJ 07962-1295
(973) 326–7600

19 Paulinskill Valley Trail

Endpoints: Sparta Junction,
Columbia
Mileage: 27
Surface: ballast, dirt, cinder

Location: Warren; Sussex
Contact: Park Superintendent
Kittatinny Valley State Park
P.O. Box 621
Andover, NJ 07821-0621
(973) 786–6445
kittvlly@warwick.net

20 Pemberton Rail-Trail

Endpoints: Pemberton
Mileage: 2.5
Surface: asphalt

Location: Burlington
Contact: Jerry Jerome
Pemberton Rotary Club
128 Hanover Street
Pemberton, NJ 08068
(609) 894–2930
TQJ@jersey.net

21 Pequest Wildlife Management Area Trail

Endpoints: Pequest
Mileage: 4.2
Surface: ballast

Location: Warren
Contact: John Piccolo
Black River Wildlife Management
Area
275 North Road
Chester, NJ 07930-2332
(908) 879–6252

22 Seashore Line Trail

Endpoints: Belleplain State
Forest, Woodbine
Mileage: 10
Surface: ballast, dirt

Location: Cape May;
Cumberland
Contact: Tom Keck
Superintendent
Belleplain State Forest
Route 550, Box 450
Woodbine, NJ 08270-0450
(609) 861–2404
belleplain.st.forest@
jerseycape.com

23 Somers Point Bike Path

Endpoints: Somers Point
Mileage: 1
Surface: asphalt

Location: Mercer
Contact: Celeste Tracy
Supervising Planner
N.J. Department of
Environmental Protection
Division of Parks and Forestry
P.O. Box 404
22 South Clinton Street
Trenton, NJ 08625-0404
(609) 984–1173
ctracy@dep.state.nj.us

24 Sussex Branch Railroad Trail

Endpoints: Byram Township,
Branchville
Mileage: 21.2
Surface: ballast, cinder

Location: Sussex

Contact: Park Superintendent
Kittatinny Valley State Park
P.O. Box 621
Andover, NJ 07821-0621
(973) 786–6445
kittvlly@warwick.net

25 Traction Line Recreation Trail

Endpoints: Morris Avenue,
Morristown, Danforth, Madison,
New Jersey
Mileage: 3
Surface: asphalt

Other use: baby carriages
Location: Morris
Contact: Janet McMillen
Trails Coordinator
Morris County Park Commission
P.O. Box 1295
Morristown, NJ 17962-1295
(973) 326–7604

26 West Essex Trail

Endpoints: Verona, Cedar Grove
Mileage: 2.2
Surface: gravel, cinder

Location: Essex
Contact: Vincent Bucci
Chief Engineer
Essex County Department of
Parks
115 Clifton Avenue
Newark, NJ 07104-1017
(973) 268–3500

NEW MEXICO

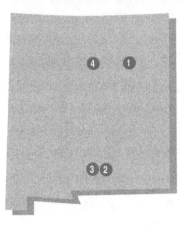

Chairperson
New Mexico Rail-Trail
Association
P.O. Box 44
Plotcroft, NM 88317-0044
(505) 682–3040
nmrails@zianet.com

3 Mexican Canyon Trestle Trail (Cloud-Climbing Trail)

Endpoints: Lincoln National
Forest
Mileage: 3.5 (3 sections)
Surface: ballast

Location: Otero
Contact: Johnny Wilson
Staff Officer
Lincoln National Forest
1101 New York Avenue
Alamagordo, NM 88310-6992
(505) 434–7200

1 Gillinas Hiking Trail

Endpoints: Las Vegas
Mileage: 1.5
Surface: asphalt

Location: San Miguel
Contact: Stella Mason
Las Vegas Recreation
Department
P.O. Box 179
Las Vegas, NM 87701-0179
(505) 454–1158

4 Santa Fe Rail-Trail

Endpoints: Santa Fe, Lamy
Mileage: 11.5
Surface: dirt

Location: Santa Fe
Contact: Lesli Kunkle-Ellis
Planner
Santa Fe County Planning
Department
102 Grant Ave.
P.O. Box 276
Santa Fe, NM 87504-0276
(505) 986–6215
lellis@co.santa-fe.nm.us

2 Grandview Trail

Endpoints: High Rolls
Mileage: 1.5
Surface: ballast

Location: Otero
Contact: Tom Springer

1 Alison Wells Ney Nature Trail

Endpoints: Brocton-Thayer Road, Bliss Road
Mileage: 5
Surface: gravel, dirt

Location: Chautauqua
Contact: Les Johnson
Hollyloft Ski and Bike
600 Fairmount Avenue
Jamestown, NY 14701-2638
(716) 483–2330
www.@cecomet.net/railtrails/

Location: Cattaraugus
Contact: George
Schanzenbacher
Chief Operating Officer
American Chamber of
Commerce
Greater Olean
120 N. Union Street
Olean, NY 14760-2735
(716) 372–4433
cooficer@Oleanny.com

2 Allegheny River Valley Trail

Endpoints: Allegany, Olean
Mileage: 5.6
Surface: asphalt

3 Auburn Trail

Endpoints: Pittsford, Farmington
Mileage: 9
Surface: gravel, grass, dirt,

crushed stone, original ballast

Location: Monroe, Ontario
Contact: David Wright
Victor Hiking Trails, Inc.
85 East Main Street
Victor, NY 14564
(716) 461–8107
dawr@juno.com
www.ggw.org/vht

4 Auburn-Fleming Trail

Endpoints: Auburn, Fleming
Mileage: 2.5
Surface: ballast, dirt

Location: Cayuga
Contact: Michele Beelman
Park Director
Cayuga County Parks and Trail
Commission
East Lake Road
Auburn, NY 13021
(315) 253–5611
www.co.cayuga.ny.lls

5 Bog Meadow Brook Trail

Endpoints: Saratoga Springs
Mileage: 1.9
Surface: ballast, grass, dirt

Location: Saratoga
Contact: Cynthia Beham
Project Director

Saratoga Springs Open Space
Project
110 Spring Street
Saratoga Springs, NY 12866-3302
(518) 587–5554

6 Canalway Trail

Mileage: 95
Surface: dirt

Location: Cayuga; Monroe;
Niagara; Onondaga; Orleans
Contact: John DiMura
Canalway Trail Program Manager
New York State Canal
Recreation Way Commission
200 Southern Boulevard
Albany, NY 12209-2098
(518) 436–3034
www.canals.state.ny.us/trail

7 Catherine Valley Trail

Endpoints: Montour Falls,
Watkins Glen
Mileage: 2
Surface: asphalt, crushed stone,
ballast

Location: Schuyler
Contact: Rick Manning
Northeast Greenways
Collaborative
114 Dey Street
Ithaca, NY 14850

(607) 277–0178
manning@lightlink.com

thiggins@co.cayuga.ny.us
www.co.cayuga.ny.us/park/trails

8 Catskill Scenic Trail

Endpoints: Bloomville, Grand Gorge
Mileage: 19
Surface: crushed stone, dirt, cinder

Location: Delaware; Schoharie
Contact: Dave Riordan
Executive Director
Catskill Revitalization
Corporation
P.O. Box 310
Railroad Avenue
Stamford, NY 12167-0310
(607) 652-2821
fun@durr.org
www.durr.org

9 Cayuga County Trail

Endpoints: Ira, Victory, Sterling
Mileage: 20
Surface: dirt, cinder

Location: Cayuga
Contact: Thomas Higgins
Principal Planner
Cayuga County Planning
Department
160 Genesee Street
Auburn, NY 13021-3424
(315) 253–1276

10 Conservation Trail

Endpoints: Allegheny State Forest, Niagara Falls
Mileage: 175 (18 are Rail-Trail)
Surface: ballast

Location: Cattaraugus; Erie; Genesse; Niagara; Wyoming
Contact: Terry Dailey
Allegheny State Park
2373 DSP Route 1
Salamana, NY 14779
(716) 354–9101

11 D&H Canal Heritage Corridor (O&W Rail-Trail)

Endpoints: Kingston, Ellensville
Mileage: 35
Surface: crushed stone, cinder

Location: Hurley; Marbleton; Rochester; Sullivan; Ulster
Contact: Rich Caraluzzo
Sullivan County Division of Public Works
P.O. Box 5012
Monticello, NY 12701
(914) 794–3000

12 Dryden Lake Park Trail

Endpoints: Dryden, Harford
Mileage: 3.3
Surface: ballast, grass

Location: Cortland, Tompkins
Contact: James Schug
Supervisor
Town of Dryden
65 East Main St.
Dryden, NY 13053-9505
(607) 844–8619
drydent@lightlink.com

13 East Ithaca Recreation Way

Endpoints: Ithaca, Dryden
Mileage: 2.2
Surface: asphalt, gravel, cinder

Location: Tompkins
Contact: George Frantz
Assistant Town Planner
Town of Ithaca
126 East Seneca Street
Ithaca, NY 14850-4352
(607) 273–1747

14 Erie Canal Trail

Endpoints: Amsterdam,
Schoharie Crossing State Historic
Site
Mileage: 90
Surface: asphalt

Location: Montgomery

Contact: Micheal Kayes
Director
Planning and Development
Department
Park Street
P.O.Box 1500
Fonda, NY 12068
(518) 853–8155

15 Genesee Valley Greenway

Endpoints: North Cuba,
Rochester
Mileage: 50
Surface: gravel, grass

Location: Livingston, Monroe
Contact: Frances Gotesik
Executive Director
Friends of the Genesee Valley
Greenway, Inc.
P.O. Box 42
Mt. Morris, NY 14510-1202
(716) 658–2569
fogvg@aol.com
www.netacc.net/~fogvg/
index.htm

16 Gorge Trail

Endpoints: Cazenovia
Mileage: 2.2
Surface: crushed stone, ballast,
cinder

Location: Madison
Contact: Gene Gissin

Cazenovia Preservation
Foundation
P.O. Box 627
Cazenovia, NY 13035-0432
(315) 655–2224

17 Groveland Secondary Trail

Endpoints: Alexander, York
Mileage: 20
Surface: ballast

Other use: ATV
Location: Genessee
Contact: Jim Peck
Supervising Forester
New York State Department of
Environmental Conservation
7291 Coon Road
Bath, NY 14810-7742
(607) 776–2165
jrpeck@gw.dec.state.ny.us

18 Harlem Valley Rail Trail

Endpoints: Millerton to Wassaic,
Alander to Copake Falls
Mileage: 15 (2 sections)
Surface: asphalt

Location: Columbia; Dutchess
Contact: Charlie Drum
Commissioner
Dutchess County Dept. of Parks,
Recreation & Conservation
85 Sheafe Road
Wappingers Falls, NY 12590-1103
(914) 297–1224
www.bmtsinc.com/clc/
hvrail.htm

19 Hojack Trail

Endpoints: Redcreek, Hannibal
Mileage: 8
Surface: crushed stone, gravel,
ballast

Location: Cayuga
Contact: Michele Beilman
Parks Director
Cayuga County Parks and Trails
Commission
Emerson Park, East Lake Road
Auburn, NY 13021
(312) 253–5611
www.co.cayuga.ny.us

20 John Kieran Nature Trail

Endpoints: Bronx (Van Cortlandt
Park)
Mileage: 1
Surface: wood chips, dirt

Location: Bronx
Contact: Marianne Anderson
Van Cortlandt and Pelham Bay
Parks Administration
1 Bronx River Parkway
Bronx, NY 10462-2869
(718) 430–1890
www.nycparks.org

21 Joseph Clarke Rail-Trail

Endpoints: Tappan, Blauvelt
Mileage: 3
Surface: crushed stone, dirt

Location: Rockland
Contact: Richard Rose
Supervisor of Parks
Town of Orangetown
81 Hunt Road
Orangeburg, NY 10962
www.orangetown.com

22 Lehigh Memory Trail

Endpoints: Amherst
Mileage: 0.75
Surface: asphalt

Location: Erie
Contact: William Wutz
Trustee
Municipality of Village of
Williamsville
5565 Main Street
Williamsville, NY 142217
(716) 632–4120
www.williamsvill.org

23 Lehigh Valley Trail

Endpoints: Victor, Genesee River
near Rush
Mileage: 12
Surface: ballast

Location: Monroe, Ontario

Contact: David Wright
Victor Hiking Trails, Inc.
85 East Main Street
Victor, NY 14564
(716) 461–8107
dawr@juno.com
www.ggw.org/vht

24 Maple City Trail

Endpoints: Ogdensburg
Mileage: 1.8
Surface: asphalt

Location: St. Lawrence
Contact: John Rishe
Ogdensburg Planning
Department
330 Ford Street
Ogdensburg, NY 13669-1626
(315) 393–7150

25 Maybrook Rail-Trail

Endpoints: East Fishkill
Mileage: 12
Surface: ballast

Location: Dutchess
Contact: Brad Barclay
Senior Planner
Duchess County Department of
Public Works
County Office Building
22 Market Street
Poughkeepsie, NY 12601
(914) 486–2900

26 Mohawk-Hudson Bikeway

Endpoints: Albany, Rotterdam Junction
Mileage: 41
Surface: asphalt, crushed stone

Location: Albany; Schenectady
Contact: Kathleen DeCataldo
Supervisor
Town of Niskayuna
One Niskayuna Circle
Schenectady, NY 12309
(518) 386–4503
nisky@crisny.org
www.canals.state.ny.us

27 North County Trailway

Endpoints: Eastview to Hawthorne; Briarcliff Law Memorial Park; Mt. Pleasant to Kitchiawan
Mileage: 15
Surface: asphalt

Location: Westchester
Contact: David DeLucia
Director of Park Facilities
Westchester County Parks & Recreation
25 Moore Avenue
Mount Kisco, NY 10549-3102
(914) 242–6300

28 Old Putnam Trail

Endpoints: Van Cortland Park
Mileage: 1.25
Surface: dirt

Location: Bronx
Contact: Marianne Anderson
Van Cortland and Pelham Bay
Parks Administration
1 Bronx River Parkway
Bronx, NY 10462-2869
(718) 430–1890

29 Ongiara Trail System

Endpoints: Whirlpool State Park, Devil's Hole State Park
Mileage: 1.5
Surface: crushed stone, grass, dirt

Other use: Birdwatching
Location: Niagara
Contact: James Ford
Regional Manager
New York State Parks—Niagara Region
Niagara Reservation State Park
P.O. Box 1132
Niagara Falls, NY 14303-0132
(716) 285–3891

30 Ontario Pathway

Endpoints: Canandaigua to Stanley with spur to Phelps
Mileage: 4.5
Surface: dirt

Location: Ontario
Contact: Ontario Pathways Inc.
P.O. Box 996
Canandaigua, NY 14424

31 Orange Heritage Trail

Endpoints: Goshen, Monroe
Mileage: 10.5
Surface: asphalt, crushed stone

Location: Orange
Contact: Graham Skea
Commissioner
Orange County Dept of Parks,
Recreation & Conservation
211 Route 416
Montgomery, NY 12549-9803
(914) 457–4900
ocgparks@warwick.net
www.ocgovernment1home.html

32 Oswego Recreational Trail

Endpoints: Fulton, Cleveland
Mileage: 26
Surface: ballast

Other use: ATV
Location: Oswego
Contact: Edward Marx
Director of Planning
Oswego County Planning
Department
46 East Bridge Street

Oswego, NY 13126-2123
(315) 349–8292
marxe@co.oswego.ny.us

33 Outlet Trail

Endpoints: Penn Yan, Dresden
Mileage: 7.5
Surface: asphalt, ballast, cinder

Location: Yates
Contact: Philip Whitman
President
Friends of the Outlet Trail Inc.
1939 Perry Point Road
P.O. Box 231
Dresden, NY 14441
(315) 536–2701

34 Pittsford Trail System (Railroad Loop Trail)

Endpoints: Pittsford
Mileage: 11.4
Surface: asphalt, crushed stone,
ballast

Location: Monroe
Contact: Mary Ann Burdett
Pittsford Parks and Recreation
Department
35 Lincoln Avenue
Pittsford, NY 14534
(716) 248–6280

35 Ralph C. Sheldon Nature Trail

Endpoints: Sherman-Titus Road,
Summerdale Road

Mileage: 6
Surface: gravel, grass, dirt

Location: Chautauqua
Contact: Les Johnson
Chautauqua Rails to Trails
P.O. Box 151
Mayville, NY 14757-0151
(716) 483–2330
www2.cecomet.net/
railtrails/

36 Raymond G. Esposito Trail

Endpoints: South Nyack, Village
of So. Nyack
Mileage: 1
Surface: crushed stone, gravel,
dirt

Location: Rockland
Contact: Irene Murphy
Deputy Village Clerk
Village of South Nyack
282 South Broadway
South Nyack, NY 10960-4639
(914) 358–0287

37 Remsen–Lake Placid Travel Corridor

Endpoints: Lake Placid, Remsen
Mileage: 119
Surface: ballast

Location: Essex; Franklin;
Hamilton; Herkimer; Oneida; St.
Lawrence

Contact: Rick Fenton
Supervising Forester
New York State Dept. of
Environmental Conservation
P.O. Box 458
Northville, NY 12134
(518) 863–4545
rtfenton@gw.dec.state.ny.us

38 Ridgeway Trail

Endpoints: Caroline
Mileage: 3.3
Surface: crushed stone

Location: Tomkins
Contact: Tompkins County
Greenway Coalition
1456 Hanshaw Road
Ithaca, NY 14850-2754
(607) 257–6220

39 Rivergate Trail

Endpoints: Clayton to
La Fargeville, Theresa to
Philadelphia
Mileage: 13.5
Surface: ballast

Other use: ATV
Location: Jefferson
Contact: Thousand Islands Land
Trust
P.O. Box 238
Clayton, NY 13624-0238
(315) 686–5345

40 Rochester, Syracuse and Eastern Trail

Endpoints: Perinton, Fairport
Mileage: 6
Surface: crushed stone

Location: Monroe
Contact: David Morgan
Director of Parks
Town of Perinton
1350 Turk Hill Road
Fairport, NY 14450-8751
(716) 223–5050

41 Saratoga Springs Bicycle/Pedestrian Path

Endpoints: Saratoga Springs
Mileage: 39.6
Surface: asphalt

Location: Saratoga
Contact: Cynthia Beham
Project Director
Saratoga Springs Open Space
Project
110 Spring Street
Saratoga Springs, NY 12866-3302
(518) 587–5554

42 Shawmut Recreational Trail

Endpoints: Hornell, Town of
Hornellsville
Mileage: 1.3
Surface: gravel

Location: Steuben
Contact: Shawn Hogan
Mayor
City of Hornell
82 Main Street
Hornell, NY 14843
(607) 324–7421
mayor@infoblvd.net

43 Skaneateles Nature Trail (Charlie Major Nature Trail)

Endpoints: Skaneateles
Mileage: 2
Surface: dirt, cinder

Location: Onondaga
Contact: Matthew Major
Recreation Supervisor
Town of Skaneateles
Recreation Dept.
24 Jordan Street
Skaneateles, NY 13152-1110
(315) 685-5607

44 South Hill Recreation Way

Endpoints: Ithaca
Mileage: 3.3
Surface: grass

Location: Tompkins
Contact: George Frantz
Assistant Town Planner

Town of Ithaca
126 East Seneca Street
Ithaca, NY 14850-4352
(607) 273–1747

45 Sullivan County Rail-Trail—Hurleyville to Mountain Dale

Endpoints: Hurleyville to
Woodridge, Mountain Dale
Mileage: 9
Surface: gravel, dirt

Location: Sullivan
Contact: Dennis Hewston
Sullivan County Rails-to-Trails
Conservancy, Inc.
195 Lake Louise Marie Road
Rock Hill, NY 12775-6613
(914) 796–2100

46 Sullivan County Rail-Trail—Monticello to Hartwood

Endpoints: Monticello,
Hartwood
Mileage: 5
Surface: gravel, dirt

Location: Sullivan
Contact: Dennis Hewston
Sullivan County Rails-to-Trails
Conservancy, Inc.
195 Lake Louise Marie Road
Rock Hill, NY 12775-6613
(914) 796–2100

47 Sullivan County Rail-Trail—Summitville to Westbrookville

Endpoints: Summitville to
Wurtsboro, Westbrookville
Mileage: 10
Surface: gravel, dirt

Location: Sullivan
Contact: Steve Levine
Town Supervisor
Railroad Plaza
South Fallsburg, NY 12779
(914) 434–8810

48 Uncle Sam Bikeway

Endpoints: Troy
Mileage: 3.5
Surface: asphalt

Location: Rensselaer
Contact: Bob Barns
Recreation Supervisor
City of Troy Bureau of Parks and
Recreation
1 Movement Square
Troy, NY 12180
(518) 270–4553

49 Verona Beach State Park Trail

Endpoints: Verona Beach State
Park
Mileage: 8

Surface: grass, dirt

Location: Oneida
Contact: Al Gorton
Verona Beach State Park
P.O. Box 245
Verona Beach, NY 13162-0245
(315) 762–4463

50 Wallkill Valley Rail-Trail

Endpoints: Gardiner, Rosendale
Mileage: 12.5
Surface: crushed stone, ballast

Location: Ulster
Contact: George Danskin
Wallkill Valley Rail Trail
Association Inc.
P.O. Box 1048
New Paltz, NY 12561-0020
(914) 255–3842
www.gorailtrail.com

51 Warren County Bikeway

Endpoints: Lake George, Glens
Falls
Mileage: 11
Surface: asphalt

Location: Warren
Contact: Patrick Beland

Director
Warren County Parks and
Recreation Department
261 Main Street, Box 10
Warrensburg, NY 12885-1122
(518) 623–5576

52 White Plains Greenway

Endpoints: White Plains
Mileage: 0.7
Surface: wood chips

Location: Westchester
Contact: Michael Graessle
Commissioner of Planning
City of White Plains
Planning Department
255 Main Street
White Plains, NY 10601
(914) 422–1374
Trailnet88@aol.com

NORTH CAROLINA

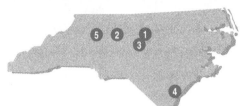

1 American Tobacco Trail

Endpoints: Durham, Cary near Apex, Bonsal and New Hill
Mileage: 23
Surface: asphalt

Location: Chatham; Durham; Wake
Contact: Christy Cornell
Wake County Parks and Recreation
P.O. Box 550, Suite 1000
Raleigh, NC 27602
(919) 856–6673
ccornell@co.wake.nc.us
www.ncrail-trails.org/trtc/

2 Lake Brandt Greenway

Endpoints: Guilford Courthouse National Military Park, Bur-Mil Park
Mileage: 3.5
Surface: asphalt

Location: Guilford

Contact: Mike Simpson
Lakes, Trails & Greenways Director
Greensboro Parks and Recreation Department
5834 Owls Roost Road
Greensboro, NC 27410
(336) 545–5955
mike.simpson@ci.greensboro.nc.us

3 Libba Cotton Trail

Endpoints: Carrboro
Mileage: 0.4
Surface: asphalt

Location: Orange
Contact: Kenneth Withrow
Transportation Planner
Town of Carrboro
3071 West Main Street
Carrboro, NC 27510
(919) 968–7713
carrplan@redial.net

4 River to Sea Bikeway

Endpoints: Wilmington, Wrightsville Beach
Mileage: 12
Surface: asphalt, concrete

Location: New Hanover
Contact: Bill Austin
Senior Transportation Planner
City of Wilmington
P.O. Box 1810
Wilmington, NC 28402-1810
(910) 341–5891
www.co.newhanover.nc.us/plan/
menu.html

5 Strollway

Endpoints: Winston-Salem
Mileage: 1
Surface: crushed stone

Location: Forsyth
Contact: Nick Jameson
Recreation and Parks Director
Winston-Salem Recreation and
Parks Department
City of Winston-Salem
P.O. Box 2511
Winston-Salem, NC 27102
(336) 727–2227
www.ci.winston-salem.nc.us

NORTH DAKOTA

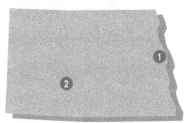

1 Grand Forks—East Grand Forks Bikeway

Endpoints: Grand Forks, East Grand Forks
Mileage: 4
Surface: asphalt

Location: Grand Forks
Contact: Charles Durrenburger
Senior Planner
Grand Forks–East Grand Forks
Metropolitan Planning
Organization
255 North Fourth Street
P.O. Box 5200
Grand Forks, ND 58206-5200
(701) 746–2656

2 Roughrider Trail

Endpoints: Mandan, Fort Rice
Mileage: 22
Surface: gravel, grass, dirt

Other use: ATV
Location: Morton
Contact: Randy Harmon
Trail Coordinator
Department of Parks and
Recreation
1835 East Bismarck Expressway
Bismarck, ND 58504-6708
(701) 328–5357
rharmon@state.nd.us

OHIO

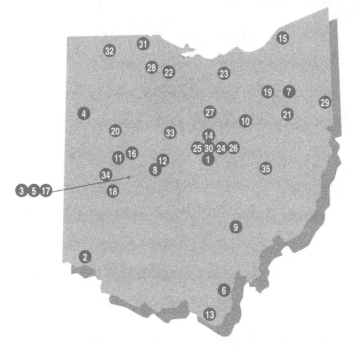

1 Blackhand Gorge Bikeway

Endpoints: Blackhand Gorge
State Nature Preserve
Mileage: 4.5
Surface: asphalt

Location: Licking
Contact: Greg Seymour
Preserve Manager
Blackhand Gorge State Nature
Preserve
5213 Rockhaven Road SE
Newark, OH 43055
(614) 763–4411

2 California Junction Trail

Endpoints: California Woods
Nature Preserve
Mileage: 1
Surface: ballast, wood chips, dirt

Location: Hamilton
Contact: Clare Thorn
Director
Cincinnati Park Board
California Woods Nature
Preserve
5400 Kellogg Avenue
Cincinnati, OH 45228
(513) 231–8678

3 Cedarville Trail (Ohio to Erie Trail)

Endpoints: Cedarville, Xenia
Mileage: 8.6
Surface: asphalt

Location: Greene
Contact: Jim Schneider
Assistant Director
Greene County Parks
651 Dayton-Xenia Road
Xenia, OH 45385-2699
(937) 376–7440
gcparktrail@dayton.net

4 Celina-Coldwater Bikeway

Endpoints: Celina, Coldwater
Mileage: 4.6
Surface: asphalt

Location: Mercer
Contact: Mike Sovinski
Celina Engineering Dept
426 West Market Street
Celina, OH 45822-2127
(419) 586–1144

5 Creekside Trail (H-Connector)

Endpoints: Dayton, Xenia
Mileage: 10.81
Surface: asphalt

Location: Montgomery; Greene
Contact: Jim Schneider
Assistant Director
Greene County Parks
651 Dayton-Xenia Road
Xenia, OH 45385-2699
(937) 376–7440

6 Gallia County Hike and Bike Trail

Endpoints: Bidwell to Kerr;
Gallipolis to Spring Valley, Spring
Valley
Mileage: 7
Surface: asphalt, crushed stone

Location: Gallia
Contact: Josette Baker
Director
O.O. McIntyre Park District
18 Locust Street
Gallipolis, OH 45631-1262
(614) 446–6275

7 Headwaters Trail

Endpoints: Garrettsville, Hiram
Station
Mileage: 3
Surface: crushed stone

Location: Portage
Contact: Christine Craycroft
Director
Portage County Park District

449 South Meridian Street
Ravenna, OH 44266
(330) 673–9404
ccraycr@earthlink.net

8 Heritage Trail

Endpoints: Hilliard
Mileage: 2.5
Surface: asphalt

Location: Franklin
Contact: Phyllis Ernst
Director
Hilliard Parks & Recreation
3800 Cherry Tree Drive
Hilliard, OH 43026-1348
(614) 876–5200

9 Hockhocking—Adena

Endpoints: Athens, Nelsonville
Mileage: 17
Surface: asphalt

Location: Athens
Contact: Athens County
Commissioner's Office
15 South Court Street
Athens, OH 45701
(740) 592–3219

10 Holmes County Trail

Endpoints: Holmesville,
Millersburg

Mileage: 6
Surface: crushed limestone

Other use: Amish buggy
Location: Holmes
Contact: Shelly Venis
Holmes County Rails to Trails
Coalition
P.O. Box 95
Millersburg, OH 44654
(330) 674–5773

11 Huffman Prairie Overlook Trail

Endpoints: Bath Township
Mileage: 6
Surface: ballast, grass

Location: Greene
Contact: Elwood Ensor
Miami Valley Regional Bicycle
Committee
1304 Horizon Drive
Fairborn, OH 45324-5816
(937) 879–2068
ejensor@prodigy.com

12 Interstate-670 Bikeway

Endpoints: Columbus
Mileage: 3
Surface: asphalt

Location: Franklin
Contact: Dale Hooper
City of Columbus
Division of Traffic Engineering

109 North Front Street
Columbus, OH 43215-2835
(614) 645–7790

13 Ironton Rail-Trail

Endpoints: Ironton
Mileage: 3
Surface: dirt

Location: Lawrence
Contact: Joe Unger
Ironton Chamber of Commerce
P.O. Box 488
South Point, OH 45680
(740) 532–0908

14 Kokosing Gap Trail

Endpoints: Mt. Vernon, Danville
Mileage: 14
Surface: asphalt

Location: Knox
Contact: Phil Samuell
President
Kokosing Gap Trail
P.O. Box 129
Gambier, OH 43022-0129
(740) 427–4509
Samuell@denison.edu
www.railtrails.org/
kokosinggap

15 Lake County Metroparks Greenway

Endpoints: Painesville, Concord
Mileage: 4.5

Surface: ballast, dirt

Location: Lake
Contact: Chuck Kenzig
Chief Landscape Architect
Lake Metroparks
11211 Spear Road
Concord Township, OH
44077-9542
(800) 227–7275

16 Little Miami Scenic Trail

Endpoints: Springfield, Yellow
Springs
Mileage: 9
Surface: asphalt

Location: Clark
Contact: Tim Smith
Director
Springfield Parks and Recreation
City Hall
76 East High Street
Springfield, OH 45502-1236
(513) 324–7348

17 Little Miami Scenic Trail

Endpoints: South of Xenia,
Yellow Springs
Mileage: 15
Surface: asphalt

Location: Greene

Contact: Jim Schneider
Assistant Director
Greene County Parks
651 Dayton-Xenia Road
Xenia, OH 45385-2699
(937) 376–7440
gcparktrail@dayton.net

Metro Parks (serving Summit
County)
975 Treaty Line Road
Akron, OH 44313-5898
(330) 867–5511
ametropa@neo.rr.com
www.neo.rr.com/Metro Parks

18 Little Miami State Park Trail

Endpoints: Millford, Spring
Valley
Mileage: 50
Surface: asphalt, ballast

Location: Greene; Warren;
Clermont; Hamilton
Contact: Chuck Thiemann
Manager
Little Miami Scenic State Park
8570 East State Route 73
Waynesville, OH 45068-9719
(513) 897–3055
www.greenlink.org/miami/
lmtrail.html

19 Metro Parks Bike and Hike Trail

Endpoints: Walton Hills, Kent
and Stow
Mileage: 27
Surface: asphalt, crushed stone

Location: Summit
Contact: Keith Shy
Director

20 Miami & Erie Canal

Endpoints: Cross Trace, Laramie
Creek
Mileage: 9
Surface: dirt

Location: Lucas; Miami
Contact: John Neilson
Manager
Piqua Historical Area State
Memorial
9845 North Hardin Road
Piqua, OH 45356-9707
(513) 773–2522

21 Nickelplate Trail

Endpoints: Louisville
Mileage: 3
Surface: asphalt

Location: Stark
Contact: Darrin Metzger
Parks Supervisor
City of Louisville Parks
Department
215 South Mill Street
Louisville, OH 44641-1665
(216) 875–5644

22 North Coast Inland Trail

Endpoints: Clyde, Fremont
Mileage: 6.5
Surface: asphalt

Location: Huron; Lorain; Ottawa;
Sandusky; Wood
Contact: Steve Gruner
Director-Secretary
Sandusky County Park District
1970 Countyside Drive
Freemont, OH 43430-9574
(419) 334–4495

23 North Coast Inland Trail– Lorain County

Endpoints: Elyria, Kipton
Mileage: 14
Surface: asphalt

Location: Lorain
Contact: Dan Martin
Executive Director
Lorain County Metropolitan Park
District
12882 Diagonal Road
La Grange, OH 44050-9728
(440) 458–5121

24 Ohio Canal Greenway

Endpoints: Hebron, Licking
county line
Mileage: 2.8
Surface: crushed stone

Location: Licking
Contact: Russell Edgington
Director
Licking Park District
P.O. Box 590
Granville, OH 43023-0590
(740) 587–2535

25 Olentangy-Scioto Bike Path

Endpoints: Columbus
Mileage: 17
Surface: asphalt, concrete

Location: Franklin
Contact: Mollie O'Donnell
Landscape Architect
City of Columbus Recreation and
Parks Department
200 Greenlawn Avenue
Columbus, OH 43223
(614) 645–3300

26 Panhandle Trail

Endpoints: Newark, Licking
county line
Mileage: 10
Surface: dirt

Location: Newark
Contact: Russell Edgington
Licking Park District
P.O. Box 590
Granville, OH 43023
(614) 587–2538
1pd@msmisp.com
www.msmisp.com/1pd

27 Richland B&O Trail

Endpoints: Butler, Mansfield
Mileage: 18.4
Surface: asphalt

Location: Richland
Contact: Steve McKee
Director
Richland County Park District
2295 Lexington Avenue
Mansfield, OH 44907-3027
(419) 884–3764

28 Slippery Elm Trail

Endpoints: Bowling Green,
Baltimore
Mileage: 13
Surface: asphalt

Location: Wood
Contact: Andrew Kalmar
Director
Wood County Park District
18729 Mercer Road
Bowling Green, OH 43402-9688
(419) 353–1897
wcpd@wcnet.org
wcnet.org/ wcpd/

29 Stavich Bicycle Trail

Endpoints: Struthers, New
Castle, PA
Mileage: 11

Surface: asphalt

Location: Mahoning; Lawrence
Contact: Gary Slaven
Falcon Foundry
Sixth and Water Street
Lowellville, OH 44436
(330) 536–6221

30 Thomas J. Evans Bike Trail

Endpoints: Newark, Johnstown
Mileage: 14.5
Surface: asphalt

Location: Licking
Contact: Russell Edgington
Director
Licking Park District
P.O. Box 590
Granville, OH 43023-9509
(614) 587–2535
1pd@msmisp.com
www.msmisp.com/1pd

31 University-Parks Bike-Hike Trail

Endpoints: Toledo
Mileage: 8.5
Surface: asphalt

Location: Lucas
Contact: Jean Ward

Director
Metroparks—Toledo Area
5100 West Central
Toledo, OH 43615-2100
(419) 535–3050

32 Wabash Cannonball Trail

Endpoints: Maumee to
Montpelier, spur to Liberty
Center
Mileage: 28
Surface: cinder

Location: Fulton; Henry;
Williams; Lucas
Contact: Gene Markley
Vice President
Northwestern Ohio Rails-to-Trails
Association
P.O. Box 234
Delta, OH 43515-0234
(800) 951–4788
140years@powersupply.net
www.toltbbs.com/~norta/

33 Westerville Bikeway

Endpoints: Westerville
Mileage: 1

Location: Franklin
Contact: Jody Stower
Director
Westerville Parks and Recreation
64 East Walnut Street
Westerville, OH 43081
(614) 890–8544
www.ci.westervill.oh.us

34 Wolf Creek Bikeway

Endpoints: Trotwood, Verona
Mileage: 13
Surface: asphalt

Location: Montgomery
Contact: Dick Peddemors
Superintendent of Parks
Five Rivers Metro Parks
1375 East Siebenthaler Avenue
Dayton, OH 45414
(937) 222–2291
www.intellweb.com/trails/

35 Zanesville Riverfront Bikepath

Endpoints: Zanesville
Mileage: 2.9
Surface: asphalt

Location: Muskingum
Contact: Ernest Bynum
Recreation Director
City of Zanesville
401 Market Street
Zanesville, OH 43701-3520
(614) 455–0609
Recreation@co2.org

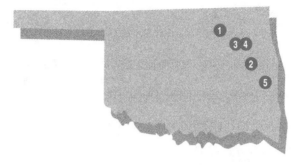

1 Cleveland Trail

Endpoints: Cleveland, Osage
Mileage: 3
Surface: asphalt

Location: Pawnee
Contact: Ed Callison
City Manager
City of Cleveland
P.O. Drawer 190
Cleveland, OK 74020-3829
(918) 358-3600

2 Indian Nations Recreation Trail

Endpoints: Stigler, Porum, Warner
Mileage: 39 (3 sections)
Surface: asphalt, ballast

Location: Haskell
Contact: Paul West
President
Indian Nations Recreation Trail, Inc.
P.O. Box 945
Warner, OK 74469-0945
(918) 463-2931

3 Katy Trail

Endpoints: Sand Springs, Tulsa
Mileage: 6.5
Surface: asphalt

Location: Tulsa
Contact: Jackie Bubenik
Executive Director
River Parks Authority
717 South Houston, Suite 510
Tulsa, OK 74127-9000
(918) 596-2006
jbubenik@ci.tulsa.ok.us

4 Midland Valley Trail & River Parks Pedestrian Bridge

Endpoints: Tulsa
Mileage: 2
Surface: asphalt

Location: Tulsa
Contact: Jackie Bubenik
Executive Director
River Parks Authority
707 South Houston, Suite 202
Tulsa, OK 74127-9000
(918) 596–2006
jbubenik@ci.tulsa.ok.us

5 Old Frisco Trail

Endpoints: Poteau, Wister
Mileage: 8.2
Surface: gravel

Location: Le Flore
Contact: Esther Canada
Director, Old Frisco Trail
Lake Wister Association
P.O. Box 890
Wister, OK 74966-0890
(918) 655–7216

OREGON

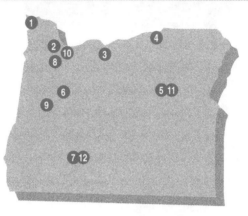

1 Astoria Riverwalk

Endpoints: Astoria—Smith Point, Tongue Point
Mileage: 5.1
Surface: asphalt, gravel, ballast, grass, concrete

Location: Clatsop
Contact: Paul Benoit
Community Development
Director
City of Astoria
City Hall
1095 Duane Street
Astoria, OR 97103-4524
(503) 325–5821
bencliff@seasurf.com

2 Banks-Vernonia State Trail

Endpoints: Banks, Vernonia
Mileage: 21
Surface: asphalt, gravel

Location: Columbia; Washington
Contact: Scott Green
Park Ranger
Banks/Veronia State Trail
24600 N.W. Bacona Road
Buxton, OR 97109
(503) 324–06061

3 Deschutes River Trail

Endpoints: Deschutes State
Park, Mac's Canyon Campground
Mileage: 17
Surface: dirt

Location: Sherman
Contact: Peter Bond
State Trail Coordinator
Oregon Parks and Recreation
Department
1115 Commercial Street NE

Salem, OR 97310-1000
(503) 378–6378
peter.d.bond@state.or.us

4 Lake Wallula Scenic River Hiking Trail

Endpoints: Hat Rock State Park, McNary Beach Park
Mileage: 4.9
Surface: gravel

Location: Umatilla
Contact: Jeff Phillip
Park Ranger
Corps of Engineers
McNary Dam
P.O. Box 1230
Umatilla, OR 97882-1230
(503) 922–3211

5 Malheur Trail

Endpoints: Malheur National Forest
Mileage: 12.5
Surface: ballast

Location: Grant
Contact: Tim Kimble
Recreation Staff Officer
Malheur National Forest
139 N.E. Dayton Street
John Day, OR 97845-1202
(503) 575–1731

6 Mill City

Endpoints: Mill City
Mileage: 2
Surface: asphalt, gravel

Location: Linn
Contact: Roel Lundquist
City Administrator
City of Mill City
252 S.W. Cedar Street
P.O. Box 256
Mill City, OR 97360-2466
(503) 897–2302
millcity@wvi.com

7 OC&E Woods Line State Trail

Endpoints: Bly, Klamath Falls, Sprague River
Mileage: 100
Surface: asphalt, gravel, ballast, dirt

Location: Klamath
Contact: Jim Beauchemin
Park Manager
Oregon State Parks and
Recreation Department
Collier State Park
4600 Highway 97 North
Chiloquin, OR 97624
(541) 783–2471
www.u-rhere.com/OCE

8 Oregon Electric ROW Trail and Linear Park

Endpoints: Beaverton
Mileage: 1
Surface: asphalt, wood chips

Location: Washington
Contact: Jim McElhinny
Director
Planning and Natural Resources
Tualatin Hills Parks and
Recreation District
15707 Southwest Walker Road
Beaverton, OR 97006-5941
(503) 645–6433

9 Row River Trail

Endpoints: Culp Creek, Mosby
Creek
Mileage: 14
Surface: asphalt, crushed stone

Location: Lane
Contact: Bryant Smith
Outdoor Recreation Planner
Eugene District Bureau of Land
Management
2890 Chad Drive
P.O. Box 10226
Eugene, OR 97408-7336
(503) 683–6600
or090mb@or.blm.gov
http://158.68.104.192/rec/
row_trail/index.html

10 Springwater Corridor

Endpoints: Boring, Portland
Mileage: 16.5
Surface: asphalt

Location: Multnomah;
Clackamas
Contact: George Hudson
Landscape Architect
City of Portland
Parks & Recreation Department
1122 S.W. Fifth Avenue, #1302
Portland, OR 97204-1933
(503) 823–6183
pkgeorge@ci.portland.or.us

11 Sumpter Valley Interpretive Trail

Endpoints: Malheur National
Forest
Mileage: 0.2
Surface: dirt

Location: Grant
Contact: Ivan Mulder
Trail Manager
Malheur National Forest
139 N.E. Dayton Street
John Day, OR 97845-1202
(503) 575–1731

12 Woods Line Trail

Endpoints: Beatty, Fremont
National Forest (Sycan)
Mileage: 47
Surface: asphalt, gravel, wood
chips

Location: Klamath
Contact: Angela Roufs
Collier State Park
4600 Highway 97-N
Chiloquin, OR 97624
(541) 783–2471

PENNSYLVANIA

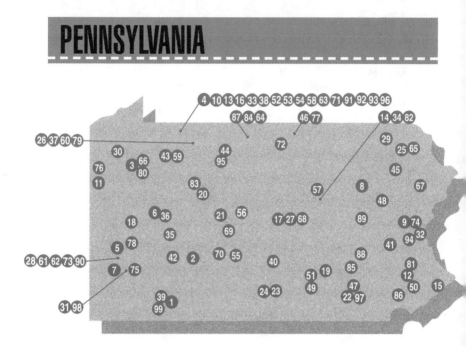

1 Allegheny Highlands Trail

Endpoints: Garrett, Markleton
Mileage: 21
Surface: crushed stone

Location: Somerset
Contact: Hank Parke
President
Somerset County Rails to Trails
829 North Center Avenue
Somerset, PA 15501-1029
(814) 445–6431
www.westol.com/tat/updates/
alleg.htm

2 Allegheny Portage Railroad Trace

Endpoints: Allegheny Portage
RR National Historic Site
Mileage: 7 (1.5 miles are
Rail-Trail)
Surface: ballast, grass, wood
chips

Location: Blair; Cambria
Contact: Joanne Hanley
Superintendent
Allegheny Portage RR National
Historic Site
116 Federal Park Road
Gallitzin, PA 16640
(814) 886–6150
www.nps.gov/alpo

3 Allegheny River Trail

Endpoints: Franklin, Kennerdell Tunnel
Mileage: 15
Surface: asphalt, cinder

Location: Venango
Contact: James Holden
President
Allegheny Valley Trails
Association
P.O. Box 264
Franklin, PA 16323-1322
(814) 437–5621
holden@csonline.net

4 Allegheny Snowmobile Trails

Endpoints: Allegheny National Forest
Mileage: 115
Surface: gravel, ballast, grass, dirt

Location: Elk; Forest; Mc Kean; Warren
Contact: Mary Hosmer
Recreation Specialist
Allegheny National Forest
P.O. Box 847
Warren, PA 16365-0847
(814) 723–5150

5 Arboretum Trail

Endpoints: Oakmont
Mileage: 1
Surface: asphalt

Location: Allegheny
Contact: Kitty Vagley
Director
Garden Club
830 Fifteenth Street
Oakmont, PA 15139-1008
(412) 828–5203

6 Armstrong Trail

Endpoints: Schenley, Upper Hillville
Mileage: 52.5
Surface: asphalt, crushed stone, gravel, ballast

Location: Armstrong; Clarion
Contact: Timothy Kelly
Executive Director
Allegheny Valley Land Trust
P.O. Box 777
Kittanning, PA 16201
(412) 543–4478
ISEAN@aol.com
www.trfn.clpgh.org/avlt

7 Arrowhead Trail

Endpoints: Thompsonville to Library Junction
Mileage: 3.5
Surface: asphalt, ballast

Location: Washington
Contact: Joanne Nelson
Director
Peters Township
Department of Parks &
Recreation
610 East McMurray Road
McMurray, PA 15317-3420
(724) 942–5000
www.atatrail.org

8 Back Mountain Trail

Endpoints: Luzerne, Trucksville
Mileage: 2.5
Surface: crushed stone, ballast

Location: Luzerne
Contact: Judith Rimple
President
Anthracite Scenic Trails
Association
P.O. Box 212
96 Hildebrandt Road
Dallas, PA 18612-9806
(570) 675–9016
jcbbr@aol.com

9 Bath-Allen Trail (Nor-Bath Trail)

Endpoints: Jacksonville,
Weaversville
Mileage: 5.2
Surface: asphalt

Location: Northampton

Contact: Gordon Heller
Superintendent
County of Northampton
Division of Parks and Recreation
RD #4, Greystone Building
Nazareth, PA 18064-9278
(610) 746–1975

10 Beaver Meadows Trail System

Endpoints: Allegheny National
Forest
Mileage: 5.5
Surface: dirt
Location: Forest
Contact: Mary Hosmer
Recreation Specialist
Allegheny National Forest
P.O. Box 847
Warren, PA 16365-0847
(814) 723–5150

11 Beaver to Erie Canal Trail (Shenango Trail)

Endpoints: Big Bend, Kids Mill
Bridge
Mileage: 8
Surface: dirt

Location: Mercer
Contact: Mike Cummings
Resource Manager
Army Corps of Engineers
Shenango Reservoir
2442 Kelly Road
Sharpsville, PA 16150-8208
(724) 962–7746
shenango.ranger@usace.army.mil

12 Betzwood Rail Trail

Endpoints: Valley Forge National Historic Park
Mileage: 2
Surface: asphalt, crushed stone, grass, dirt

Location: Montgomery
Contact: Scott Kalbach
Chief Park Ranger
Valley Forge National Historic Park
P.O. Box 953
Valley Forge, PA 19482-0953
(610) 783–1046

13 Big Side Loop of Hickory Trail

Endpoints: Allegheny National Forest
Mileage: 11.2
Surface: dirt

Location: Forest
Contact: Mary Hosmer
Recreation Specialist
Allegheny National Forest
P.O. Box 847
Warren, PA 16365-0847
(814) 723–5150

14 Black Forest Trail

Endpoints: Black Forest
Mileage: 30
Surface: ballast

Location: Lycoming
Contact: Jim Hyland
Recreation Forester
Tiadaghton Forest Fire Fighters Association
c/o Bureau of Forestry
423 East Central Ave.
South Williamsport, PA 17702

15 Bristol Spurline Park

Endpoints: Bristol
Mileage: 2.5
Surface: asphalt

Location: Bucks
Contact: Fidel Esposito
Manager
Borough of Bristol
250 Pond Street
Bristol, PA 19007-4937
(215) 788–3828

16 Brush Hollow Cross-Country Ski Trail

Endpoints: Allegheny National Forest
Mileage: 6.9
Surface: gravel, ballast, dirt

Location: Elk
Contact: Mary Hosmer
Recreation Specialist
Allegheny National Forest
P.O. Box 847

Warren, PA 16365-0847
(814) 723–5150

17 Brush Hollow Trail

Endpoints: Bald Eagle State
Forest
Mileage: 1.3
Surface: crushed stone, dirt

Location: Union
Contact: Amy Griffith
District Forester
Bald Eagle State Forest
P.O. Box 147
Laurelton, PA 17835
(570) 922–3344
www.dcnr.state.pa.us

18 Butler-Freeport Community Trail

Endpoints: Butler, Freeport
Mileage: 12
Surface: crushed stone, ballast

Location: Butler; Armstrong
Contact: Ron Bennettz
President
Butler-Freeport Community
Trail Council
P.O. Box 533
Saxonburg, PA 16056-0533
(412) 352–4783

19 Capital Area Greenbelt

Endpoints: Loop around
Harrisburg

Mileage: 20 (2 are Rail-Trail)
Surface: wood chips, asphalt,
grass, stone

Location: Danphen County
Contact: Norman Laccase
Capital Area Greenbelt Assoc.
2415 Patton Road
Harrisburg, PA 17112
(717) 652–4079

20 Clarion/Little Toby Creek Trail

Endpoints: DuBois, Ridgway
Mileage: 27
Surface: crushed stone, cinder

Location: Clearfield; Elk;
Jefferson
Contact: Dave Love
Director
Tri-County Rails-to-Trails
Association
c/o Love's Canoe
Main Street
Ridgway, PA 15853
(814) 776–6285
dlove@ncentral.com

21 Clearfield-Grampian Trail

Endpoints: Clearfield, Grampian
Mileage: 10.2
Surface: crushed stone, ballast,
dirt

Location: Clearfield;

Curwensville; Grampion
Contact: Benny Irwin
Secretary
Clearfield County Rails to Trails
Association
310 East Cherry Street
Clearfield, PA 16830
(814) 236–0894

22 Conewago Trail

Endpoints: Elizabethtown,
Lebanon county line
Mileage: 5
Surface: dirt, cinder

Location: Lancaster
Contact: John Gerencser
Recreation Coordinator
Lancaster County Parks and
Recreation
1050 Rockford Road
Lancaster, PA 17602-4624
(717) 299–8215
www.co.lancaster.pa.us/
parks.htm

23 Cumberland County Biker/Hiker Trail

Endpoints: Pine Grove Furnace
State Park, Mt. Creek
Campground
Mileage: 5.5
Surface: crushed stone

Location: Cumberland
Contact: William Rosevear
Park Manager

Pine Grove Furnace State Park
1100 Pine Grove Road
Gardeners, PA 17324-9802
(717) 486-7174

24 Cumberland Valley Rail-Trail

Endpoints: Newville,
Shippensburg
Mileage: 10.8
Surface: ballast, dirt

Location: Cumberland
Contact: Jerry Angulo
Cumberland Valley Rails-to-Trails
Council
P.O. Box 531
Shippensburg, PA 17257
(717) 860–0444
ajangulo@innernet.net

25 D&H Rail-Trail

Endpoints: Simpson, Steven's
Point
Mileage: 38
Surface: ballast, cinder

Location: Lackawanna;
Susquehanna; Wayne
Contact: Lynn Conrad
Rail-Trail Council of
Northeast Pennsylvania
P.O. Box 123
Forest City, PA 18421-0123
(717) 785–7245
tccrail@epix.net
www.neparailtrails.org

26 Deerlick Cross-Country Ski Trail

Endpoints: Allegheny National Forest
Mileage: 9
Surface: ballast, grass, dirt

Location: Warren
Contact: Jeff Stevenson
District Ranger
Allegheny National Forest
Sheffield Ranger District
Route 6
Sheffield, PA 16347
(814) 968–3232

27 Duncan Trail

Endpoints: Bald Eagle State Forest
Mileage: 1.8
Surface: crushed stone, dirt

Location: Union
Contact: Amy Griffith
District Forester
Bald Eagle State Forest
P.O. Box 147
Laurelton, PA 17835
(570) 922–3344

28 Eliza Furnace Trail

Endpoints: Pittsburgh
Mileage: 2.43
Surface: asphalt, crushed stone

Location: Allegheny
Contact: Darla Cravotta
Office of the Mayor
414 Grant Street
Room 512, City County Building
Pittsburgh, PA 15219
(412) 255–2626

29 Endless Mountains Riding Trail

Endpoints: Alford, Montrose
Mileage: 14
Surface: ballast

Location: Susquehanna
Contact: Roy Brown
President
Bridgewater Riding Club
RR 4
Montrose PA 18801
(717) 278–9406

30 Ernst Bike Trail

Endpoints: Meadville, Watson Run
Mileage: 5
Surface: crushed stone

Location: Crawford
Contact: Tom McNally
Chairperson
Crawford County Visitors Bureau
211 Chestnut Street
Meadville, PA 16335
(800) 332–2338
www.mooshaus.com/fcrt/index.html

31 Five Star Trail

Endpoints: Greensburg, Youngwood
Mileage: 7.5
Surface: asphalt, crushed stone

Location: Westmoreland
Contact: Robert McKinley
Trail Manager
Regional Trail Council
101 N. Water Street
P.O. Box 95
West Newton, PA 15089-1535
(412) 872–5586
www.westol.com/tat/updates/5star.htm

32 Forks Township Recreation Trail

Endpoints: Forks Township, Palmer Township
Mileage: 7
Surface: asphalt, gravel

Location: Northampton
Contact: Robert Fretz
Road Supervisor
Forks Township Recreation Board
1606 Sullivan Trail
Easton, PA 18040
(610) 252–0785

33 Gamelands Trail

Endpoints: Allegheny National Forest
Mileage: 2.3

Surface: dirt

Location: Warren
Contact: Mary Hosmer
Recreation Specialist
Allegheny National Forest
P.O. Box 847
Warren, PA 16365-0847
(814) 723–5150

34 George B. Will Trail

Endpoints: Tiadaghton State Forest
Mileage: 5
Surface: ballast, grass

Location: Lycoming
Contact: Jim Hyland
Recreation Forester
Tiadaghton Forest Fire Fighters Association
Bureau of Forestry
423 East Central Avenue
South Williamsport, PA 17702
(570) 327–3450
www.dcnr.state.pa.us

35 Ghost Town Trail

Endpoints: Nanty Glo, Dilltown
Mileage: 16
Surface: crushed stone

Location: Indiana; Cambria
Contact: Indiana County Parks
Blue Spruce Park Road

Indiana, PA 15701-9802
(724) 463–8636
http://cpcug.org/user/warholic/
ghost.html

36 Great Shamokin Path

Endpoints: Yatesboro, Numine
Mileage: 4.5
Surface: gravel, ballast, grass,
cinder

Location: Armstrong
Contact: Pam Meade
President
Cowanshannock Creek
Watershed Association
P.O. Box 307
Rural Valley, PA 16249-0307
(412) 783–6692

37 Heart's Content Cross-Country Ski Trail

Endpoints: Allegheny National
Forest
Mileage: 7.7
Surface: grass, dirt

Location: Warren
Contact: Jeff Stevenson
District Ranger
Allegheny National Forest
Sheffield Ranger District
Route 6
Sheffield, PA 16347
(814) 968–3232

38 Hickory Creek Trail

Endpoints: Allegheny National
Forest
Mileage: 11.5
Surface: dirt

Location: Forest
Contact: Mary Hosmer
Recreation Specialist
Allegheny National Forest
P.O. Box 847
Warren, PA 16365-0847
(814) 723–5150

39 Indian Creek Valley Hiking and Biking Trail

Endpoints: Indian Head,
Champion
Mileage: 5
Surface: crushed stone, ballast

Location: Fayette
Contact: Megan Hess-Kalp
Secretary/Treasurer
Salt Lick Township
147 Municipal Building Road
P.O. Box 403
Melcroft, PA 15462-0403
(724) 455–2866
saltlick@hhs.net

40 Iron Horse Trail

Endpoints: Big Spring State
Park, Tuscarora State Forest
Mileage: 10

Surface: crushed stone, ballast, dirt

Location: Perry
Contact: Bob Beleski
Forester
DCNR Bureau of Forestry
RD 1, Box 42 A
Blain, PA 17006
(717) 536–3191

41 Ironton Rail-Trail

Endpoints: Whitehall, North Whitehall
Mileage: 9
Surface: crushed stone, dirt

Location: Lehigh
Contact: Scott Cope
Bureau Chief of Recreation
Whitehall Township
3219 MacArthur Road
Whitehall, PA 18052-2900
(610) 437–5524

42 Jim Mayer Riverwalk

Endpoints: Johnstown
Mileage: 1.8
Surface: crushed stone

Location: Cambria
Contact: Lisa Dailey
Cambria County Tourist Council
111 Market Street

Johnstown, PA 15902-2901
(814) 536–7993

43 Kellettville to Nebraska Trace Trail

Endpoints: Kellettville, Nebraska Recreation Area
Mileage: 12.2
Surface: grass, dirt

Location: Forest
Contact: Rodney Daum
Park Ranger
US Army Corps of Engineers
1 Tionesta Lake
Tionesta, PA 16353-9613
(814) 755–3311

44 Kinzua Bridge Trail

Endpoints: Kinzua Bridge State Park
Mileage: 1
Surface: wood chips, dirt

Location: McKean
Contact: Trail Manager
Kinzua Bridge State Park
c/o Bendigo State Park
P.O. Box A
Johnsonburg, PA 15845-0016
(814) 965–2646

45 Lackawanna River Heritage Trail

Endpoints: Pittston, Scranton and Carbondale
Mileage: 40
Surface: crushed stone, gravel

Location: Lackawanna; Luzerne; Susquehanna; Wayne
Contact: Bernie McGurl
Executive Director
Lackawanna River Heritge Trail
P.O. Box 368
Scranton, PA 15501
(570) 347–6311
1rea@epix.net

46 Lambs Creek Hike and Bike Trail

Endpoints: Mansfield, Lamb's Creek Recreation Area
Mileage: 3.7
Surface: asphalt

Location: Tioga
Contact: Richard Koeppel
Park Manager
Tioga-Hammond Lakes
RR #1, Box 65
Tioga, PA 16946-9733
(570) 835–5281

47 Lancaster Junction Trail

Endpoints: Lancaster Junction, Landisville
Mileage: 2.5
Surface: dirt, cinder

Location: Lancaster
Contact: John Gerencser
Recreation Coordinator

Lancaster County Parks and Recreation
1050 Rockford Road
Lancaster, PA 17602-4624
(717) 299–8215
www.xo.lancaster.pa.us/parks.htm

48 Lehigh Gorge State Park Trail

Endpoints: Jim Thorpe, White Haven
Mileage: 26
Surface: crushed stone, ballast

Location: Carbon; Luzerne
Contact: Kevin Fazzini
Park Manager
Lehigh Gorge State Park
RR 1, Box 81
White Haven, PA 18661-9712
(717) 443–0400
www.dcnr.state.pa.us

49 LeTort Spring Run Nature Trail

Endpoints: Carlisle, South Middleton
Mileage: 1.4
Surface: ballast, grass

Location: Cumberland
Contact: Rian Fischbach
Executive Director
LeTort Regional Authority
415 Franklin Street
Carlisle, PA 17013-1859
(717) 245–0508
blfisch@epix.net

50 Lititz-Warwick Trailway

Endpoints: Lititz, Warwick
Mileage: 1.4
Surface: asphalt

Location: Chester
Contact: Dan Zimmerman
Warwick Township
P.O. Box 308
Lititz, PA 17543
(717) 626–8900

51 Little Buffalo State Park Trail

Endpoints: Shoeff's Mill to western boundary
Mileage: 2.5
Surface: dirt, gravel

Location: Perry
Contact: Little Buffalo State Park
RD2 Box 256A
Newport, PA 17074
(717) 567–9255
www.dcnr.state.pa.us

52 Little Drummer Historic Pathway

Endpoints: Allegheny National Forest
Mileage: 3.1
Surface: grass, dirt

Location: Elk
Contact: Mary Hosmer
Recreation Specialist
Allegheny National Forest

P.O. Box 847
Warren, PA 16365-0847
(814) 723–5150

53 Little Side Loop of Hickory Trail

Endpoints: Allegheny National Forest
Mileage: 3.9
Surface: dirt

Location: Forest
Contact: Mary Hosmer
Recreation Specialist
Allegheny National Forest
P.O. Box 847
Warren, PA 16365-0847
(814) 723–5150

54 Loleta Hiking Trail

Endpoints: Allegheny National Forest
Mileage: 3
Location: Forest
Contact: Mary Hosmer
Recreation Specialist
Allegheny National Forest
P.O. Box 847
Warren, PA 16365-0847
(814) 723–5150

55 Lower Trail

Endpoints: Alexandria, Williamsburg
Mileage: 11
Surface: crushed stone, ballast

Other use: wagon
Location: Blair; Huntingdon
Contact: Jennifer Barefoot
President
Central Pennsylvania Rails-to-
Trails
P.O. Box 592
Hollidaysburg, PA 16648-0592
(814) 832–2400

56 LR 651

Endpoints: Osceola Mills, West
Moshannon
Mileage: 4.5
Surface: ballast

Location: Clearfield
Contact: Clearfield County Rails
to Trails Association
310 East Cherry Street
Clearfield, PA 16830-2319

57 Lycoming Creek Bikeway

Endpoints: Williamsport,
Loyalsock
Mileage: 3.3
Surface: asphalt

Location: Lycoming
Contact: Mark Murawski
Transportation Planner
Lycoming County Planning
48 West Third Street
Williamsport, PA 17701-6536
(570) 320–2130

58 Marienville ATV/Bike Trail

Endpoints: Allegheny National
Forest
Mileage: 36.7
Surface: crushed stone, gravel,
grass, dirt

Other use: ATV
Location: Forest
Contact: Mary Hosmer
Recreation Specialist
Allegheny National Forest
P.O. Box 847
Warren, PA 16365-0847
(814) 723–5150

59 Mill Creek Loop Trail

Endpoints: Allegheny National
Forest
Mileage: 16.7
Surface: grass, dirt

Location: Elk
Contact: Allegheny National
Forest
Marienville Ranger District
HC 2, Box 130
Marienville, PA 16239
(814) 927–6628

60 Minister Creek Trail

Endpoints: Allegheny National
Forest
Mileage: 6.6
Surface: grass, dirt

Location: Warren; Forest
Contact: Jeff Stevenson
District Ranger
Allegheny National Forest
Sheffield Ranger District
Route 6
Sheffield, PA 16347
(814) 968–3232

61 Montour Trail—Cecil

Endpoints: Cecil Township,
Venice to Hendersonville
Mileage: 5.7
Surface: crushed stone

Location: Washington
Contact: Don Berty
Montour Trail Council
P.O. Box 11866
Pittsburgh, PA 15228-0866
(412) 221–6406
www.atatrail.org

62 Montour Trail— Coraopolis to Champion

Endpoints: Coraopolis,
Champion
Mileage: 18.5
Surface: crushed stone

Location: Allegheny
Contact: Tom Fix
Montour Trail Council
P.O. Box 11866
Pittsburgh, PA 15228-0866
(412) 831–2030
www.atatrail.org

63 North Country National Scenic Trail

Endpoints: Allegheny National
Forest, New York State Line
Mileage: 86.8 (several sections)
Surface: ballast, grass, dirt

Location: Elk; Forest; Mc Kean;
Warren
Contact: Mary Hosmer
Recreation Specialist
Allegheny National Forest
P.O. Box 847
Warren, PA 16365-0847
(814) 723–5150

64 North Link Trail

Endpoints: Susquehannock State
Forest
Mileage: 9.3
Surface: dirt

Location: Potter
Contact: David Schiller
District Forester
Susquehannock State Forest
3150 East Second Street
P.O. Box 673
Coudersport, PA 16915-0673
(814) 274–600
fd15.coudersport@a1.dcnr.state.
pa.us

65 O&W Trail

Endpoints: Simpson, Stillwater
Mileage: 8
Surface: gravel, dirt

Location: Wayne
Contact: Lynn Conrad
Rail-Trail Council of Northeast
Penn.
P.O. Box 123
Forest City, PA 18421-0123
(717) 785–7245
tccrail@epix.net
www.neparailtrails.org

66 Oil Creek State Park Trail

Endpoints: Petroleum Centre,
Titusville
Mileage: 9.7
Surface: asphalt

Location: Venango; Crawford
Contact: Marcia Baker
Park Manager
Oil Creek State Park
RR 1, Box 207
Oil City, PA 16301-9733
(814) 676–5915
www.dcnr.state.pa.us

67 Old Railroad Trail

Endpoints: Big Pocono State
Park, Crescent Lake
Mileage: 8.4
Surface: ballast

Location: Monroe

Contact: Ronald Dixon
Park Manager
Big Pocono State Park
c/o Tobyhanna State Park
P.O. Box 387
Tobyhanna, PA 18466-0387
(717) 894–8336
www.dcnr.state.pa.us

68 Old Tram Trail

Endpoints: Bald Eagle State
Forest
Mileage: 1.2
Surface: crushed stone, dirt

Location: Union
Contact: Amy Griffith
District Forester
Bald Eagle State Park
P.O. Box 147
Laurelton, PA 17835
(570) 922–3344

69 Penns Creek Path (Mid State Trail)

Endpoints: Poe Paddy State Park
Mileage: 2.9
Surface: ballast

Location: Centre; Mifflin
Contact: Thomas Thwaites
President
Mid State Trail Association
P.O. Box 167
Boalsburg, PA 16827-0167
(814) 237–7703

70 Pennsylvania Mainline Canal

Endpoints: Alexandria, Huntingdon county line
Mileage: 5
Surface: crushed stone

Location: Huntingdon
Contact: Richard Stahl
Planning Director, Huntingdon
County Planning Commission
Courthouse
Huntingdon, PA 16652
(814) 643–5091
hcpc@penn.com

71 Pigeon Run Falls Trail

Endpoints: Allegheny National Forest
Mileage: 5.9
Surface: dirt

Location: Forest
Contact: Mary Hosmer
Recreation Specialist
Allegheny National Forest
P.O. Box 847
Warren, PA 16365-0847
(814) 723–5150

72 Pine Creek Trail

Endpoints: Wellsboro, Avis
Mileage: 62.2
Surface: ballast

Location: Tioga; Lycoming
Contact: District Forester
Bureau of Forestry
Department of Conservation and
Natural Resources
One Nessmuk Lane
Route 287 South
Wellsboro, PA 16901
(570) 724–2868

73 Pittsburgh Riverwalk at Station Square

Endpoints: Pittsburgh
Mileage: 1.5
Surface: asphalt

Location: Allegheny
Contact: Darla Cravotta
Trails and Parks Coordinator
Office of the Mayor
414 City-County Building
Room 512
Pittsburgh, PA 15219
(412) 255–4768
darla.cravotta@city.pittsburgh.
pa.us

74 Plainfield Township Recreation Trail

Endpoints: Plainfield
Mileage: 6.7
Surface: crushed stone, gravel

Location: Northampton
Contact: Jenny Koehler
Treasurer
Plainfield Township
6292 Sullivan Trail
Nazareth, PA 18064-9334
(610) 759–6944

75 PW&S Railroad Hiking-Biking Trail

Endpoints: Forbes State Forest, Lynn Run State Park
Mileage: 36
Surface: gravel, dirt

Location: Westmoreland; Somerset
Contact: Thomas Grote
Executive Director
Loyalhanna Watershed Assn.
P.O. Box 561
Ligonier, PA 15658-0561
(412) 238–7560

76 Pymatuning State Park Trail

Endpoints: Pymatuning State Park
Mileage: 2.9
Surface: ballast

Location: Crawford
Contact: Dennis Mihoci
Park Manager
Pymatuning State Park
2660 Williamsfield Road
Jamestown, PA 16134-0425
(724) 932–3141
Pymatuning.sp@a1.dcnr.
state.pa.us

77 Railroad Grade Trail

Endpoints: Ives Run Recreation Area
Mileage: 2.6

Surface: ballast

Location: Tioga
Contact: Terry Anderson
Trails Coordinator
U.S. Army Corps of Engineers
RD 1, Box 65
Tioga, PA 16946-9733
(570) 835–5281

78 Roaring Run Trail

Endpoints: Kiskiminetas
Mileage: 3.7
Surface: crushed stone

Location: Armstrong
Contact: Don Stevenson
President
Roaring Run Watershed
Association
P.O. Box 333
Apollo, PA 15613
(724) 727–7360
don_stevenson@hotmail.com
www.roaring.run.org

79 Rocky Gap ATV/Bike Trail

Endpoints: Allegheny National Forest
Mileage: 15.5
Surface: grass, dirt

Other use: ATV
Location: Warren
Contact: Jeff Stevenson
District Ranger
Allegheny National Forest
Sheffield Ranger District
Route 6
Sheffield, PA 16347
(814) 968–3232

80 Samuel Justus Recreation Trail

Endpoints: Franklin, Oil City
Mileage: 5.8
Surface: asphalt

Location: Venango
Contact: Frank Pankratz
Secretary
Cranberry Township
P.O. Box 378
Seneca, PA 16346-0378
(814) 676–8812

81 Schuylkill River Trail

Endpoints: Philadelphia, Valley
Forge
Mileage: 22
Surface: asphalt

Location: Montgomery;
Philadelphia
Contact: John Wood
Chief of Open Space Planning
Montgomery County Planning
Commission

P.O. Box 311 Courthouse
Norristown, PA 19404-0311
(610) 278–3736
j.wood@montcopa.org

82 Sentiero Di Shay Trail

Endpoints: Tiadaghton State
Forest
Mileage: 13
Surface: ballast, grass

Location: Lycoming
Contact: Tiadaghton Forest Fire
Fighters Association
c/o Bureau of Forestry
423 East Central Ave.
South Williamsport, PA 17702
(570) 327–3450
www.dcnr.state.pa.us

83 Snowshoe Trail

Endpoints: Clarence (Snowshoe),
Winburne
Mileage: 19
Surface: ballast

Location: Centre; Clearfield
Contact: Erin Freer
Program Specialist
Headwaters Charitable Trust
478 Jeffers
Du Bois, PA 15801
(814) 375–1372
Headwatr@PENN.com

84 South Link Trail

Endpoints: Susquehannock State Forest
Mileage: 6
Surface: dirt

Location: Potter
Contact: David Schiller
District Forester
Susquehannock State Forest
P.O. Box 673
Coudersport, PA 16915-0673
(814) 274–7459

85 Stony Valley Railroad Grade

Endpoints: Ellendale Forge, Lebanon Reservoir
Mileage: 22
Surface: cinder

Other use: hunting
Location: Dauphin; Lebanon; Schuylkill
Contact: Roland Bergner
Chief
Federal-State Coordination Division
Pennsylvania Game Commission
2001 Elmerton Avenue
Harrisburg, PA 17110-9797
(717) 787–9612

86 Struble Trail

Endpoints: Downingtown
Mileage: 2.5
Surface: crushed stone

Location: Chester
Contact: Chester County Parks and Recreation Department
601 Westtown Road, Suite 160
P.O. Box 2747
West Chester, PA 19380-0990
(610) 344–6415
www.chesco.org/ccparks.html

87 Susquehannock Trail System

Endpoints: Susquehannock State Forest
Mileage: 89 (30 are Rail-Trail)
Surface: dirt

Location: Clinton; Potter
Contact: David Schiller
District Forester
Susquehannock State Forest
P.O. Box 673
Coudersport, PA 16915-0673
(814) 274–7459

88 Swatara Multi-Use Trail

Endpoints: Lickdale, Suedberg
Mileage: 9
Surface: dirt

Location: Lebanon, Schuylkill

Contact: Pennsylvania
Department of Conservation and
Natural Resources
Swatara State Park
c/o Memorial Lake State Park
R.R. 1, Box 7045
Grantville, PA 17028-9682
(717) 865–6470
memorial.sp@a1.dcnr.state.pa.us
www.dcnr.state.pa.us

89 Switchback Railroad Trail

Endpoints: Summit Hill, Jim
Thorpe
Mileage: 18
Surface: crushed stone, ballast

Location: Carbon
Contact: Dennis DeMara
Park Director
Carbon County Park and
Recreation Department
625 Lentz Trail Road
Jim Thorpe, PA 18229
(570) 325–3669
www.dcnr.state.pa.us

90 Three Rivers Heritage Trail

Endpoints: Pittsburgh
Mileage: 12
Surface: asphalt, crushed stone

Location: Allegheny
Contact: John Stephen
Friends of the Riverfront
P.O. Box 42434
Pittsburgh, PA 15203-0434
(412) 488–0212
jsdi@andrew.comm.edu
www.atatrail.org

91 Thun Trail

Endpoints: Reading, Stowe
Mileage: 15
Surface: ballast

Location: Berks
Contact: Dixie Swenson
Managing Director
Schuylkill River Greenway
Association
The Old Mill
960 Old Mill Road
Wyomissing, PA 19610
(610) 372–3916
info@schuylkillriver.org

92 Tidioute Riverside RecTrek Trail

Endpoints: Allegheny National
Forest
Mileage: 4.5
Surface: ballast

Location: Warren
Contact: Mary Hosmer
Recreation Specialist
Allegheny National Forest
P.O. Box 847
Warren, PA 16365-0847
(814) 723–5150

93 Tom Run Loop Trail

Endpoints: Allegheny National
Forest
Mileage: 3.6
Surface: dirt

Location: Warren
Contact: Mary Hosmer
Recreation Specialist
Allegheny National Forest
P.O. Box 847
Warren, PA 16365-0847
(814) 723–5150

94 Towpath Bike Trail (National Trails Towpath Bike Trail)

Endpoints: Bethlehem, Palmer Township
Mileage: 7.8
Surface: asphalt

Location: Northampton
Contact: Jeffery Young
Chairman
Palmer Township Board of Supervisors
3 Weller Place, P.O. Box 3039
Palmer, PA 18043-3039
(610) 253–7191

95 Twin Lakes Trail

Endpoints: Allegheny National Forest
Mileage: 14.7
Surface: grass, dirt

Location: Elk; Warren
Contact: Leon Blashock
District Ranger
Allegheny National Forest

Ridgway Ranger District
RD 1, Box 28A
Ridgway, PA 15853
(814) 776–6172

96 Warren–North Warren Bike Trail

Endpoints: Warren, North Warren
Mileage: 2
Surface: asphalt

Location: Warren
Contact: Dan Glotz
Warren County Planning Commission
207 West Fifth Avenue
Warren, PA 16365
(814) 726–3861

97 York County Heritage Rail-Trail

Endpoints: New Freedom, Hanover Junction
Mileage: 10.7
Surface: crushed stone

Location: York
Contact: Gwen Loose
Project Coordinator
York County Trail Authority
5922 Nixon Drive
York, PA 17403-9677
(717) 428–2586
www.southernyorkcounty.com/org/railtrail/

98 Youghiogheny River Trail—North

Endpoints: Connellsville, McKeesport
Mileage: 43
Surface: crushed stone, ballast

Location: Fayette;
Westmoreland; Allegheny
Contact: Robert McKinley
Trail Manager
Regional Trail Council
101 North Water Street
P.O. Box 95
West Newton, PA 15089-1535
(412) 872–5586
yrt@nb.net
www.youghrivertrail.com

99 Youghiogheny River Trail—South

Endpoints: Confluence, Connellsville
Mileage: 28
Surface: crushed stone

Location: Fayette
Contact: Douglas Hoehn
Park Operations Manager
Ohiopyle State Park
P.O. Box 105
Ohiopyle, PA 15470-0105
(412) 329–8591
ohiopyle.sp@a1.dcnr.state.pa.us
www.atatrail.org

RHODE ISLAND

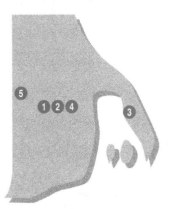

Location: Kent
Contact: Guy Lefebvre
Director of Parks and Recreation
Parks & Recreation Department
1670 Flat River Road
Coventry, RI 02816
(401) 822–9107

1 Arkwright Riverwalk

Endpoints: Coventry
Mileage: 1.5
Surface: wood chips, dirt

Location: Kent
Contact: Jeffrey Kos
Chairperson
Pawtuxet River Authority
P.O. Box 336
West Warwick, RI 02893-0336
(401) 828–5650

2 Coventry Greenway

Endpoints: Coventry, West
Warwick Border
Mileage: 5
Surface: asphalt, ballast

3 East Bay Bicycle Path

Endpoints: Bristol, Providence
Mileage: 14.5
Surface: asphalt

Location: Bristol
Contact: Kevin O'Malley
Regional Manager
Colt State Park
Bristol, RI 02809
(401) 253–7482
www.riparks.com

4 Phenix-Harris Riverwalk

Endpoints: West Warwick
Mileage: 0.5
Surface: dirt

Location: Kent
Contact: Jeffrey Kos
Chairperson
Pawtuxet River Authority
P.O. Box 336
West Warwick, RI 02893
(401) 828–5650

5 Trestle Trail (Charter Oak Greenway)

Endpoints: Coventry Center, Connecticut state line
Mileage: 10
Surface: gravel, ballast, dirt

Location: Kent
Contact: Bob Sutton
Chief of Planning and
Development
Rhode Island Department of
Environmental Management
235 Promenade Street
Providence, RI 02908
(401) 222–2776

SOUTH CAROLINA

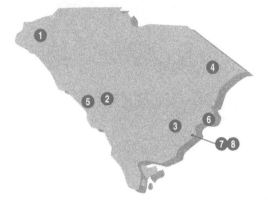

1 Blue Ridge Railroad Historical Trail

Endpoints: Stumphouse Tunnel, Walhalla
Mileage: 5
Surface: wood chips, dirt

Location: Oconee
Contact: Hurley Badders
Executive Director
Pendleton Historic and
Recreational Commission
P.O. Box 565
Pendleton, SC 29670-0565
(803) 646–3782

2 Cathedral Aisle Trail

Endpoints: Aiken
Mileage: 1
Surface: dirt

Location: Aiken
Contact: Gary Burger
Forest Manager
Hitchcock Foundation
P.O. Box 1702
Aiken, SC 29802-1702
(803) 648–8085

3 Edisto Nature Trail

Endpoints: Colleton
Mileage: 1.5
Surface: grass, dirt

Location: Jacksonboro
Contact: Westuaco Corporation
Public Affairs
P.O. 1950
Summerville, SC 29484
(843) 871–5000

4 Marion Hike and Bike Trail

Endpoints: Marion
Mileage: 0.25

Surface: asphalt, dirt

Location: Marion
Contact: Ronny Pridgen
Recreation Director
City of Marion Parks and
Recreation Department
P.O. Box 1190
Marion, SC 29571-1190
(843) 423–5410

5 North Augusta Greeneway

Endpoints: North Augusta
Mileage: 5.2
Surface: asphalt, gravel

Location: Aiken
Contact: Robert Brooks
Director
North Augusta Parks &
Recreation
P.O. Box 6400
North Augusta, SC 29841-0400
(803) 441–4300
bbrooks@mail.n-augusta.sc.us
www.nirthaugusta.net

6 Swamp Fox National Recreation Trail

Endpoints: Francis Marion
National Forest, Awendaw-
Withenbee
Mileage: 27
Surface: dirt

Location: Berkeley; Charleston
Contact: Cheron Rhodes
Recreation Forester
Francis Marion National Forest
P.O. Box 788
McClellanville, SC 29458-0788
(803) 887–3257

7 West Ashley Bikeway

Endpoints: Charleston
Mileage: 2
Surface: asphalt

Location: Charleston
Contact: Amanda Barton
Charleston Department of Parks
823 Meeting Street
Charleston, SC 29403-3108
(843) 724–7321

8 West Ashley Greenway

Endpoints: Charleston
Mileage: 8.5
Surface: crushed stone, grass,
dirt

Location: Charleston
Contact: Dave Eason
Recreation Services
Superintendent
City of Charleston Recreation
Department
823 Meeting Street
Charleston, SC 29403
(843) 724-7327
easond@ci.charleston.sc.us

1 George S. Mickelson Trail

Endpoints: Deadwood, Edgemont
Mileage: 114
Surface: crushed stone, gravel

Location: Lawrence; Custer; Pennington; Fall River
Contact: Dan Simon
Trails Program Specialist
South Dakota Department of Game, Fish, and Parks
523 East Capitol Avenue
Pierre, SD 57501-3182
(605) 773–3930
dans@gfp.state.sd.us

2 Spearfish Recreational Trail

Endpoints: Spearfish
Mileage: 2.8
Surface: concrete

Location: Lawrence
Contact: Keith Hepper
City of Spearfish
625 Fifth Street
Spearfish, SD 57783-2311
(605) 642–1333
keithh@spearfish.sd.us

TENNESSEE

1 Bald River Trail

Endpoints: Cherokee National Forest
Mileage: 5.6
Surface: dirt

Location: Monroe
Contact: Larry Fleming
District Ranger
Cherokee National Forest
Tellico Ranger District
250 Ranger Station Road
Tellico Plains, TN 37385-5804
(423) 253–2520

2 Betsy Ligon Park & Walking Trail

Endpoints: Erin
Mileage: 2
Surface: asphalt

Location: Houston
Contact: Linda Bratchi
Recorder Erin City Hall
P.O. Box 270
Erin, TN 37061-0270
(931) 289–4108

3 Conasauga River Trail

Endpoints: Cherokee National Forest
Mileage: 4.5
Surface: dirt

Location: Monroe
Contact: Larry Fleming
District Ranger
Cherokee National Forest
Tellico Ranger District
250 Ranger Station Road
Tellico Plains, TN 37385-5804
(423) 253–2520

4 Crowder Branch Trail

Endpoints: Cherokee National Forest
Mileage: 2.6
Surface: dirt

Location: Monroe
Contact: Larry Fleming
District Ranger
Cherokee National Forest
Tellico Ranger District
250 Ranger Station Road
Tellico Plains, TN 37385-5804
(423) 253–2520

5 Cumberland River Bicentennial Trail

Endpoints: Ashland City, Sycamore Recreation Area
Mileage: 4
Surface: asphalt, gravel, ballast

Location: Cheatham
Contact: Tony Young
Director
Ashland City Parks and
Recreation
P.O. Box 36
Ashland City, TN 37015-0036
(615) 792–2655

6 Grassy Branch Trail

Endpoints: Cherokee National Forest
Mileage: 3.2
Surface: dirt

Location: Monroe
Contact: Larry Fleming
District Ranger
Cherokee National Forest
Tellico Ranger District
250 Ranger Station Road
Tellico Plains, TN 37385-5804
(423) 253–2520

7 Hemlock Trail

Endpoints: Cherokee National Forest
Mileage: 3
Surface: dirt

Location: Monroe
Contact: Larry Fleming
District Ranger
Cherokee National Forest
Tellico Ranger District
250 Ranger Station Road
Tellico Plains, TN 37385-5804
(423) 253–2520

8 Laurel Branch Trail

Endpoints: Cherokee National Forest
Mileage: 3
Surface: dirt

Location: Monroe
Contact: Larry Fleming
District Ranger
Cherokee National Forest
Tellico Ranger District
250 Ranger Station Road
Tellico Plains, TN 37385-5804
(423) 253–2520

9 Long Branch Trail

Endpoints: Cherokee National Forest
Mileage: 2.7
Surface: dirt

Location: Monroe
Contact: Larry Fleming
District Ranger
Cherokee National Forest
Tellico Ranger District
250 Ranger Station Road
Tellico Plains, TN 37385-5804
(423) 253–2520

10 McNabb Creek Trail

Endpoints: Cherokee National Forest
Mileage: 3.9
Surface: ballast

Location: Monroe
Contact: Larry Fleming
District Ranger
Cherokee National Forest
Tellico Ranger District
250 Ranger Station Road
Tellico Plains, TN 37385-5804
(423) 253–2520

11 North Fork Citico Trail

Endpoints: Cherokee National Forest
Mileage: 5
Surface: ballast

Location: Monroe
Contact: Larry Fleming
District Ranger
Cherokee National Forest
Tellico Ranger District
250 Ranger Station Road
Tellico Plains, TN 37385-5804
(423) 253–2520

12 South Fork Citico Trail

Endpoints: Cherokee National Forest
Mileage: 8.1
Surface: dirt

Location: Monroe
Contact: Larry Fleming
District Ranger
Cherokee National Forest
Tellico Ranger District
250 Ranger Station Road
Tellico Plains, TN 37385-5804
(423) 253-2520

13 Tellico Plains Rail-Trail

Endpoints: Tellico Plains
Mileage: 0.85
Surface: asphalt

Location: Monroe
Contact: Sam Stamey
Mayor
City Hall
201 Southard St.
Tellico Plains, TN 37385-5125
(423) 253–2333
wn.cityhall.com

14 V&E Greenline

Endpoints: Memphis
Mileage: 1.7
Surface: grass, dirt, original ballast

Location: Shelby
Contact: Michael Kirby
V&E Greenline
VECA CDC
1680 Jackson Avenue
Memphis, TN 38107
(901) 276–1782
mkirby@ionictech.com
www.geocities.com/VEGreenline

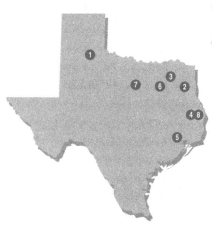

2 Cargill Long Park Trail

Endpoints: Longview
Mileage: 2.2
Surface: asphalt

Location: Gregg
Contact: Terry Owens
Manager
Longview Parks and Recreation
P.O. Box 1952
Longview, TX 75606-1952
(903) 237–1391
tgowens@internetwork.net

1 Caprock Canyons State Park Trailway

Endpoints: Estelline, South Plains
Mileage: 64.2
Surface: ballast

Location: Briscoe; Floyd; Hall
Contact: Geoffrey Hulse
Park Manager
Caprock Canyons State Park &
Canyonlands Trailway Complex
Texas Parks & Wildlife
Department
P.O. Box 204
Quitaque, TX 79255-0204
(806) 455–1332

3 Chaparral Trail

Endpoints: Farmersville, Ladonia
Mileage: 20
Surface: dirt

Location: Collin; Fannin; Hunt
Contact: Joe Barton
Constable
P.O. Box 367
Farmersville, TX 75442
(972) 782–7211

4 Four-C Hiking Trail

Endpoints: Davy Crockett National Forest
Mileage: 20
Surface: ballast, dirt

Location: Houston
Contact: Duane Strock
Landscape Architect
Davy Crockett National Forest
701 North First Street
Lufkin, TX 75901-3057
(409) 639–8529

5 Harrisburg and Sunset Rail-Trails

Endpoints: Houston (Commerce Street, Hidalgo Park)
Mileage: 5.9
Surface: asphalt

Location: Harris
Contact: Mignette Dorsey
Public Works and Engineering
611 Walker
Houston, TX 77002
(713) 837–0003

6 Katy Trail

Endpoints: Dallas
Mileage: 2.3
Surface: concrete

Location: Dallas
Contact: Darryl Baker
Dallas Parks and Recreation
New City Hall
Room 6F South
Dallas, TX 75201
(214) 670–4282

7 Lake Mineral Wells State Trailway

Endpoints: Mineral Wells, Weatherford
Mileage: 20
Surface: asphalt, crushed stone

Location: Palo Pinto, Parker
Contact: Lee Ellis
Assistant Superintendant
Texas Parks and Wildlife
RR4, Box 39C
Mineral Wells, TX 76967
(940) 328–1171

8 Sawmill Hiking Trail

Endpoints: Angelina National Forest
Mileage: 5.5
Surface: dirt

Location: Jasper
Contact: Catherine Albers
Resource Forester
Angelina National Forest
Angelina Ranger District
Lufkin, TX 75904
(409) 639–8620

UTAH

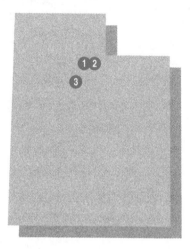

1 Historic Union Pacific Rail Trail

Endpoints: Echo Junction, Park City
Mileage: 28
Surface: asphalt, crushed stone

Location: Summit; Wasatch
Contact: Troy Duffin
Mountain Trails Foundation
P.O. Box 754
Park City, UT 84060
(435) 649–6839

2 Olympic Parkway

Endpoints: Park City
Mileage: 1
Location: Summit
Contact: Jennifer Harrington

Senior Landscape Architect
Park City Municipal Corporation
P.O. Box 1480
445 Marsac Avenue
Park City, UT 84060-1480
(801) 645–5016

3 Provo Jordan River Parkway Trail

Endpoints: Provo, Provo Canyon
Mileage: 43
Surface: asphalt

Location: Utah
Contact: Clyde Naylor
Engineer
Utah County
2855 South State
Provo, UT 84606-6502
(801) 370–8600

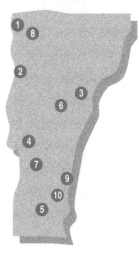

2 Burlington Waterfront Bikeway

Endpoints: Burlington
Mileage: 7.6
Surface: asphalt

Location: Chittenden
Contact: Robert Whalen
Superintendent
Burlington Department of Parks
& Recreation
1 LaValley Lane
Burlington, VT 05401-2779
(802) 865–7247

1 Alburg Recreational Rail-Trail

Endpoints: Alburg Village, East
Alburg
Mileage: 3.5
Surface: ballast, cinder

Location: Grand Isle
Contact: Charles Vile
Forestry District Manager North
Vt. Department of Forests, Parks
& Recreation
111 West Street
Essex Junction, VT 05452-4615
(802) 879–6565
cvile@anressex.anr.state.vt.us
www.members.tripod.com/ keny-
on_karl

3 Cross Vermont Trail (Montpelier & Wells River Trail)

Endpoints: Burlington, Wells
River
Mileage: 75
Surface: gravel, ballast

Location: Caledonia; Chittenden;
Washington
Contact: David Willard
Trails Coordinator
Vermont Agency of Natural
Resources
Department of Forests, Parks &
Recreation
184 Portland Street

St. Johnsbury, VT 05819-2099
(802) 751–0110

4 Delaware and Hudson Rail-Trail

Endpoints: West Rupert, Castleton
Mileage: 19.8 (two sections)
Surface: ballast

Location: Rutland; Bennington
Contact: Gary Salmon
Trails Coordinator
Dept. of Forests, Parks and Recreation
317 Sanitorium Road, West Wing
Pittsford, VT 05763-9802
(802) 483–2733
gsalmon@anrpitts.anr.state.vt.us

5 East Branch Trail

Endpoints: Green Mountain National Forest
Mileage: 5.1
Surface: gravel

Location: Windham
Contact: John Ragonese
Recreation Planner
New England Power Company
33 West Lebanon Road
P.O. Box 528
Lebanon, NH 03784-1917
(603) 448–2200

6 Graniteville Trails

Endpoints: Websterville, Graniteville
Mileage: 1.4
Surface: asphalt, ballast

Location: Washington
Contact: Cail Rogers
Town Manager
Town of Berrytown
Municipal Building
Websterville, VT 05678
(802) 479–9331

7 Lye Brook Trail

Endpoints: Green Mountain National Forest
Mileage: 9.7
Surface: gravel

Location: Bennington; Windham
Contact: Robert Pramuk
Recreation Forester
Green Mountain National Forest
231 North Main Street
Rutland, VT 05701-2412
(802) 747–6700

8 Missisquoi Valley Rail-Trail

Endpoints: St. Albans, Richford
Mileage: 26.4
Surface: crushed stone

Location: Franklin
Contact: Bonnie Waninger
Special Projects Planner
Northwest Regional Planning
Commission
140 S. Main Street
St. Albans, VT 05478-1850
(802) 524–5958
nrpcvt@together.net
www.members.tripod.com/
kenyon_karl

Location: Windham
Contact: Rick White
Trails Coordinator
Vermont Agency of Natural
Resources
Department of Forests, Parks &
Recreation
100 Mineral Street, Suite 304
Springfield, VT 05156
(802) 885–8824
rick.white@anr.state.vt.us

9 Springfield Trail

Endpoints: Springfield, VT;
Charleston, NH
Mileage: 3
Surface: asphalt

Location: Windsor
Contact: Bettina McCrady
Springfield Trails and Greenways
Committee
108 Summer Street
Springfield, VT 05156-3539
(802) 885–9687

10 West River Trail (Railroad Bed Trail)

Endpoints: South Londonderry,
Townshend
Mileage: 11
Surface: gravel, ballast

VIRGINIA

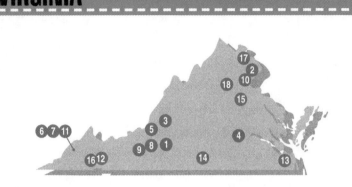

1 Blackwater Creek Natural Area Bikeway

Endpoints: Lynchburg
Mileage: 18
Surface: asphalt, gravel

Location: Lynchburg
Contact: Andy Reeder
Parks Manager
City of Lynchburg Parks and
Recreation Division
301 Grove Street
Lynchburg, VA 24501
(804) 847–1640
reedeah@ci.lynchburg.va.us

2 Bluemont Junction Trail

Endpoints: Bluemont Park,
Ballston
Mileage: 1.3
Surface: asphalt

Location: Arlington
Contact: Ritch Viola
Arlington County Department of
Public Works
2100 Clarendon Blvd, Suite 717
Arlington, VA 22201-5445
(703) 358–3699

3 Chessie Nature Trail

Endpoints: Lexington, Buena
Vista
Mileage: 7.5
Surface: crushed stone, gravel,
grass, dirt, cinder and sand

Location: Rockbridge
Contact: Louise Dooley
Assistant Vice President
VMI Foundation
P.O. Box 932
Lexington, VA 24450-0932
(540) 464–7221

4 Chester Linear Park

Endpoints: Chester
Mileage: 1

Surface: crushed stone

Location: Chesterfield
Contact: Mike Golden
Director
Chesterfield Parks & Recreation
Box 40
Chesterfield, VA 23832
(804) 748–1623

5 Craig Valley Scenic Trail

Endpoints: Eagle Rock, Horton;
Oriskany, Charlton
Mileage: 15 (in two segments)
Surface: dirt, crushed stone

Location: Botetourt, Craig
Contact: Jerry Jacobsen
Recreation Forester
U.S. Forest Service
P.O. Box 246
New Castle, VA 24127-0246
(540) 864–5195
jljacobsen@fs.fed.us

6 Devils Fork Loop Trail

Endpoints: Dungannon, George
Washington National Forest
Mileage: 5.1
Surface: dirt

Location: Scott
Contact: John Stallard
Recreation Forester
USDA Forest Service/Clinch

Ranger District
9416 Darden Drive
Wise, VA 24293
(540) 328–2931
www.fsfed.us\gwjnf

7 Guest River Gorge Trail

Endpoints: Coeburn, Jefferson
National Forest
Mileage: 5.5
Surface: crushed stone

Location: Scott; Wise
Contact: Jim McIntyre
Clinch Ranger District
Jefferson National Forest
9416 Darden Drive
Wise, VA 24293-5900
(540) 328–2931

8 Hanging Rock Battlefield Trail

Endpoints: Salem, Hanging Rock
Mileage: 1.6
Surface: gravel

Location: Roanoke
Contact: David Robbins
Hanging Rock Battlefield and
Railway Preservation
620 High Street
Salem, VA 24153-2830

9 Huckleberry Trail

Endpoints: Blacksburg, Christiansburg
Mileage: 6
Surface: asphalt

Location: Montgomery
Contact: Joe Powers
Planning Director
Montgomery County Planning
Department
County Courthouse
P.O. Box 6126
Christiansburg, VA 24068
(540) 382–5750
www.mfrl.org/compages/
huckleberry

10 Lake Accotink Trail

Endpoints: Springfield
Mileage: 6
Surface: crushed stone, gravel

Location: Fairfax
Contact: Tawny Hammond
Park Manager
Fairfax County Park Authority
Lake Accotink Park
7500 Accotink Park Road
Springfield, VA 22150
(703) 569–3464

11 Little Stony National Recreation Trail

Endpoints: Dungannon, George Washington National Forest
Mileage: 2.8
Surface: dirt

Location: Scott
Contact: Jim McIntyre
Clinch Ranger District
Jefferson National Forest
9416 Darden Drive
Wise, VA 24293-5900
(540) 328–2931

12 New River Trail State Park

Endpoints: Pulaski to Galax, spur to Fries
Mileage: 57
Surface: gravel, dirt, cinder

Location: Pulaski; Carroll; Grayson; Wythe
Contact: Eric Houghland
Chief Ranger
Virginia Department of
Conservation and Recreation
Division of State Parks
Route 2 Box 126F
Foster Falls, VA 24360
(540) 699–6778
www.chr.vt.edu/Colors/nrt/NRTS.
html.nrt.org

13 Park Connector Bikeway

Endpoints: Mt. Trashmore, Princess Anne Park
Mileage: 4.9
Surface: asphalt

Location: Virginia Beach
Contact: Travis Campbell
Planner
Department of Planning
Room 115, Operations Building
2405 Courthouse Road
Virginia Beach, VA 23456-9121
(804) 427–4621
teampbel@city.
virginiabeach.va.us

14 Patrick Henry Trail

Endpoints: Staunton River
Battlefield
Mileage: 0.8
Surface: crushed stone

Location: Halifax
Contact: Jim Zanarihi
Chief Ranger
Staunton River Bridge Battlefield
State Park
1035 Fort Hill Trail
Randolph, VA 23962
(804) 454–4312

15 Virginia Central Railway Trail

Endpoints: Salem Church Road,
Gordon Road
Mileage: 1.2
Surface: asphalt

Location: Spotsylvania
Contact: Joe Lerch
Planning Department
Spotsylvania Co.
P.O. Box 876
Spotsylvania, VA 22553
(540) 582–7040
jlerch@spotsylvania.va.us

16 Virginia Creeper National Recreation Trail

Endpoints: Abingdon, White Top
Mileage: 34.1
Surface: gravel, dirt

Location: Washington; Grayson
Contact: Tina Counts
Abingdon Convention and
Visitors Bureau
335 Cummings Street
Abingdon, VA 24210-3207
(540) 676–2282
www.his.com/~jmenzies
/urbanatb/rtrails/creeper/
creeper.htm

17 W&OD Railroad Regional Park

Endpoints: Arlington, Purcellville
Mileage: 45
Surface: asphalt, crushed stone

Location: Arlington; Fairfax;
Loudoun
Contact: Paul McCray
Park Manager

Northern Virginia Regional Park
Authority
21293 Smiths Switch Road
Ashburn, VA 20147
(703) 729–0596
wodtrail@erols.com
www.geocities.com/yosemite/
trails/9401/

18 Warrenton Branch Greenway

Endpoints: Warrenton (Fourth
Street), Calverton
Mileage: 1.5
Surface: asphalt

Location: Fauquier
Contact: Larry Miller
Director
Fauquier County Parks and
Recreation
62 Culpeper Street
Warrenton, VA 20186-3289
(540) 347–6896
parks@crosslink.net
http://cofauguier.va.us/services/
parks/greenway

WASHINGTON

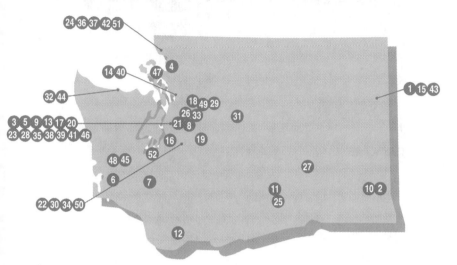

1 Benn Burr Trail

Endpoints: Spokane
Mileage: 1.1
Surface: crushed stone, gravel, dirt

Location: Spokane
Contact: Taylor Bressler
Division Manager
City of Spokane Parks Dept.
North 809 Washington Street
Spokane, WA 99201-2233
(509) 625–6655

2 Bill Chipman Palouse Trail

Endpoints: Pullman, WA, Moscow, ID
Mileage: 7.5
Surface: asphalt

Location: Whitman, Latah
Contact: Roger Marens
Whitman County Parks
310 North Main Street
Colfax, WA 99111
(509) 397–6238
ranger@co.whitman.wa.us

3 Burke-Gilman Trail

Endpoints: Seattle, Bothell
Mileage: 18
Surface: asphalt

Location: King
Contact: Peter Lagerwey

Bicycle/Pedestrian Coordinator
Seattle Engineering Department
708 Municipal Building
600 Fourth Avenue
Seattle, WA 98104-1879
(206) 684–5108
pete.lagerwey@ci.seattle.wa.us
www.ci.seattle.wa.us/seattle/td/
bikeprog/bg-trail.html

4 Cascade Trail

Endpoints: Burlington-Regent
Street, Peter-Anderson Street
Mileage: 1.5
Surface: crushed stone

Location: Skagit
Contact: Peter Mayer
Operations Manager
Skagit County Parks, Recreation
and Fair Department
315 South Third Street
Mount Vernon, WA 98273-3822
(360) 336–9414
peterm@co.skagit.wa.us

5 Cedar River Trail

Endpoints: North Bend, Renton
Mileage: 17.5
Surface: asphalt, crushed stone

Location: King
Contact: Tom Eksten
Trails Coordinator
King County Office of Open Space
2040 Eighty-fourth Avenue SE
Mercer Island, WA 98040-2222
(206) 296–7808

www.metrokc.gov/parks/trails/
trails/cedar.htm

6 Chehalis to Raymond (Raymond to Southbend Riverfront Trail)

Endpoints: Raymond, Southbend
Mileage: 3.5
Surface: asphalt

Location: Pacific; Lewis
Contact: Rebecca Chafee
City Engineer
City of Raymond
230 Second Street
Raymond, WA 98577-2420
(360) 942–3451

7 Chehalis Western Trail (Woodard Bay Trail)

Endpoints: Woodard Bay
Natural Resource Conservation
Area, Martin Way (Lacey), Vail
Mileage: 13
Surface: asphalt

Location: Thurston
Contact: Michael Welter
Thurston County Parks and
Recreation
2617-A Court, SW
Olympia, WA 98502
(360) 786–5595

8 City of Snoqualmie Centennial Trail

Endpoints: Snoqualmie
Mileage: 0.5

Surface: asphalt

Location: King
Contact: Jeff Mumma
Superintendent of Parks
City of Snoqualmie
P.O. Box 987
Snoqualmie, WA 98065-0987
(206) 888–5337
jeff@ci.snoqualmie.wa.us
www.ci.snoqualmie.wa.us

9 Coal Creek Park Trail

Endpoints: Coal Creek Park
Mileage: 3
Surface: ballast, grass, dirt

Location: King
Contact: Tom Eksten
Trails Coordinator
King County Office of Open Space
2040 Eighty-fourth Avenue SE
Mercer Island, WA 98040-2222
(206) 296–7808
tom.eksten@metrokc.gov
www.metroke.gov/parks

10 Colfax Trail

Endpoints: Colfax
Mileage: 3
Surface: dirt

Location: Whitman
Contact: Tim Myers
Superintendent of Parks
Whitman County Parks and
Recreation

310 North Main
Colfax, WA 99111-1850
(509) 397–6238

11 Cowiche Canyon Trail

Endpoints: Yakima
Mileage: 2.9
Surface: gravel, dirt

Location: Yakima
Contact: Ray Paolella
President
Cowiche Canyon Conservancy
P.O. Box 877
Yakima, WA 98907-0877
(509) 577–9585

12 Dry Creek Trail

Endpoints: Gifford Pinchot
National Forest
Mileage: 4
Surface: dirt

Location: Skamania
Contact: Jim Slagle
Trails Coordinator
Gifford Pinchot National Forest
6926 E. Fourth Plain Boulevard
P.O. Box 8944
Vancouver, WA
98661-7254
(360) 750–5011

13 Duwamish Bikeway

Endpoints: Seattle
Mileage: 4.5
Surface: asphalt

Location: King
Contact: Peter Lagerwey
Bicycle/Pedestrian Coordinator
Seattle Engineering Dept
708 Municipal Building
600 Fourth Avenue
Seattle, WA 98104-1879
(206) 684-5108
pete.lagerwey@ci.seattle.wa.us

14 Everett-Shoreline Interurban

Endpoints: Everett, Mt. Lake Terrace
Mileage: 8.5
Surface: asphalt, gravel

Location: Snohomish
Contact: Marc Krandel
Trail Manager
Snohomish County Parks &
Recreation Department
3000 Rockefeller Avenue, MS 303
Everett, WA 98201-4060
(206) 339-1208
planning@premier1.net

15 Fish Lake Trail

Endpoints: Fish Lake, Cheney
Mileage: 7
Surface: asphalt

Location: Spokane
Contact: Robert Hudson
City of Cheney Parks and
Recreation

520 4th Street
Cheney, WA 99004
(509) 235-7295

16 Foothills Trail

Endpoints: Buckley, Orting
Mileage: 8
Surface: asphalt, ballast

Location: Pierce
Contact: Ernest Bay
President
Foothills Rails-to-Trails Coalition
P.O. Box 192
Puyallup, WA 98371-0021
(206) 841-2570
BUGTRAIL@aol.com
www.colpierce.wa.us\parkstrails

17 Green to Cedar River Trail (Lake Wilderness Trail)

Endpoints: Maple Valley, Lake Wilderness
Mileage: 4
Surface: ballast

Location: King
Contact: Tom Eksten
Trails Coordinator
King County Office of Open Space
2040 Eighty-fourth Avenue SE
Mercer Island, WA 98040-2222
(206) 296-7808

18 Iron Goat Trail

Endpoints: Mt. Baker Snoqualmie National Forest
Mileage: 6
Surface: crushed stone, ballast

Location: King
Contact: Ian Ritchie
Archaeologist
Mt. Baker Snoqualmie National Forest
Skykomish Ranger District
P.O. Box 305
Skykomish, WA 98288-0305
(206) 677–2412

19 Iron Horse State Park

Endpoints: North Bend, Vantage
Mileage: 82
Surface: gravel, ballast

Other use: dogsledding; llamas
Location: King; Kittitas
Contact: Keith Wersland
Park Ranger Iron Horse State Parks
P.O. Box 26
Easton, WA 98925-0026
(509) 656–2586

20 Issaquah Creek Trail

Endpoints: High Point, Issaquah
Mileage: 2
Surface: ballast

Location: King
Contact: Tom Eksten
Trails Coordinator
King County Office of Open Space
2040 Eighty-fourth Avenue SE
Mercer Island, WA 98040-2222
(206) 296–7808

21 Issaquah Trail

Endpoints: Issaquah
Mileage: 2
Surface: concrete

Location: King
Contact: Margaret McCleod
Issaquah Parks and Recreation Department
P.O. Box 1307
Issaquah, WA 98027
(425) 837–3322
margm@ci.issaquah.wa.us

22 Iverson Railroad Grade Trail

Endpoints: Tiger Mountain State Forest
Mileage: 2
Surface: dirt

Location: King
Contact: Jim Matthews
Recreation Forester
Tiger Mountain State Forest
P.O. Box 68
Enumclaw, WA 98022-0068
(360) 825–1631

23 King County Interurban Trail

Endpoints: Tuckwila, Pacific
Mileage: 15
Surface: asphalt

Location: King
Contact: Tom Eksten
Trails Coordinator
King County Office
of Open Space
2040 Eighty-fourth Avenue SE
Mercer Island, WA 98040-2222
(206) 296–7808

24 Lower Padden Creek Trail

Endpoints: Bellingham
Mileage: 1
Surface: crushed stone

Location: Whatcom
Contact: Leslie Bryson
Design & Development Manager
Bellingham Parks and
Recreation Department
3424 Meridian
Bellingham, WA 98225-1764
(360) 676–6985

25 Lower Yakima Valley Pathway

Endpoints: Grandview, Sunnyside
Mileage: 6.4
Surface: asphalt

Location: Yakima
Contact: Dave Veley
Assistant Director
Yakima County Parks
1000 Ahtanum Road
Union Gap, WA 98903-1202
(509) 574–2430

26 Middle Fork Snoqualmie River Trail

Endpoints: Mt. Baker–
Snoqualmie National Forest
Mileage: 14.5
Surface: dirt, gravel

Location: King
Contact: William S. Sobieralski
Forestry Technician
Mt. Baker–Snoqualmie
National Forest
North Bend Ranger District
42404 S.E. North Bend Way
North Bend, WA 98045-9545
(425) 744–3563
bsobieralski@fs.fed.us

27 Milwaukee Road Corridor (John Wayne Pioneer Trail)

Endpoints: Iron Horse State Park, Tekoa
Mileage: 145
Surface: crushed stone, ballast, dirt

Location: Grant; Adams; Whitman; Spokane
Contact: James Munroe
Recreation Land Mgr. S.E. Region
Washington Department of
Natural Resources
713 Bowers Road
Ellensburg, WA 98926
(509) 925–8510

28 Myrtle Edwards Park Trail

Endpoints: Seattle
Mileage: 2.5
Surface: asphalt

Location: King
Contact: Peter Lagerwey
Bicycle/Pedestrian Coordinator
Seattle Transportation
Municipal Building, Room 410
600 Fourth Avenue
Seattle, WA 98104-1879
(206) 684–5108
pete.lagerwey@ci.seattle.wa.us

29 Necklace Valley Trail

Endpoints: Skykomish
Mileage: 8
Surface: dirt

Location: King
Contact: Tom Davis
Trail Specialist
Snoqualmie National Forest
Skykomish Ranger District
P.O. Box 305
Skykomish, WA 98288-0305
(206) 677–2414

30 Northwest Timber Trail

Endpoints: North Bend
Mileage: 2.5
Surface: gravel, dirt

Location: King
Contact: Shirley Shuttle
Washington State Department of
Natural Resources
P.O. Box 68
Enumclaw, WA 98022
(360) 825–1631

31 Pacific Crest National Scenic Trail

Endpoints: Stevens Pass, Yodelin
Mileage: 36
Surface: dirt

Location: Chelan
Contact: Roger Ross
Trails/Wilderness Coordinator
U.S. Forest Service
22976 Highway 207
Leavenworth, WA 98826
(509) 763–3103

32 Port Angeles Waterfront Trail

Endpoints: Port Angeles
Mileage: 5
Surface: asphalt

Location: Clallam
Contact: Scott Brodhun

Director
City of Port Angeles
Parks and Recreation
321 East Fifth Street
Port Angeles, WA 98362-3206
(360) 417–4551

33 Pratt River Trail

Endpoints: Mt. Baker–
Snoqualmie National Forest
Mileage: 7.5
Surface: ballast

Location: King
Contact: Thomas Quinsey
Forestry Technician
Mt. Baker–Snoqualmie
National Forest
North Bend Ranger District
42404 S.E. North Bend Way
North Bend, WA 98045-9545
(425) 888–1421

34 Preston Railroad Trail

Endpoints: Tiger Mountain State
Forest
Mileage: 32
Surface: crushed stone, gravel,
dirt

Location: King
Contact: Jim Matthews
Recreation Forester
Tiger Mountain State Forest
P.O. Box 68
Enumclaw, WA 98022-0068
(360) 825–1631

35 Preston-Snoqualmie Trail

Endpoints: Preston, Snoqualmie
Mileage: 6.5
Surface: asphalt

Location: King
Contact: Tom Eksten
Trails Coordinator
King County Office
of Open Space
2040 Eighty-fourth Ave. SE
Mercer Island, WA 98040-2222
(206) 296–7808

36 Railroad Trail

Endpoints: Bellingham,
Memorial Park
Mileage: 4
Surface: crushed stone

Location: Whatcom
Contact: Leslie Bryson
Design & Development Manager
Bellingham Parks and Recreation
Department
3424 Meridian
Bellingham, WA 98225-1764
(360) 676–6985

37 Scudder Pond Trail

Endpoints: Bellingham
Mileage: 0.5
Surface: crushed stone

Location: Whatcom
Contact: Leslie Bryson
Design & Development Manager
Bellingham Parks and Recreation
Department
3424 Meridian
Bellingham, WA 98225-1764
(360) 676–6985

38 Seattle Waterfront Pathway

Endpoints: Seattle
Mileage: 0.8
Surface: asphalt

Location: King
Contact: Peter Lagerwey
Bicycle/Pedestrian Coordinator
Seattle Transportation
Seattle Municipal Building
600 Fourth Avenue, Room 410
Seattle, WA 98104-1879
(206) 684–5108
pete.lagerwey@ci.seattle.wa.us

39 Ship Canal Trail

Endpoints: Seattle
Mileage: 2
Surface: asphalt

Location: King
Contact: Peter Lagerwey
Bicycle/Pedestrian Coordinator
Seattle Transportation
600 Fourth Avenue, Room 410
Seattle, WA 98104-1879
(206) 684–5108
pete.lagerwey@ci.seattle.wa.us

40 Snohomish County Centennial Trail

Endpoints: Arlington,
Snohomish/King county line
Mileage: 17
Surface: asphalt, dirt

Location: Snohomish
Contact: Mark Krandel
Senior Planner
Snohomish County Parks &
Recreation Department
3000 Rockefeller Avenue, MS 303
Everett, WA 98201-4060
(425) 388–6621
planning@premier1.net
www.co.snohomish.wa.us/parks

41 Snoqualmie Valley Trail

Endpoints: Carnation,
Snoqualmie Falls
Mileage: 27.9
Surface: ballast

Location: King
Contact: Tom Eksten
Trails Coordinator
King County Office
of Open Space
2040 Eighty-fourth Ave. SE
Luther Burbank Park
Mercer Island, WA 98040-2222
(206) 296–7808
www.metrokc.gov/parks/

42 South Bay Trail

Endpoints: Bellingham
Mileage: 4
Surface: asphalt, crushed stone, concrete

Location: Whatcom
Contact: Leslie Bryson
Design & Development Manager
Bellingham Parks and
Recreation Department
3424 Meridian
Bellingham, WA 98225-1764
(360) 676–6985

43 Spokane River Centennial Trail

Endpoints: Washington, Idaho state line
Mileage: 39
Surface: asphalt

Location: Spokane
Contact: Charlie Karb
Park Ranger 2
Riverside State Park
North 4427 A.L. White Parkway
Spokane, WA 99205
(509) 456–3964

44 Spruce Railroad Trail (Lake Crescent Trail)

Endpoints: Olympic National Park
Mileage: 4

Surface: gravel, dirt

Location: Clallam
Contact: Polly Angelakis
Supervisor, Visitor Center
Olympic National Park
600 East Park Avenue
Port Angeles, WA 98362
(360) 452–0330
www.nps.gov/olym

45 Sylvia Creek Forestry Trail

Endpoints: Montesano
Mileage: 2.3
Surface: asphalt, dirt

Location: Gray's Harbor
Contact: Dan Kincaid
Park Manager
Lake Sylvia State Park
P.O. Box 701
Montesano, WA 98563
(360) 249–3621

46 Terminal 91 Bike Path (Elliot Bay Bike Trail)

Endpoints: Seattle
Mileage: 1
Surface: asphalt

Location: King
Contact: Bill Health
Property Manager
Port of Seattle
P.O. Box 1209
Seattle, WA 98111-1209
(206) 728–3379

47 Tommy Thompson Parkway

Endpoints: Anacortes
Mileage: 1
Surface: asphalt

Location: Skagit
Contact: Gary Robinson
Parks and Recreation Director
City of Anacortes
P.O. Box 547
Anacortes, WA 98221
(360) 293–1918
gary@cityofanacortes.org

48 Two Mile Trail

Endpoints: Montesano
Mileage: 2
Surface: gravel, dirt

Location: Gray's Harbor
Contact: Dan Kincaid
Park Manager Lake Sylvia State
Park
P.O. Box 701
Montesano, WA 98563
(360) 249–3621

49 Wallace Falls Railway Trail

Endpoints: Wallace Falls State
Park
Mileage: 2.5
Surface: grass, dirt

Location: Snohomish
Contact: Susan Evans

Park Ranger
Washington State Parks and Rec.
Commission
P.O. Box 230
Gold Bar, WA 98251-0230
(360) 793–0420

50 West Tiger Railroad Grade

Endpoints: West Tiger State
Forest
Mileage: 4
Surface: ballast, dirt

Location: King
Contact: Jim Matthews
Recreation Forester
Tiger Mountain State Forest
P.O. Box 68
Enumclaw, WA 98022-0068
(360) 825–1631

51 Whatcom County and Bellingham Interurban Trail

Endpoints: Bellingham, Larrabee
State Park
Mileage: 7
Surface: crushed stone

Location: Whatcom
Contact: Roger DeSpain
Director
Whatcom County Parks and
Recreation Board
3373 Mount Baker Highway
Bellingham, WA 98226-9522
(360) 733–2900

52 Yelm-Tenino Trail

Endpoints: Yelm, Rainier
Mileage: 7
Surface: asphalt

Location: Thurston
Contact: Michael Welter
Thurston County Parks and
Recreation
2617-A 12th Court SW
Olympia, WA 98502
(360) 786–5595
welterm@co.thurston.wa.us
www.thurston-parks.org

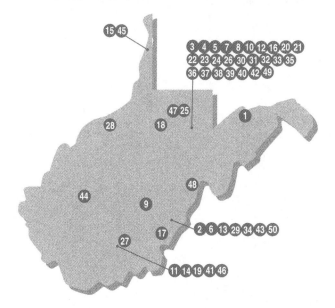

1 Barnum Trail

Endpoints: Barnum, Hampshire
Mileage: 4
Surface: gravel, ballast

Location: Mineral
Contact: Rex Riffle
Director of County Properties
Mineral County Parks &
Recreation Commission
150 Armstrong Street
Keyser, WV 26726-3500
(304) 788–5732

2 Bear Pen Ridge Trail

Endpoints: Tea Creek Recreation
Area
Mileage: 3.5
Surface: grass, dirt

Location: Pocahontas
Contact: Tim Henry
Assistant Ranger
Marlinton Ranger District
Tea Creek Recreation Area
P.O. Box 210
Marlinton, WV 24954-0210
(304) 799–4334

3 Big Stonecoal Trail

Endpoints: Monongahela
National Forest
Mileage: 4.4
Surface: dirt

Location: Tucker
Contact: Carol Rucker
Assistant Ranger
Monongahela National Forest
Cheat Ranger District
P.O. Box 368
Parsons, WV 26287-0368
(304) 478–3251

4 Black Ridge Trail

Endponts: Monongahela
National Forest
Mileage: 5
Surface: dirt

Location: Tucker
Contact: Carol Rucker
Assistant Ranger
Monongahela National Forest
Cheat Ranger District
P.O. Box 368
Parsons, WV 26287-0368
(304) 478–3251

5 Blackwater Canyon Trail

Endpoints: Monongahela
National Forest
Mileage: 10.2
Surface: gravel, dirt

Location: Tucker
Contact: Carol Rucker
Assistant Ranger
Monongahela National Forest
Cheat Ranger District
P.O. Box 368
Parsons, WV 26287-0368
(304) 478–3251

6 Boundary Trail

Endpoints: Tea Creek Recreation
Area
Mileage: 3.8
Surface: grass, dirt

Location: Pocahontas
Contact: Tim Henry
Assistant Ranger
Marlinton Ranger District
Tea Creek Recreation Area
P.O. Box 210
Marlinton, WV 24954-0210
(304) 799–4334

7 Clover Trail

Enpoints: Monongahela National
Forest
Mileage: 2
Surface: dirt

Location: Tucker
Contact: Carol Rucker
Assistant Ranger
Monongahela National Forest
Cheat Ranger District
P.O. Box 368
Parsons, WV 26287-0368
(304) 478–3251

8 County Line Trail

Endpoints: Monongahela
National Forest
Mileage: 11.2
Surface: dirt

Location: Tucker
Contact: Carol Rucker
Assistant Ranger
Monongahela National Forest
Cheat Ranger District
P.O. Box 368
Parsons, WV 26287-0368
(304) 478–3251

9 Cranberry/Tri-Rivers Rail Trail

Endpoints: Richwood, Allingdale
Mileage: 26
Surface: crushed stone

Location: Nicholas; Webster
Contact: Bruce Donaldson
Rail-Trail Chairman
Richwood Area Chamber of
Commerce
One East Main Street
Richwood, WV 26261-0796
(304) 846–6790
ktylerstirling@richwoodwv.com
www.wvrtc.org

10 Davis Trail (Engine Run Trail)

Endpoints: Monongahela
National Forest

Mileage: 2.3
Surface: dirt

Location: Tucker
Contact: Carol Rucker
Assistant Ranger
Monongahela National Forest
Cheat Ranger District
P.O. Box 368
Parsons, WV 26287-0368
(304) 478–3251
www.wvrtc.org

11 Dunloup Creek Trail (Thurmond-Minden Connector)

Endpoints: New River Gorge
National River
Mileage: 0.5
Surface: gravel, dirt

Location: Fayette
Contact: Pete Hart
Superintendent
New River Gorge National River
P.O. Box 246
Glen Jean, WV 25846-0246
(304) 465–0508
neri_interpretation@nps.gov
www.wvrtc.org

12 Flatrock Run Trail

Endpoints: Monongahela
National Forest
Mileage: 5.1
Surface: dirt

Location: Tucker
Contact: Carol Rucker
Assistant Ranger
Monongahela National Forest
Cheat Ranger District
P.O. Box 368
Parsons, WV 26287-0368
(304) 478–3251

13 Gauley Mountain Trail

Endpoints: Tea Creek Recreation Area
Mileage: 5.2
Surface: gravel, dirt

Location: Pocahontas
Contact: Tim Henry
Assistant Ranger
Marlinton Ranger District
Tea Creek Recreation Area
P.O. Box 210
Marlinton, WV 24954-0210
(304) 799–4334

14 Glade Creek Trail

Endpoints: New River Gorge National River
Mileage: 5.6
Surface: gravel, dirt

Location: Raleigh
Contact: Pete Hart
Superintendent
New River Gorge National River
P.O. Box 246
Glen Jean, WV 25846-0246
(304) 465–0508
neri_interpretation@nps.gov
www.wvrtc.org

15 Greater Wheeling Trail

Endpoints: Wheeling
Mileage: 8.5
Surface: asphalt

Location: Ohio
Contact: Tom Murphy
Planning Administrator
Department of Development
City-County Building
1500 Chapline Street
Wheeling, WV 26003-3553
(304) 234–3701
dod@hgo.net
www.cityofwheeling.com

16 Green Mountain Trail

Endpoints: Monongahela National Forest
Mileage: 4
Surface: dirt

Location: Tucker
Contact: Carol Rucker
Assistant Ranger
Monongahela National Forest
Cheat Ranger District
P.O. Box 368
Parsons, WV 26287-0368
(304) 478–3251

17 Greenbrier River Trail

Endpoints: North Caldwell, Cass
Mileage: 75
Surface: gravel, ballast

Location: Greenbrier; Pocahontas
Contact: Pocahontas County Convention and Visitors Center
P.O. Box 275
Marlinton, WV 24954
(800) 336–7009

18 Harrison County Parks & Recreation Bike and Hike Trail

Endpoints: North View
Mileage: 7
Surface: gravel, grass, cinder

Location: Harrison
Contact: Michael Book
Director
Harrison County Parks and Recreation Commission
Harrison County Courthouse
Room 238
Clarksburg, WV 26301-2980
(304) 624–8619
www.wvrtc.org

19 Kaymoor Trail

Endpoints: New River Gorge National River
Mileage: 1.8
Surface: gravel, dirt

Location: Fayette
Contact: Pete Hart
Superintendent
New River Gorge National River
P.O. Box 246
Glen Jean, WV 25846-0246
(304) 465–0508
neri_interpretation@nps.gov
www.wvrtc.org

20 Laurel Fork River Trail—South

Endpoints: Monongahela National Forest
Mileage: 9.6
Surface: dirt

Location: Tucker
Contact: Carol Rucker
Assistant Ranger
Monongahela National Forest
Cheat Ranger District
P.O. Box 368
Parsons, WV 26287-0368
(304) 478–3251

21 Laurelly Branch

Endpoints: Monongahela National Forest
Mileage: 3.4
Surface: dirt

Location: Tucker
Contact: Carol Rucker
Assistant Ranger
Monongahela Nationa Forest
Cheat Ranger District
P.O. Box 368
Parsons, WV 26287-0368
(304) 478–3251

22 Limerock Trail

Endpoints: Monongahela National Forest
Mileage: 4.1
Surface: dirt

Location: Tucker
Contact: Carol Rucker
Assistant Ranger
Monongahela National Forest
Cheat Ranger District
P.O. Box 368
Parsons, WV 26287-0368
(304) 478–3251

23 Little (Black) Fork Trail

Endpoints: Monongahela National Forest
Mileage: 3.5
Surface: dirt

Location: Tucker
Contact: Carol Rucker
Assistant Ranger
Monongahela National Forest
Cheat Ranger District
P.O. Box 368
Parsons, WV 26287-0368
(304) 478–3251

24 Lumberjack Trail

Endpoints: Monongahela National Forest
Mileage: 3.3
Surface: dirt

Location: Tucker
Contact: Carol Rucker
Assistant Ranger
Monongahela National Forest
Cheat Ranger District
P.O. Box 368
Parsons, WV 26287-0368
(304) 478–3251

25 Marion County Trail (MCTRAIL)

Endpoints: Prikets Fort State Park, Fairmont
Mileage: 2
Surface: gravel, cinder

Location: Marion
Contact: Park
Marion County Parks and Recreation Commission
P.O. Box 1258
Fairmont, WV 26555-1258
(304) 363–7037
mcparc@access.mountain.net
www.wvtrc.org

26 Moore Run Trail

Endpoints: Monongahela National Forest
Mileage: 4.1
Surface: dirt

Location: Tucker
Contact: Carol Rucker
Assistant Ranger
Monongahela National Forest
Cheat Ranger District
P.O. Box 368

Parsons, WV 26287-0368
(304) 478–3251

27 Narrow Gauge Trail

Endpoints: Babcock State Park,
Old Sewell Road
Mileage: 2.5
Surface: crushed stone, dirt

Location: Fayette
Contact: Richard Morris
Superintendent
Babcock State Park
HC-35, Box 150
Clifftop, WV 25831-9000
(304) 438–3004
www.wvtrc.org

28 North Bend State Park Rail-Trail

Endpoints: Parkersburg, Walker
Mileage: 72
Surface: crushed stone, gravel,
dirt

Other use: horse-drawn carriage
Location: Harrison; Doddridge;
Ritchie; Wood
Contact: Scott Fortney
Supervisor
North Bend State Park Rails to
Trails
P.O. Box 221
Cairo, WV 26337
(304) 643–2931
www.wvweb.com/www/travel_
recreation/state_parks/north_
bend_rail/north_bend_rail.htm

29 North Face Trail

Endpoints: Tea Creek Recreation
Area
Mileage: 3.1
Surface: grass, dirt

Location: Pocahontas
Contact: Tim Henry
Assistant Ranger
Marlinton Ranger District
Tea Creek Recreation Area
P.O. Box 210
Marlinton, WV 24954-0210
(304) 799–4334

30 Otter Creek Trail

Endpoints: Monongahela
National Forest
Mileage: 11.4
Surface: dirt

Location: Tucker
Contact: Carol Rucker
Assistant Ranger
Monongahela National Forest
Cheat Ranger District
P.O. Box 368
Parsons, WV 26287-0368
(304) 478–3251

31 Possession Camp Trail

Endpoints: Monongahela
National Forest
Mileage: 3.3
Surface: dirt

Location: Tucker
Contact: Carol Rucker
Assistant Ranger
Monongahela National Forest
Cheat Ranger District
P.O. Box 368
Parsons, WV 26287-0368
(304) 478–3251

32 Railroad Grade Trail

Endpoints: Elkins, Davis
Mileage: 4
Surface: dirt

Location: Randolph; Tucker
Contact: Carol Rucker
Recreation Manager
USDA Forest Service
P.O. Box 368
Parsons, WV 26287
(304) 478–3251

33 Red Creek Trail

Endpoints: Monongahela
National Forest
Mileage: 6.1
Surface: dirt

Location: Tucker
Contact: Carol Rucker
Assistant Ranger
Monongahela National Forest
Cheat Ranger District
P.O. Box 368
Parsons, WV 26287-0368
(304) 478–3251

34 Red Run Trail

Endpoints: Tea Creek Recreation
Area
Mileage: 2.5
Surface: grass, dirt

Location: Pocahontas
Contact: Tim Henry
Assistant Ranger
Marlinton Ranger District
Tea Creek Recreation Area
P.O. Box 210
Marlinton, WV 24954-0210
(304) 799–4334

35 Rocky Point Trail

Endpoints: Monongahela
National Forest
Mileage: 1.8
Surface: dirt

Location: Tucker
Contact: Carol Rucker
Assistant Ranger
Monongahela National Forest
Cheat Ranger District
P.O. Box 368
Parsons, WV 26287-0368
(304) 478–3251

36 Rohbaugh Plains Trail

Endpoints: Monongahela
National Forest
Mileage: 3.5
Surface: dirt

Location: Tucker
Contact: Carol Rucker
Assistant Ranger
Monongahela National Forest
Cheat Ranger District
P.O. Box 368
Parsons, WV 26287-0368
(304) 478–3251

37 Rough Run Trail

Endpoints: Monongahela
National Forest
Mileage: 3
Surface: dirt

Location: Tucker
Contact: Carol Rucker
Assistant Ranger
Monongahela National Forest
Cheat Ranger District
P.O. Box 368
Parsons, WV 26287-0368
(304) 478–3251

38 Senaca Creek Trail

Endpoints: Monongahela
National Forest
Mileage: 5
Surface: dirt

Location: Tucker
Contact: Carol Rucker
Assistant Ranger
Monongahela National Forest
Cheat Ranger District
P.O. Box 368
Parsons, WV 26287-0368
(304) 478–3251

39 Shingletree Trail

Endpoints: Monongahela
National Forest
Mileage: 1.4
Surface: dirt

Location: Tucker
Contact: Carol Rucker
Assistant Ranger
Monongahela National Forest
Cheat Ranger District
P.O. Box 368
Parsons, WV 26287-0368
(304) 478–3251

40 South Prong Trail

Endpoints: Monongahela
National Forest
Mileage: 5.9
Surface: dirt

Location: Tucker
Contact: Carol Rucker
Assistant Ranger
Monongahela National Forest
Cheat Ranger District
P.O. Box 368
Parsons, WV 26287-0368
(304) 478–3251

41 Southside Junction– Brooklyn Trail

Endpoints: New River Gorge
National River
Mileage: 6.4
Surface: gravel, dirt

Location: Fayette
Contact: Pete Hart
Superintendent
New River Gorge National River
P.O. Box 246
Glen Jean, WV 25846-0246
(304) 465–0508
neri_interpretation@nps.gov
www.wvrtc.org

42 Stone Camp Run Trail

Endpoints: Monongahela
National Forest
Mileage: 1.5
Surface: dirt

Location: Tucker
Contact: Carol Rucker
Assistant Ranger
Monongahela National Forest
Cheat Ranger District
P.O. Box 368
Parsons, WV 26287-0368
(304) 478–3251

43 Tea Creek Trail

Endpoints: Tea Creek Recreation
Area
Mileage: 7
Surface: grass, dirt

Location: Pocahontas
Contact: Tim Henry
Assistant Ranger
Marlinton Ranger District
Tea Creek Recreation Area
P.O. Box 210
Marlinton, WV 24954-0210
(304) 799–4334

44 The Elk River Trail

Endpoints: Coonskin Park
Mileage: 1
Surface: gravel

Location: Kanawha
Contact: Tom Raker
Director
Kanawha County Parks and
Recreation Commission
2000 Coonskin Drive
Charleston, WV 25311-1087
(304) 341–8000
www.wvrtc.org

45 The Greater Wheeling Trail

Endponts: Wheeling
Mileage: 4
Surface: asphalt

Location: Ohio
Contact: Thomas Murphy
Planning Administrator
Economic and Community
Development
City-County Building
1500 Chapline Street, Room 305
Wheeling, WV 26003-3553
(304) 234–3701
dod@hgo.net
www.cityofwheeling.com

46 Thurmond-Minden Trail

Endpoints: New River Gorge
National River
Mileage: 3.2
Surface: gravel, dirt

Location: Fayette
Contact: Pete Hart
Superintendent
New River Gorge National River
P.O. Box 246
Glen Jean, WV 25846-0246
(304) 465–0508
neri_interpretation@nps.gov

47 West Fork Rail-Trail

Endpoints: Fairmont, Shinnston
Mileage: 16
Surface: crushed stone, cinder

Location: Harrison; Marion
Contact: Marion County Park
Marion County Parks and
Recreation Commission
P.O. Box 1258
Fairmont, WV 26555-1258
(304) 363–7037
mcparc@access.mountain.net
www.wvrtc.org

48 West Fork Trail

Endpoints: Durbin, Glady
Mileage: 24
Surface: crushed stone, ballast

Location: Pocahontas; Randolph
Contact: Gary Willison
Assistant District Ranger
Monongahela National Forest
Greenbrier Ranger District
P.O. Box 67
Bartow, WV 24920-0067
(304) 456–3335

49 Whitemeadow Ridge Trail

Endpoints: Monongahela
National Forest
Mileage: 4.6
Surface: dirt

Location: Tucker
Contact: Carol Rucker
Assistant Ranger
Monongahela National Forest
Cheat Ranger District
P.O. Box 368
Parsons, WV 26287-0368
(304) 478–3251

50 Williams River Trail

Endpoints: Tea Creek Recreation Area
Mileage: 2.5
Surface: gravel, dirt

Location: Pocahontas
Contact: Tim Henry
Assistant Ranger
Marlinton Ranger District
Tea Creek Recreation Area
P.O. Box 210
Marlinton, WV 24954-0210
(304) 799–4334
Trailnet88@aol.com

WISCONSIN

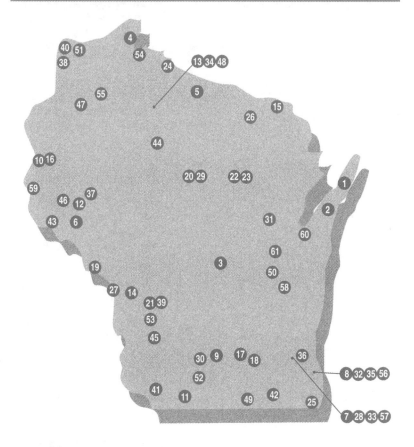

1 Ahnapee State Park Trail

Endpoints: Algoma, Sturgeon Bay
Mileage: 15.3
Surface: crushed stone

Location: Door; Kewaunee
Contact: Jean Romback-Bartels

Park Manager
Ahnapee State Park Trail
c/o Potawatomi State Park
3740 Park Drive
Sturgeon Bay, WI 54235-9091
(920) 746–2890

2 Algoma to Casco Junction

Endpoints: Algoma, Casco Junction
Mileage: 12.4
Surface: crushed stone

Location: Kewaunee
Contact: Jean Romback-Bartels
Park Manager
Ahnapee State Park Trail
c/o Potawatomi State Park
3740 Park Drive
Sturgeon Bay, WI 54235-9091
(920) 746–2890

3 Bannerman Trail

Endpoints: Red Granite, 5 miles
south of Wautoma
Mileage: 7
Surface: grass, dirt

Location: Waushara
Contact: Scott Schuman
Parks Superintendent
Waushara County Parks
Wautoma, WI 54982
(414) 787–7037

4 Bayfield County Snowmobile Trail

Endpoints: Washburn, Hayward
Mileage: 65
Surface: ballast

Location: Bayfield; Sawyer
Contact: Patricia Thornton
Snowmobile Coordinator
Bayfield County Tourism and
Recreation

P.O. Box 832
Washburn, WI 54891
(800) 472–6338
tourbc@win.bright.net
www.travelbayfieldcounty.com

5 Bearskin State Park Trail

Endpoints: Minocqua, Highway
K; Heafford Junction, Tomahawk
Mileage: 24.7 (in two sections)
Surface: red granite

Location: Oneida, Lincoln
Contact: John Brandenburg
Trails Manager
Wisconsin Department of Natural
Resources
4125 Highway M
Boulder Junction, WI 54548
(715) 385–2727

6 Buffalo River State Park Trail

Endpoints: Fairchild, Mondovi
Mileage: 36.4
Surface: gravel, ballast, dirt

Other use: ATV
Location: Eau Claire; Jackson;
Trempealeau; Buffalo;
Contact: Jean Rygiel
Trails Coordinator
Wisconsin DNR, Western Division
1300 West Clairmont Avenue
P.O. Box 4001
Eau Claire, WI 54701-6127
(715) 839–1607
rygiej@dnr.state.wi.us

7 Bugline Trail

Endpoints: Menomonee Falls, Merton
Mileage: 13
Surface: crushed stone

Location: Waukesha
Contact: David Burch
Senior Landscape Architect
Waukesha County Dept. of Parks and Land Use
1320 Pewaukee Road, Room 230
Waukesha, WI 53188-3868
(414) 548–7790
dburch@groupwise.co.
waukesha.wi.us

8 Burlington Trail

Endpoints: Burlington, Rochester
Mileage: 4
Surface: crushed stone, gravel

Location: Racine
Contact: Tom Statz
Park Planning & Program Director
Racine County Public Works Department
14200 Washington Avenue
Sturtevant, WI 53177-1253
(414) 886–8440

9 Capital City Trail

Endpoints: Madison, Fitchburg
Mileage: 3.9
Surface: asphalt, crushed stone

Location: Dane
Contact: Ken Lepine
Director
Dane County Parks
4318 Robertson Road
Madison, WI 53714-3123
(608) 246–3896
www.co.dane.wi.us/parks

10 Cattail Trail

Endpoints: Almena, Amery
Mileage: 17.8
Surface: gravel, ballast, dirt

Other use: ATV
Location: Barron; Polk
Contact: Sue Mathews
Manager
Polk County Information Center
710 Highway 35 South
St. Croix Falls, WI 54024
(800) 222–7655

11 Cheese Country Recreation Trail

Endpoints: Mineral Point, Monroe
Mileage: 47
Surface: crushed stone

Other use: ATV
Location: Iowa; Green; Lafayette
Contact: Mike Doyle
Trail Coordinator
Tri-County Trail Commission
Courthouse Green County
Monroe, WI 53530
(608) 328–9430
www.state.wi.us/agencies/
tourism.html

12 Chippewa River State Trail

Endpoints: Eau Claire, Caryville
Mileage: 20
Surface: asphalt

Location: Eau Claire; Dunn
Contact: Jean Rygiel
Trails Coordinator
Wisconsin DNR, Western Division
1300 West Clairmont Avenue
P.O. Box 4001
Eau Claire, WI 54701-6127
(715) 839–1607
rygiej@dnr.state.wi.us

13 Clover Creek Trail

Endpoints: Chequamegon
National Forest
Mileage: 15.8
Surface: grass, dirt

Other use: ATV
Location: Price
Contact: Victor Peterson
Forestry Technician
Chequamegon National Forest
1170 Fourth Avenue South
Park Falls, WI 54552-1921
(715) 762–2461

14 Elroy-Sparta State Park Trail

Endpoints: Elroy, Sparta
Mileage: 32
Surface: crushed stone

Location: Monroe; Juneau
Contact: Lenore Schroeder
Sub-Team Supervisor
Wisconsin Department of Natural
Resources
c/o Wildcat Mountain State Park
P.O. Box 99
Ontario, WI 54651
(608) 337–4775

15 Florence County Snowmobile Trail

Endpoints: Nicolet National
Forest
Mileage: 130
Surface: gravel, dirt

Location: Florence
Contact: Jeffrey Herrett
Assistant District Ranger
Nicolet National Forest
USFS, Florence Ranger District
HC 1, Box 83
Florence, WI 54121-9764
(715) 528–4464

16 Gandy Dancer Trail

Endpoints: St. Croix Falls, Superior
Mileage: 97
Surface: crushed stone, ballast

Other use: ATV
Location: Burnett; Douglas; Polk
Contact: Debbie Peterson
Director
Polk County Parks Department
100 Polk County Plaza, Suite 10
Balsam Lake, WI 54810
(715) 485–9272

17 Glacial Drumlin State Park Trail

Endpoints: Cottage Grove, Waukesha
Mileage: 51.6
Surface: asphalt, crushed stone

Location: Dane; Jefferson; Waukesha
Contact: Brian Hefty
Glacial Drumlin State Park
W329 N846 Co. C
Delafield, WI 53018
(262) 646–3025

18 Glacial River Trail

Endpoints: Fort Atkinson, Koshkonong
Mileage: 6.5
Surface: asphalt, crushed stone

Location: Jefferson
Contact: Joe Nehmer
Director
Jefferson County Parks
Department
Courthouse
320 South Main Street
Jefferson, WI 53549-1718
(920) 674–7260
joen@co.jefferson.wi.us

19 Great River State Park Trail

Endpoints: Onalaska, Trempealeau National Wildlife Refuge
Mileage: 4
Surface: crushed stone

Location: Buffalo; La Crosse; Trempealeau
Contact: Lois Isaacson
Ranger
Perrot State Park
P.O. Box 407
Trempealeau, WI 54661-0407
(608) 534–6409

20 Hiawatha Trail (Bearskin-Hiawatha State Trail)

Endpoints: Tomahawk, Sara Park
Mileage: 5.6
Surface: crushed stone

Location: Lincoln
Contact: William Wengeler
County Forestry Administrator
Lincoln County Forestry Land and Parks
1106 East Eighth Street
Merrill, WI 54452-1100
(715) 536–0327

21 Hillsboro Trail

Endpoints: Hillsboro, Union Center
Mileage: 4.3
Surface: crushed stone

Location: Juneau
Contact: Dale Dorow
Administrator
Juneau County Forest and Parks Department
250 Oak Street
Mauston, WI 53948-1365
(608) 847–9390

22 Ice Age Trail—Lumber Camp Segment

Endpoints: Langlade County Forest
Mileage: 9.2

Surface: gravel, ballast

Location: Langlade
Contact: Michael Sohasky
County Forest Admin.
Langlade County Forestry Dept.
P.O. Box 460
Antigo, WI 54409-0460
(715) 627–6236

23 Ice Age Trail—Old RR Segment

Endpoints: Langlade County Forest
Mileage: 9.2
Surface: gravel, ballast

Location: Langlade
Contact: Michael Sohasky
County Forest Admin.
Langlade County Forestry Dept.
1633 Neva Road
Antigo, WI 54409-0460
(715) 627–6300

24 Iron Horse Trail

Endpoints: Manitowish Frontier Campground
Mileage: 55
Surface: gravel

Other use: ATV
Location: Iron
Contact: Tom Salzmann

Forest Administrator
Iron County Forestry Office
603 Third Avenue
Hurley, WI 54534-1012
(715) 561–2697

25 Kenosha County Bike Trail

Endpoints: Racine county line, Illinois state line
Mileage: 14.2
Surface: asphalt, crushed stone

Location: Kenosha
Contact: Ric Ladine
Director of Parks
Kenosha County Parks
P.O. Box 549
Bristol, WI 53104-0549
(414) 857–1862

26 Kimball Creek Trail

Endpoints: Nicolet National Forest
Mileage: 12
Surface: ballast

Other use: Dog sledding
Location: Forest
Contact: Bill Reardon
Forestry Technician
Nicolet National Forest
Eagle River Ranger District
P.O. Box 1809
Eagle River, WI 54521-1809
(715) 479–2827

27 La Crosse River State Park Trail

Endpoints: Sparta, La Crosse
Mileage: 23
Surface: crushed stone

Location: Monroe; La Crosse
Contact: Jim Moorhead
Park Ranger
Wildcat Mountain State Park
Work Unit
P.O. Box 99
Ontario, WI 54651-0099
(608) 337–4775

28 Lake Country Recreation Trail

Endpoints: Delafield, Waukesha
Mileage: 8
Surface: asphalt, crushed stone

Location: Waukesha
Contact: David Burch
Senior Landscape Architect
Waukesha County Dept. of Parks and Land Use
1320 Pewaukee Road, Room 230
Waukesha, WI 53188-3868
(414) 548–7790
dburch@groupwise.co.waukesha.wi.us

29 Lincoln County Snowmobile Trail

Endpoints: Tomahawk, Lincoln/Price County Line
Mileage: 15
Surface: ballast

Location: Lincoln
Contact: William Wengeler
County Forestry Administrator
Lincoln County Forestry
Land and Parks
1106 East Eighth Street
Merrill, WI 54452-1100
(715) 536–0327

30 Military Ridge State Park Trail

Endpoints: Dodgeville, Verona
Mileage: 39.6
Surface: crushed stone

Location: Iowa; Dane
Contact: Cindy Delkamp
Manager
Wisconsin Department
of Natural Resources
c/o Blue Mounds State Park
4350 Mounds Park/P.O. Box 98
Blue Mounds, WI 53517-0098
www.military.ridge@mail01.dnr.
state.wi.us

31 Mountain-Bay State Trail (Delly Trail)

Endpoints: Duck Creek, Kelly
Mileage: 83.4
Surface: crushed stone

Other use: ATV

Location: Brown; Marathon;
Shawano
Contact: Pat Vail
Shawno County Parks
Department
311 North Main Street
Shawno, WI 54166
(715) 526–6766

32 MRK Trail

Endpoints: Racine, Caledonia
Mileage: 5
Surface: crushed stone, gravel,
ballast

Location: Racine
Contact: Tom Statz
Park Plan. & Prog. Director
Racine County Public Works
Department
14200 Washington Avenue
Sturtevant, WI 53177-1253
(414) 886–8440

33 New Berlin Trail

Endpoints: Waukesha, West Allis
Mileage: 7
Surface: crushed stone

Location: Waukesha
Contact: David Burch
Senior Landscape Architect
Waukesha County Dept. of Parks
and Land Use
1320 Pewaukee Road, Room 230
Waukesha, WI 53188-3868
(414) 548–7790
dburch@groupwise.co.
waukesha.wi.us

34 North Flambeau Cycle Trail

Endpoints: Chequamegon
National Forest
Mileage: 23
Surface: dirt

Other use: ATV
Location: Price
Contact: Victor Peterson
Forestry Technician
Chequamegon National Forest
1170 Fourth Avenue South
Park Falls, WI 54552-1921
(715) 762–2461

35 North Shore Trail

Endpoints: Racine, Kenosha
county line
Mileage: 3
Surface: crushed stone, gravel

Location: Racine
Contact: Tom Statz
Park Plan. & Prog. Director
Racine County Public Works
Department
14200 Washington Avenue
Sturtevant, WI 53177-1253
(414) 886–8440

36 Oakleaf Trail (old-76 bike tour)

Endpoints: Milwaukee
Mileage: 96.41
Surface: asphalt

Location: Milwaukee
Contact: Paul Hathaway
Associate Director of Parks
Milwaukee County Parks
9480 Watertown Plank Road
Wauwatosa, WI 53226-3560
(414) 257–6100
parksmke@execpc.com

37 Old Abe Trail

Endpoints: Chippewa Falls,
Cornell
Mileage: 19.7
Surface: asphalt, ballast

Location: Chippewa
Contact: Jean Rygiel
Trails Coordinator
Wisconsin DNR, Western Division
1300 West Clairmont Avenue
P.O. Box 4001
Eau Claire, WI 54701-6127
(715) 839–1607
rygiej@dnr.state.wi.us

38 Oliver-Wrenshall Trail

Endpoints: Oliver-Wrenshall,
Minn.
Mileage: 12
Surface: grass, dirt

Other use: ATV
Location: Carlton; Douglas
Contact: Mark Schroeder
Resource & Recreation Manager
Douglas County Forestry
Department
P.O. Box 211
Solon Springs, WI 54873-0211
(715) 378–2219

39 Omaha Trail

Endpoints: Camp Douglas, Elroy
Mileage: 12.5
Surface: asphalt, gravel

Location: Juneau
Contact: Dale Dorow
Administrator
Juneau County Forest and Parks
Department
250 Oak Street
Mauston, WI 53948-1365
(608) 847–9390
dottsl@yahoo.com

40 Osaugie Trail

Endpoints: Superior
Mileage: 2.2
Surface: asphalt, gravel

Location: Douglas
Contact: Superior Parks and

Recreation Department
1409 Hammond Avenue
Superior, WI 54880
(715) 394–0270

41 Pecatonica State Park Trail

Endpoints: Calamine, Belmont
Mileage: 13.5
Surface: crushed stone

Other use: ATV, golf carts
Location: Lafayette; Grant
Contact: Mike Doyle
Trail Coordinator
Tri-County Trail Commission
Green County Courthouse
Monroe, WI 53530
(608) 328–9430

42 Pelishek Nature Trail

Endpoints: Clinton, Allens
Grove, Darien
Mileage: 7
Surface: gravel, ballast, sand

Location: Rock; Walworth
Contact: Tom Kautz
Director
County of Rock Parks and
Conservation Div.
3715 Newville Road
Janesville, WI 53545-8844
(608) 757–5450
kautz@co.rock.wi.us

43 Pierce County Snowmobile Trail

Endpoints: Plum City, River Falls
Mileage: 221
Surface: ballast, grass

Location: Pierce
Contact: Scott Schoepp
Snowmobile Coordinator
Pierce County Snowmobile Trail
c/o Nugget Lake County Park
N4351 County Road HH
Plum City, WI 54761
(715) 639–5611

44 Pine Line Trail (Taylor County Snowmobile Trail)

Endpoints: Medford, Prentice
Mileage: 25.9
Surface: grass, gravel, crushed stone

Location: Price, Taylor
Contact: Brad Ruesch
Taylor County Recreation
224 South Second
Medford, WI 54451
(715) 748–1486
BRuesch@mail.co.taylor.wi.us

45 Pine River Trail

Endpoints: Lone Rock, Richland Center
Mileage: 14.2
Surface: crushed stone

Location: Richland
Contact: Steve, Kohlstendt
UW-Extension
1100 Highway 14 West
Richland Center, WI 53581-1314
(608) 647–6148
steve.kohlstedt@ces.uwex.edu

46 Red Cedar State Trail

Endpoints: Menomonie, The Dunnville Wildlife Area
Mileage: 14.5
Surface: crushed stone

Location: Dunn; Eau Claire
Contact: James Janowak
Manager
Red Cedar State Trail
921 Brickyard Road
Menomonie, WI 54751-9100
(715) 232–1242

47 Rice Lake to Superior Trail (Chippewa Falls to Superior)

Endpoints: Rice Lake, Superior
Mileage: 90
Surface: ballast

Location: Barron; Douglas; Washburn
Contact: Terry Jordan
Northern Regional Trails Coord.
Wisconsin Dept. of Natural
Resources—Northern Region

810 West Maple
Spooner, WI 54801
(715) 635–4121
jordat@mail01.dnr.state.wi.us

48 Riley Lake Snowmobile Trail

Endpoints: Chequamegon
National Forest
Mileage: 23
Surface: grass, dirt

Other use: ATV
Location: Price
Contact: Victor Peterson
Forestry Technician
Chequamegon National Forest
1170 Fourth Avenue, South
Park Falls, WI 54552-1921
(715) 762–2461

49 Rock River Parkway Trail

Endpoints: Janesville, Beloit
Mileage: 1.9
Surface: crushed stone

Location: Rock
Contact: Tom Presny
Director of Parks
Janesville Leisure Services
17 North Franklin Street
Janesville, WI 53545-2917
(608) 755–3025

50 Rush Lake Trail (Greenlake, Winnebago, Ripon Trails)

Endpoints: Berlin, Ripon
Mileage: 10.3
Surface: ballast

Location: Winnebago
Contact: Jeffrey Christensen
Parks Director
Winnebago County Parks
Department
500 E. County Road Y
Oshkosh, WI 54901-9774
(920) 424–0042

51 Saunders Grade Recreation Trail

Endpoints: Superior, Douglas
Mileage: 8.4
Surface: ballast

Location: Douglas
Contact: Mark Schroeder
Resource & Recreation Manager
Douglas County Forestry
Department
P.O. Box 211
Solon Springs, WI 54873-0211
(715) 378–2219

52 Sugar River State Park Trail

Endpoints: New Glarus,
Brodhead
Mileage: 23.5
Surface: crushed stone

Location: Green
Contact: Steve Colden
Park Manager
Sugar River State Park Trail
W5446 City Highway NN
P.O. Box 805
New Glarus, WI 53574
(608) 527–2335
coldes@dnr.state.wi.us

53 The 400 State Trail

Endpoints: Elroy, Reedsburg
Mileage: 22.3
Surface: crushed stone

Location: Juneau; Sauk
Contact: Jim Moorhead
Park Ranger
Wildcat Mountian State Park
Work Unit
P.O. Box 99
Ontario, WI 54651-0099
(608) 337–4775

54 Tri-County Corridor

Endpoints: Ashland, Superior
Mileage: 61.8
Surface: crushed stone, ballast

Other use: ATV, hunting

Location: Ashland; Bayfield;
Douglas
Contact: Richard Mackey
Executive Director
Tri-County Recreational Corridor
Commission
Ashland, WI 54806
(800) 472–6338

55 Tuscobia State Trail

Endpoints: Park Falls, Rice Lake
Mileage: 74
Surface: gravel, ballast, grass

Other use: ATV
Location: Barron; Price; Sawyer;
Washburn
Contact: Raymond Larsen
Superintendent
Tuscobia State Park Trail
10220 North State Road 27
Hayward, WI 54843-9505
(715) 634–6513

56 Waterford-Wind Lake Trail

Endpoints: Waterford, Wind
Lake
Mileage: 5
Surface: crushed stone, gravel

Location: Racine
Contact: Tom Statz
Park Plan. & Prog. Director
Racine County Public Works
Dept.
14200 Washington Avenue
Sturtevant, WI 53177-1253
(414) 886–8440

57 Waukesha Bike Trails

Endpoints: Milwakee, Madison
Mileage: 200
Surface: asphalt, crushed stone

Location: Waukesha
Contact: David Kopp
City Planner
Waukesha City Planning
Room 200
201 Delafield Street
City Hall
Waukesha, WI 53188-3690
(414) 524–3752

58 Wild Goose State Trail

Endpoints: Clyman Junction,
Fond du Lac
Mileage: 34
Surface: asphalt, crushed stone

Location: Dodge; Fond du Lac
Contact: Sam Tobias
Director
Fond du Lac County Planning &
Parks Department
160 South Macy Street
Fond du Lac, WI 54935-4241
(920) 929–3135
joanne.nitz@co.fond-du-lac.wt.us
www.dodgecountywi.com

59 Wildwood Trail

Endpoints: Woodville, St. Croix
county line
Mileage: 7.6
Surface: gravel, dirt, cinder

Location: St. Croix
Contact: Sue Nelson
County Clerk
Government Center
1101 Carmichael Road
Hudson, WI 54016
(715) 386–4600
suen@co.saint-croix.wi.us

60 WIOUWASH Trail— North

Endpoints: Aniwa, New London
Mileage: 20
Surface: crushed stone

Location: Outagame; Shawano;
Waupaca
Contact: Gary Hanson
Regional Trails Coordinator
Wisconsin Department of Natural
Resources
1125 N. Military Avenue
Green Bay, WI 54303-4413
(920) 492–5823
hansog@dnr.state.wi.us

61 WIOUWASH Trail— South

Endpoints: Hortonville, Oshkosh
Mileage: 20.3
Surface: crushed stone, ballast

Location: Winnebago;
Outagamie
Contact: Christopher Brandt
Director
Outagamie County Parks
1375 East Broadway Drive,
Plamann Park
Appleton, WI 54915
(414) 832–4790
cbrandt48@aol.com

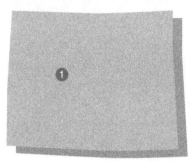

1 Wyoming Heritage Trail

Endpoints: Riverton, Shoshoni
Mileage: 22
Surface: asphalt, ballast

Other use: ATV
Location: Fremont
Contact: Lewis Diehn
Fremont County Recreation
Board
213 East Lincoln
Riverton, WY 82501

Appendix: State Trail Planners

Alabama
Jon Strickland
Recreation Programs Manager
Department of Economic and
Community Affairs
401 Adams Avenue, Suite 580
P.O. Box 5690
Montgomery, AL 36103-5690
(334) 242–5483
jons@adeca.state.al.us

Alaska
Ron Crenshaw
Trails Administrator
Alaska Department of Natural
Resources
Division of Parks and Outdoor
Recreation
3601 C Street, Suite 1280
Anchorage, AK 99503-5921
(907) 269–8704
ronc@dnr.state.ak.us

Arkansas
Steve Weston
Trans. Study Coordinator
Arkansas Highway and
Transportation Department
P.O. Box 2261
Little Rock, AR 72203-2261
(501) 569–2020
srwd165@ahd.stste.ar.us

Arizona
Eric Smith
State Trails Coordinator
Arizona State Parks
1300 West Washington
Phoenix, AZ 85007
(602) 542–7116
esmith@pr.state.az.us

California
Odel King, Jr.
Manager
Dept. of Parks & Recreation
Local Assistance Section
1416 Ninth Street, Room 1311
P.O. Box 942896
Sacramento, CA 94296-0001
(916) 653–8758
oking@parks.ca.gov

Colorado
Stuart Macdonald
State Trails Coordinator
Colorado Division of Parks and
Outdoor Recreation
1313 Sherman Street, Room 618
Denver, CO 80203-2240
(303) 866–3203
mactrail@aol.com

Connecticut
David Stygar
Environmental Analyst
Dept. of Environmental Protection
State of Connecticut
79 Elm Street
Hartford, CT 06106
(860) 424–3081
david.stygar@po.state.ct.us

Delaware
Susan Moerschel
Division of Parks & Recreation
P.O. Box 1401
Dover, DE 19903-1401
(302) 739–5285
smoerschel@state.de.us

District of Columbia
Theodore Pochter
Chief
Department of Recreation and
Parks, Policy and Planning Division
3149 Sixteenth Street, NW, 4th
Floor
Washington, DC 20010-3302
(202) 673–7692

Florida
Alexandra Weiss
Community Assistance Consult.
Office of Greenways and Trails
325 John Knox
Woodcrest Office Park
Building 500
Tallahassee, FL 32303-4113
(904) 488–7896
weiss_a@dep.state.fl.us

Georgia
Alicia Soriano
Trails Coordinator, Planning
Dept. of Natural Resources
205 Butler Street SE, Suite 1352
Atlanta, GA 30334-4910
(404) 656–6530
alicias@mail.dnr.state.ga.us

Hawaii
Curt Cottrell
Program Manager
Department of Land and Natural
Resources
888 Mililani Street
Kendall Building, Suite 700
Honolulu, HI 96813
(808) 587–0062

Idaho
Jeff Cook
State Trails Coordinator
Idaho Department of Parks and
Recreation

5657 Warm Springs Avenue
P.O. Box 83720
Boise, ID 83720-0065
(208) 334–4180
jcook@idpr.state.id.us

Illinois
Bill Yuskus
Chief, Statewide Prgm. Planning
Department of Transportation
(ILDOT)
2300 South Dirksen Parkway
Room 307, Transp. Adm. Bldg.
Springfield, IL 62764-0001
(217) 785–9109

Indiana
Bob Bronson
Chief/Outdoor Rec. Planning
Indiana Department of Natural
Resources
402 West Washington Street,
Room W271
Indianapolis, IN 46204-2212
(317) 232–4070
bbronson@dnr.state.in.us

Iowa
Nancy Burns
Enhancements Coordinator
Iowa Dept. of Transportation
800 Lincoln Way
Ames, IA 50010-6993
(515) 239–1621
nburns@iadot.email.com

Kansas
Gerald Hover
Director of State Parks
Kansas State Parks
512 SE Twenty-fifth Avenue
Pratt, KS 67124-8174
(316) 672–5911
JerryRH@wp.state.ks.us

Kentucky
Jim Barker
Recreation Programs
Dept. of Local Government
Division of Development and
Finance
1024 Capital Center Drive,
Suite 340
Frankfort, KY 40601-8204
(502) 573–2382
jbarker@mail.state.ky.us

Louisiana
Don Terry
Field Coordinator
Louisiana Office of Rural
Development
P.O. Box 94004
Baton Rouge, LA 70804
(225) 342–1618
ordresearch@linknet.net

Maine
Mike Gallagher
Grants & Community Rec, Div.
Maine Bureau of Parks and Land
Department of Conservation
State House Station #22
Augusta, ME 04333
(207) 287–2163
mike.gallagher@state.me.us

Maryland
Charles Adams
Director
MD State Highway Administration
Office of Environmental Design
707 N. Calvert Street
Mailstop C-303
P.O. Box 717
Baltimore, MD 21203-0717
(301) 545–8640
cadams@sha.state.md.us

Massachusetts
Peter Brandenburg
State Trails Coordinator
Department of Environmental
Management
100 Cambridge Street Room 1901
Boston, MA 02202-0020
(617) 727–3180
peter.brandenburg@state.ma.us

Michigan
Hector Chiunti
State Trails Coordinator
Department of Natural Resources
Stevens T. Mason Building
P.O. Box 30452
Lansing, MI 48909-7952
(517) 335–3040

Minnesota
Dan Collins
Recreation Services Supervisor
Minnesota Department of Natural
Resources
500 Lafayette Road
St. Paul, MN 55126
(612) 296–6048
dan.collins@dnr.state.mn.us

Mississippi
Jimmy Graves
Administrator
Department of Wildlife, Fisheries,
and Parks
Recreation Grants Office
P.O. Box 451
Jackson, MS 39205-0451
(601) 364–2155

Missouri
Steve Burdic
Grants Administrator
Department of Natural Resources
P.O. Box 176
Jefferson City, MO 65102

(573) 751–8560
nrburds@mail.dnr.state.mo.us

Montana
Bob Walker
Trails Coordinator
Montana Department of Fish,
Wildlife, and Parks
1420 East Sixth Avenue
P.O. Box 200701
Helena, MT 59620-0701
(406) 444–4585
bwalker@mt.gov

Nebraska
Larry Voecks
State Trail Coordinator
Nebraska Games and Parks
Commission, District 3 Office
2201 N. Thirteenth
Norfolk, NE 68701-2267
(402) 370–3374
lvoecks@ngpc.state.ne.us

Nevada
Steve Weaver
Chief, Planning & Development
Nevada Division of State Parks
1300 S. Curry Street
Carson City, NV 89706-0818
(702) 687–1693
stparks@govmail.state.nv.us

New Hampshire
Paul Gray
Chief, Bureau of Trails
Division of Parks and Recreation
172 Pembroke Road
P.O. Box 1865
Concord, NH 03302-1856
(603) 271–3254

New Jersey
Celeste Tracy
Supervising Planner
NJ DEPE Division of Parks and
Forestry
22 South Clinton Street, CN 404
P.O. Box 404
Trenton, NJ 08625-0404
(609) 984–1173
ctracy@dep.state.nj.us

New Mexico
Sandra Massengill
Planner Director
State Park and Recreation
Department
2040 S. Pacheco Street, Room 107
Santa Fe, NM 87505
(505) 827–9463
smassengill@stae.nm.us

New York
Robert Reinhardt
Director of Planning
Parks and Historic Preservation
Empire State Plaza, Building #1
Albany, NY 12238
(518) 474–0415
rreinhar@nysnet.net

North Carolina
Darrell McBane
State Trails Coordinator
Division of Parks & Recreation
12700 Bayleaf Church Road
P.O. Box 27687
Raleigh, NC 27614-9633
(919) 846–9991
darrell_mcbane@mail.enr.state.
nc.us

North Dakota
Randy Harmon
Trail Coordinator
Department of Parks and
Recreation

1835 East Bismarck Expressway
Bismarck, ND 58504-6708
(701) 328–5369
rharmon@state.nd.us

Ohio
William Daehler
Research Administrator
DNR, Division of Real Estate and
Land Management
1952 Belcher
Columbus, OH 43224
(614) 265–6395
bill.daehler@state.oh.us

Oklahoma
Susan Henry
Planning Coordinator
Oklahoma Tourism & Rec. Dept.
Planning and Development Division
15 North Robinson, Suite 100
Oklahoma City, OK 73102
(405) 521–2904
pdplan@otrd.state.ok.us

Oregon
Peter Bond
State Trail Coordinator
Oregon Parks and Recreation
Department
1115 Commercial Street NE
Suite 1
Salem, OR 97310-1000
(503) 378–6378
pete.bond@state.or.us

Pennsylvania
Vanyla Tierney
Env. Planning Supervisor
PA Department of Conservation
and Natural Resources
P.O. Box 8475
Harrisburg, PA 17105-8475
(717) 783–2654
tierney.vanyla@a1.dcnr.state.pa.us

Rhode Island
Richard Tierney
Trails Program Specialist
RI Department of Environmental
Management
235 Promenade Street
Providence, RI 02908
(401) 222–2776

South Carolina
Jim Schmid
Trail Coordinator
SC Department of Parks,
Recreation, and Tourism
1205 Pendleton Street, Suite 110
Columbia, SC 29201-3731
(803) 734–0130
jschmid@prt.state.sc.us

South Dakota
Dan Simon
Trails Program Specialist
South Dakota Department of
Game, Fish, and Parks
523 E. Capitol Avenue
Pierre, SD 57501-3182
(605) 773–3930
dans@gfp.state.sd.us

Tennessee
Alison Brayton
Recreation Planning Manager
Department of Environmental
Conservation
401 Church Street
L & C Tower, 10th Floor
Nashville, TN 37243
(615) 532–0755
abrayton@mail.state.tn.us

Texas
Andrew Goldbloom
Head of Greenways Program
Recreational Trails Program
Manager
4200 Smith School Road

Austin, TX 78744-3291
(512) 389–4737

Utah
John Knudson
Trails Program Coordinator
Utah Division of Parks and
Recreation
1594 West North Temple, Suite 116
Box 14001
Salt Lake City, UT 84116-3156
(801) 538–7344
nrdpr.jknudson@state.ut.us

Vermont
Laurie Adams
Rec. & Trails Admin. Assistant
Department of Forests, Parks, &
Recreation
103 South Main Street, 10 South
Waterbury, VT 05671-0604
(802) 241–3690
ladams@fpr.anr.state.vt.us

Virginia
Jerry Cassidy
Grant Administrator
Department of Conservation and
Recreation
203 Governor Street, Suite 326
Richmond, VA 23219
(804) 786–3218
jlc@dcr.state.va.us

Washington
Greg Lovelady
Recreation Resource Planner
Interagency Committee for
Outdoor Recreation
P.O. Box 40917
Olympia, WA 98504-0917
(360) 902–3008
GregL@iac.wa.gov

West Virginia
Harold Simmons
Enhancements Coordinator
WV Department of Transportation
1900 Kanawha Boulevard East
Building 5
Charleston, WV 25305
(304) 558–3165
rhartman@mail.dot.state.wv.us

Wisconsin
Larry Freidig
Manager
Motorized Rec. Grant Programs
Bureau of Community Assistance
P.O. Box 7921
Madison, WI 53707
(608) 266–5897

Wyoming
Kim Raap
Wyoming Div. of State Parks
Herschler Bldg, First NE
122 W. Twenty-fifth Street
Cheyenne, WY 82002
(307) 777–7550
kraap@missc.state.wy.us

Puerto Rico
Cesar de Jesus
Trails Coordinator
Dept. of Recreation and Sports
Box 3207
San Juan, Puerto Rico 00902-3207
(809) 721–0666

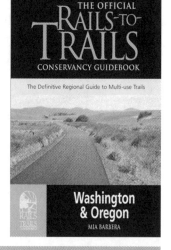

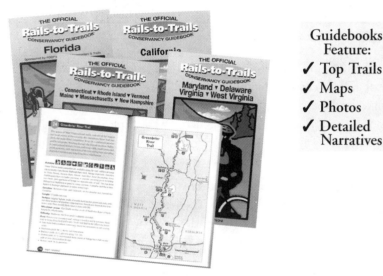

Please send me the following RTC Guidebooks!

❑ **Mid Atlantic States** (MD, DE, VA, WV)   ❑ **California**
❑ **New England States** (CT, RI, VT, MA, NH, ME)   ❑ **Florida**

Item #	Guidebooks	Member Price	Non-Member Price	Qty	Total
GPG1	Mid-Atlantic	$12.95	$14.95		$
GPG2	New England	$12.95	$14.95		
GPG3	California	$12.95	$14.95		
GPG4	Florida	$10.95	$12.95		
				Order Total	$
			Sales Tax (CA, FL, MA, MI, OH, PA)		$
				Handling Charge	$ 4.95
				Total Enclosed	$

❑   I want to join Rails-to-Trails Conservancy. My membership contribution is enclosed (amount checked below). Send me my member packet including my *Sampler of America's Rail-Trails* and one year of *Rails to Trails*, the colorful, quarterly magazine that celebrates trails and greenways. I will also receive discounts on publications and merchandise.

❑ **$18 Regular**   ❑ **$50 Patron**
❑ **$75 Benefactor**   ❑ **$1000 - Trailblazer Society level includes
                                 invitations to exclusive rail-trail excursions.**

❑ My check, payable to Rails-to-Trails Conservancy, is enclosed.

❑ Charge my Credit Card   ❑ MC ❑ VISA ❑ American Express

Card #_____ Exp._____

Signature_____

Name on card (Please Print)_____

Ship to: (Please Print)
Name_____
Street_____
City, State, Zip_____
Phone (_____)_____
Email Address_____